M. E. Thomas is the pseudonym of a practising
lawyer and law professor. She is also the founder

Praise for *Confessions of a Sociopath*

'The goal of *Confessions* is to redefine sociopathy – or at
least to shake off the stigma associated with it. And Thomas
accomplishes both. Through her honest portrayal of herself as
a highly capable yet deeply flawed individual, she demystifies
her disorder'   *Scientific American*

'Fascinating stuff, and Thomas delivers . . . riveting . . . Her
incisive observations about human nature can be breath-
takingly pointed'   *Cleveland Plain Dealer*

'Fascinating and compelling as well as chilling, Thomas'
memoir offers a window into the mind of a portion of the
population that usually remains shrouded in mystery and
fear'   *Booklist*, starred review

'[Thomas] invites us into her courtroom, classroom and bedroom to witness how her behavior has stunted her work life
and made her love life difficult . . . Much here is chilling, but
there are also cracks that make you ache for her . . . A work
of advocacy for greater awareness of sociopathy's reach and
conduct'   *Kirkus Reviews*

A SOCIOPATH

CONFESSIONS OF A SOCIOPATH

A Life Spent Hiding in Plain Sight

M. E. THOMAS

PAN BOOKS

First published 2013 by Crown Publishers, an imprint of Crown Publishing Group

First published in the UK 2013 by Sidgwick & Jackson
This paperback edition published 2014 by Pan Books
an imprint of Pan Macmillan, a division of Macmillan Publishers Limited
Pan Macmillan, 20 New Wharf Road, London N1 9RR
Basingstoke and Oxford
Associated companies throughout the world
www.panmacmillan.com

ISBN 978-1-4472-4273-4

3 5 7 9 8 6 4 2

A CIP catalogue record for this book is available from the British Library.

Printed by CPI Group (UK) Ltd, Croydon, CR0 4YY

Visit **www.panmacmillan.com** to read more about all our books
and to buy them. You will also find features, author interviews and
news of any author events, and you can sign up for e-newsletters
so that you're always first to hear about our new releases.

To Ann, who was my Virgil

Contents

AUTHOR'S NOTE

This book is a work of memoir. It is a true story according to my best recollections; however, in addition to the inevitable flaws of memory, this story is told through the lens of how I see the world, including my megalomania, single-minded focus, and a lack of understanding about the inner worlds of others.

I have chosen to publish this book under a pseudonym, and I have changed the names and identifying characteristics of my family and friends and certain other people mentioned in the book to protect their privacy. In some instances, I disguised settings and rearranged and/or compressed events and time periods in service of the narrative. Otherwise, this is a true and honest account and I have not knowingly misrepresented any material facts.

Psychological Evaluation Excerpt

Ms. Thomas is a 30-year-old Caucasian female seeking an assessment of her personality, particularly in regards to the presence or absence of psychopathic traits. Across multiple self-report inventories tapping both normal-range and pathological personality characteristics, Ms. Thomas scored beyond the 99th percentile of the community normative data. Her presentation in many regards could be considered that of a prototypical psychopathic personality. Additionally, the results of the PCL:SV assessment largely converge with this description, particularly in regards to the affective and interpersonal features displayed by Ms. Thomas, such as a pronounced lack of empathy, a ruthless and calculating attitude towards social and interpersonal relationships, and a relative immunity to experiencing negative emotions.

Most notable in Ms. Thomas's clinical presentation ... were pronounced elevations on scales tapping antisocial and psychopathic traits (particularly egocentricism and sensation-seeking characteristics), interpersonal dominance, verbal aggression, and excessive self-esteem, as well as very low scores on measures tapping negative affective experiences (e.g., phobias, traumatic stressors, depressive symptoms), interpersonal nurturance and stressful life events. Here again, her overall profile reflected a constellation of personality characteristics and interpersonal style highly consistent with current conceptualizations of psychopathy.

Although cognizant that she is "different" from most people she knows in terms of her personality structure, Ms. Thomas does not view herself as "disordered" in the sense of suffering from a form of mental illness per se. Quite the contrary, she seems content with her lifestyle and its current trajectory and rather blasé about many issues and concerns that might cause others some degree of uncertainty or distress. Of course, such attitudes are emblematic of individuals who are highly psychopathic.

By all accounts Ms. Thomas has thus far experienced relatively few objective (or subjective) negative consequences associated with being highly psychopathic—and in many regards appears to have excelled across various life domains (e.g., academic, occupational). This suggests that one might describe her as a "socialized" or "successful" psychopath, or at least a relatively non-maladaptive variant of this personality pattern.

—JOHN F. EDENS, PhD,
Professor, Department of Psychology,
Texas A&M University

CONFESSIONS

OF A

SOCIOPATH

Chapter 1

I'm a Sociopath and
So Are You

If my life were a television show it would start like this: It's a pleasantly warm summer day in a beautiful southern clime. Sunlight glints off ripples in the pool. The sliding door opens with a gentle rumble. A young woman steps out in her flip-flops and a black Speedo swimming suit. Her dark hair hits just below muscular swimmer's shoulders. Her skin is darkly tan from lifeguarding at the local municipal pool. She is neither pretty nor ugly, of medium build and with no prominent features. She looks like an athlete; there's a clumsy tomboyishness about the way she moves, an emotional disconnect with her body. She does not appear to have any feelings about her body, good or bad. She is used to being near-naked, the way athletes are.

Today she is giving a private swim lesson. She flings a towel on a deck chair and kicks off her sandals. There's a casual recklessness about the way she does these things, as if letting loose wayward objects into the world with abandon. That's when she notices the ripples on the surface of the water. She sees that there is something moving in the pool.

It is so small that she doesn't recognize it until she's close—a baby opossum, probably only a week old, its tiny pink paws frantically paddling, its even tinier pink nose struggling above the surface of the water. The poor thing must have fallen into the pool in the night. It is too little to thrust its tiny body up and over the nearest ledge. The baby's muscles quake with exhaustion. Even its tiny sparkling eyes look tired; it is on the brink of succumbing to fatigue.

The young woman moves quickly, sliding her sandals back on, and pauses for a moment at the top of the deck. She grabs a net and heads toward the opossum. The camera cuts in as the net lowers, dipping into the surface of the water, catching the baby opossum under the belly just in front of its hind legs. With a quick, almost effortless movement, the net drags the opossum under the surface until its head is fully submerged. The animal thrashes, its tired body now alert to a new threat. It struggles loudly, whimpering and squealing, until it finally manages to free its hindquarters from the lip of the net. But it's barely able to gasp a breath before the net comes down again. The angle of the net is awkward though, and the animal is able to writhe out of its trap.

The young woman sighs, and the net is lifted. The baby opossum feels relief wash over it for a fraction of a second, only to resume its desperate paddling against the water. The young woman drops the net on the ground, grabs her towel, and heads back inside. Moments later she is on the phone with her private student—today's lesson is canceled; there is something wrong with the pool. She grabs her keys, flings her front door open, and skips down the stairs to the muscle car that she's been driving since her sixteenth birthday. The V-8 engine stutters for just a moment, then roars to life. She slams the transmission into reverse, just barely dodging the other cars in the driveway, then takes off, ready to make the most of a newly free summer afternoon.

When she returns home at dusk she sees a dark shadow at the bottom of the pool. She grabs the same net, manages to scoop up the small bundle on the first try, and pitches it over the fence into her neighbor's yard. She drops an extra chlorine tablet into the pool and heads inside. The camera lingers on the placid pool, no longer interrupted by frantic waves. Fade to black.

I am a sociopath. Through dual quirks of genetics and environment, I suffer from what psychologists now refer to as antisocial personality disorder, characterized in the *Diagnostic and Statistical Manual of Mental Disorders (DSM)* as "a pervasive pattern of disregard for and violation of the rights of others." Key among the characteristics of the diagnosis are a lack of remorse, a penchant for deceit, and a failure to conform to social norms. I prefer to define my sociopathy as a set of traits that inform my personality but don't define me: I am generally free of entangling and irrational emotions, I am strategic and canny, I am intelligent and confident and charming, but I also struggle to react appropriately to other people's confusing and emotion-driven social cues. *Psychopathy* and *sociopathy* are terms with an intertwined clinical history, and they are largely now used interchangeably, though some academics distinguish between the two based on genetics, aggression, or other factors. I have chosen to call myself a sociopath because of the negative connotations of *psycho* in the popular culture. I may have a disorder, but I am not crazy.

I can trace the likely genetic link through my father to his birth father, who was known for being an exceptionally cold man. My grandfather's heavily scarred face attested to his impulsiveness and penchant for risk taking and violence. He was literally a rocket scientist but fancied himself a cowboy. He spent all of his inherited wealth on a ranch that he ran into the ground, then lost to back taxes. He knocked up my grandmother and was forced into an unwanted marriage that ended quite suddenly just months after my father was born. He gave up parental rights and never saw my father again. I don't know anything about my paternal great-grandparents, although my guess is that the apple did not fall far from the tree.

My upbringing promoted my genetic propensities, but not in the ways that you would expect from watching television or movie depictions of a sociopath. I was not a victim of child abuse, and I am not a murderer or a criminal. I have never skulked behind prison walls; I prefer mine to be covered in ivy. I am an accomplished attorney and law professor. I am a typical well-respected, young academic, regularly writing for law journals and advancing various legal theories. I donate 10 percent of my income to charity and teach Sunday school every week. I have a close circle of family and friends whom I love and who very much love me.

Does any of this sound like you? Maybe you are a sociopath too. Recent estimates say that 1 percent to 4 percent of the population, or one in every twenty-five people, is a sociopath—that's higher than the percentage of people who have anorexia or autism. You're not a serial killer? Never imprisoned? Most of us aren't. Some of you may be surprised to find that it is no defense that you're not a criminal. Only 20 percent of male and female prison inmates are sociopaths, although we are probably responsible for about half of serious crimes committed. Nor are most sociopaths incarcerated. In fact, the silent majority of sociopaths lives freely and anonymously in society, holding down jobs, getting married, having children—fitting in with varying degrees of success in a culture that easily considers sociopaths as monsters. Who then are sociopaths? We are legion and diverse. At least one of them looks like me. Does one of them look like you?

Do you have plenty of friends, paramours, or admirers? That doesn't disqualify you; in fact quite the opposite. Despite our bad reputation, sociopaths are categorically known for our exceptional, albeit superficial, charm. In a world filled with gloomy, mediocre nothings populating a go-nowhere rat race, people are attracted to the sociopath's exceptionalism like moths to a flame.

You would like me if you met me. I am quite confident about that because I have met a statistically significant sample size of the population and they were all susceptible to my charms. I have the kind of smile that is common among television show characters and rare in real life, perfect in its sparkly-teeth dimensions and ability to express pleasant invitation. I'm the sort of date you would love to bring to your ex's wedding. Fun, exciting, the perfect office escort—your boss's wife has never met anyone quite so charming. And I'm just the right amount of smart and successful so that your parents would be thrilled if you brought me home.

Do you have an inflated view of yourself? I certainly seem to, don't I? Sociopaths are known for having egos so full-bodied they could be considered Rubenesque. I exude confidence, much more than my looks or social stature would warrant. I am not very tall but present solidly with broad, strong shoulders and an angular jaw. My friends often remark on my toughness and swagger. But I am just as comfortable in summer dresses as I am in cowboy boots.

Perhaps the most noticeable aspect of my confidence is

the way I sustain eye contact. Some people have called it a "predator stare," and it appears that most sociopaths have it. Sustained eye contact can seem hostile, and so zoo visitors are frequently advised not to stare at gorillas, lest it be taken as a sign of aggression. Most humans seem to think so, too; otherwise, staring contests wouldn't present much of a challenge. Sociopaths are different. We are unfazed by uninterrupted eye contact. Our failure to look away politely is often perceived as being confident, aggressive, seductive, or predatory. It can throw people off balance, but often in an exciting way that imitates the unsettling feeling of infatuation.

Ever find yourself using that charm and confidence to get people to do things for you that they otherwise wouldn't? Some might call it manipulation, but I like to consider it simply using what God gave me. And the word *manipulation* is so ugly. It's what people say to disavow their own choices. If they end up never regretting their decision, does that mean that no one has manipulated them?

Manipulation is where the traits of a sociopath take a distinct turn for the nefarious in a lot of people's minds, but I don't see why. It is just fulfilling an exchange. People want a particular thing—to please you, to feel wanted or needed, to be seen as a good person—and manipulation is just a quick and dirty way to get both people something they want. You might call it seduction. One of my sociopathic friends gave this example. One guy wants to sell a car for $5,000, the second wants to buy it for $10,000. I am aware of the two but neither is aware of the other. I buy the car for $5,000, sell it to the second guy for $10,000, and I make $5,000. It's called arbitrage and happens on Wall Street (and a lot of other places) every day. We all get what we want, and we're all happy, as long as the two never connect the dots and never learn more than they need to. I facilitate their ignorance for the benefit of all, especially myself.

Indeed, I believe that most people who interact with sociopaths are better off than they otherwise would be. Sociopaths are part of the grease making the world go round. We fulfill fantasies, or at least the appearance of fantasies. In fact, we are sometimes the only ones attentive to providing for your deepest wants and needs, the only ones so deeply attuned to them for no ulterior motive immediately discernible by you. We observe our target and strive to become a facsimile of whatever or whoever that person wants—a good employee or boss or lover. It's not always the case that the facsimile is malicious or ill intentioned. And it makes the target feel good for the course of the transaction and usually ends without harm. Of course everything comes at a price—we wouldn't be doing it if we weren't getting something from you, often money or power or simply even the enjoyment of your admiration and desire, but this certainly does not mean that you get nothing out of it. Maybe some might think the price is too high. But the truth is that if you've made a deal with the devil, it's probably because no one else has offered you more favorable terms.

What about morality? Do you approach questions of morality with ambivalence, finding it easy to justify your own or others' behavior with a reference to "survival of the fittest"? People sometimes say that we lack remorse or guilt like it's a bad thing. They are sure that remorse and guilt are necessary to being a "good" person. But there is probably no universal, and certainly no objective, morality. Despite millennia of arguments among theologians and philosophers, no one can really agree on the contours and parameters of morality. From where I stand, it's hard to put such faith in something so wildly elastic and changeable, something associated with horrors as diverse as honor killings, "just" wars, and capital punishment. Like many people, I adhere to a religion that gives me moral guidance. The practice of it is just good sense—it keeps you out of prison and safely hidden in the crowd. But the heart of morality is something I have never understood.

My view of morality is instrumental. I abide by conventional dictates when it suits me, and otherwise, I follow my own course with little need for justification. Once I helped two elderly Holocaust survivors fill out forms for restitution funds from the German government. They were a couple: a lovely blond woman in her late seventies or early eighties who obviously spent money on her clothes and her face, and an even older man with a shock of white hair on top of his head and the sense of entitlement that you often see in Los Angeles among aging Hollywood stars. His papers seemed to be more or less in order. At one point he even belligerently rolled up his sleeve to reveal a numeric tattoo that matched his paperwork. The woman's papers were more confusing. She had dates from a previous restitution claim, but they didn't really make sense when compared with the story she told me. According to her paperwork she was in and out of camps, which seemed unusually inefficient for the Germans. I didn't really know what to put down on the form, so I stood and told her I would ask for help from the organizers sponsoring the event. She panicked, grabbed my arm, and sat me back down. What followed was a bit difficult to understand, given her old age, likely senility, and bad English. Pointing to one of the forms, she said, "This isn't me."

A story of fraud and survival rolled out before me, if not from her actual words then from my own tendency to infer deceit. With her blond hair and blue eyes, no one had suspected her of being Jewish. She was able to "pass" for the duration of the war as a seamstress and then stole the documents that corroborated her story of time spent in camps from another young woman, who had died shortly after liberation. I think that was the gist, anyway; I made it a point not to ask any questions. I wonder if her husband even knew who she really was. I wonder if it was all a figment of her imagination, or mine.

In any case, I felt no moral compunction about helping her fill out the forms. It was not my job to question her story, only to help her tell it. I was glad to do it, actually. I admired her. In the course of my travels, I had visited several Holocaust sites and been through the Anne Frank Achterhuis more times than I would have preferred. Visiting these places, I was always struck by the enormous passivity of most of the people involved: the neighbors, the townspeople, the camp guards, the fellow prisoners.

Looking at the old woman, I could not help but recognize myself. A kindred spirit. She knew what it meant to be a survivor at all costs. An elaborate identity theft to rise from oppression. I could only hope to do so well in my own life.

She was probably lucky to have been assigned to me rather than some other volunteer. It's hard to know if someone else with a firmer moral compass might have asked more questions and availed themselves of more, and thus potentially incriminating, information. A compassionate person might think that she must have suffered during the war, if not in the same ways then for the same reasons as those the restitution was meant to help. She probably lived in constant fear of being discovered. Who knows whom she had to bribe, befriend, or seduce to maintain her freedom? But yet another might not want to help someone who helped herself by breaking the rules. Shouldn't we be disgusted with those who game the system, accept government money when they're not entitled to it, and are opportunistic about social safety nets? There might even be some judgment about her choice to capitalize on her Aryan looks to avoid suffering alongside her kin. But luckily for her there was no moral conundrum for me, and I sent them both on their way in time to catch a nice lunch.

Are you good at making decisions on the fly, sometimes to the consternation of your friends and family? Sociopaths are known for being spontaneous. I get restless; I find it hard to focus on one project for a particular length of time or to keep a job for more than a few years. Sociopaths tend to crave stimulation and are easily bored, so we tend to make snap decisions. The darker side of impulsivity is that we can become fixated on an impulse to the exclusion of all else, unable to listen to reason. Whereas most people experience impulsivity as hotheadedness, I become coldhearted.

I have never killed anyone, but I have certainly wanted to, as I am sure most people have. I have rarely wanted to kill those close to me; more often it has been a chance encounter with someone who caused me consternation. Once while visiting Washington, DC, for a law conference, a metro worker tried to shame me about using an escalator that was closed. He asked in thickly accented English, "Didn't you see the yellow gate?"

ME: Yellow gate?

HIM: The gate! I just put the gate up and you had to walk around it!

Silence. My face is blank.

HIM: That's trespassing! Don't you know it is wrong to trespass! The escalator was closed, you broke the law!

I stare at him silently.

HIM: *[visibly rattled at my lack of reaction]* Well, next time, you don't trespass, okay?

It was not okay. People often say, in explaining their horrible actions, that they "just snapped." I know that feeling well. I stood there for a moment, letting my rage reach that decision-making part of my brain, and I suddenly became filled with a sense of calm purpose. I blinked my eyes and set my jaw. I started following him. Adrenaline started flowing. My mouth tasted metallic. I fought to keep my peripheral vision in focus, hyperaware of everything around me, trying to predict the movement and behavior of the crowd. I was unfamiliar with the city, a new user of the metro, and it was just before rush hour. I was hoping that he would walk into some deserted hallway or sneak away through a hidden, unlocked door where I would find him alone, waiting. I felt so sure of myself, so focused on this one thing I felt I had to do. An image sprang to my mind of my hands wrapped around his neck, my thumbs digging deeply into his throat, his life slipping away from him under my unrelenting grasp. How right that would feel.

It seems odd thinking about this now. I weigh less than 130 pounds; he probably weighed 160. I have strong hands from being a musician, but I wonder if they would be strong enough to squeeze the breath out of him in his last moments of life. Is it truly so easy to extinguish a life? When it came down to it, I couldn't even manage to drown a baby opossum. I had been caught in a fit of megalomaniacal fantasy, but in the end it didn't matter anyway. I lost him in the crowd, and just as quickly as it had arisen in me, my murderous rage dissipated.

I have wondered since, what would have happened to me had I not lost sight of him? I'm sure I wouldn't have been able to actually kill him, but I am also relatively certain I would have assaulted him. Would he have struggled? Would I have been hurt? Would police have been involved? What could I possibly have said or done to get myself off the hook? I often wonder about this and dozens of similar incidents. I realize that one day I may do something very bad. How would I react in such a situation? Would I be able to put on a sufficient show of remorse? Or would I be revealed to be a faker?

From my own observations, I have found that a sociopath's need for stimulation plays out in very person-specific ways. I'm not surprised that some sociopaths would fill this need via criminal or violent acts, particularly if these were the opportunities that regularly presented themselves. It also seems perfectly plausible that others would feed their need for stimulation via other more legitimate routes, pursuing careers in firefighting or espionage or duking it out in the boardrooms of corporate America. My thought is that sociopaths who grow up poor among drug dealers are likely to become sociopathic drug dealers; sociopaths who grow up in the middle and upper classes are likely to become sociopathic surgeons and executives.

Have you succeeded in rapidly climbing the corporate ladder in a competitive field like business, finance, or law? If charm, arrogance, cunning, callousness, and hyper-rationality are considered sociopathic traits, it's probably no surprise that many sociopaths end up as successful corporate types. In fact, as one CNN reporter opined: "Squint at the symptoms of psychopathy, and in a different light they can appear as simple office politics or entrepreneurial prowess." Dr. Robert Hare, one of the foremost researchers on sociopathy, believes that a sociopath is four times more likely to be at the top of the corporate ladder than in the janitor's closet, due to the close match between the personality traits of sociopaths and the unusual demands of high-powered jobs.

Al Dunlap, former CEO of Sunbeam and Scott Paper, was famous as a turnaround artist and downsizer until he was investigated for accounting fraud by the SEC. In the book *The Psychopath Test* by Jon Ronson, Dunlap admits to having many of the traits of a psychopath, but he redefines those traits as crucial to being a business leader. For instance, in his mind, "manipulation" can be translated to the ability to inspire and lead others. Overblown confidence is necessary to survive the hard knocks of business: "You've got to like yourself if you're going to be a success." Not to mention, due to our inability to empathize, sociopaths are perfect for all the dirty work that no one else has the stomach for, such as firing and downsizing. In fact, that ruthlessness in personnel decisions is how Dunlap earned his nickname—"Chainsaw Al."

Easily distracted? That's situational awareness. Constantly in need of stimulation and love playing games? These characteristics promote risk taking, which in business often equals reward. If you combine a propensity for manipulation, dishonesty, callousness, arrogance, poor impulse control, and the rest of the sociopathic traits, you could end up with a socially dangerous individual or the next big-thinking entrepreneur. Robert Hare says that the biggest tip-off to identifying a "successful sociopath" is a "predatory spirit," just the kind that businesses seem to love. It seems that where we do not crash and burn, we have the potential to achieve dizzying amounts of success.

I wouldn't be surprised if some of you recognize yourselves in these descriptions. It is statistically very probable that some people reading this book are sociopaths and have never realized it. If this is you, welcome home.

· · ·

B eing a sociopath doesn't define me. In a lot of ways I am ordinary. These days I lead a quiet, middle-class life in a medium-size city that looks like any number of cities across America. I accomplish errands at various strip malls on the weekends. I work more than I should, and I have trouble sleeping.

When not acting impulsively, almost everything I do is done with purpose. Things like physical appearance are most easy to manipulate. My nails are immaculately manicured and my eyebrows perfectly groomed. These days I allow my dark hair to grow just past my shoulders. It is soft and unfussy in subtle compliance with the strictures of fashion. The pleasant ordinariness of my hair brushing lightly against my eyelashes functions to neutralize the intensity of my eyes, which are shiny and flecked by jagged-edged shards of amber, as if something shattered when they first opened to the world. They are probing and merciless.

I should say something about my intelligence, which I believe to be one of the most difficult topics to navigate. While people may be forced to acknowledge their inferior physical appearances, they rarely do so in regards to their intellect, the hidden and variable nature of which allows for rampant self-deception. Even your regular junior high dropout likes to think that he could have been Steve Jobs had he chosen computer programming over meth addiction.

I think I am pretty realistic about my intelligence. I am probably smarter than you, dear reader, but I know that in the rare instance this will not be true. I accept that there are many more kinds of intelligence than just raw brainpower (which of course I have in spades), but I do not necessarily respect them all. Rather, I believe that true, worthwhile intelligence is characterized by an innate and superior awareness of surroundings and an ability and desire to learn. This type is rare in the general populace. I was very young when I realized I was smarter than most everyone else, and I felt at once victorious and isolated.

It is not always clear what sets people like me apart from other members of society. Sociopathy cannot be diagnosed based solely on a person's behavior but must focus on their internal motivations. Take for instance my story about drowning an opossum. It is not, in itself, a sociopathic act. Killing a small, cute animal might be cruel or sadistic, which is not necessarily sociopathic. In my case, it was merely expedient. It was an act of dispassion.

In letting the baby opossum die a slow and horrible death, I didn't feel morally justified. I didn't think about having to justify myself at all. I didn't feel sad or happy about it. I took no pleasure in its suffering; I did not give it a thought. I didn't feel anything other than a desire to solve my problem in the simplest way possible. I was concerned only for myself. There wasn't much chance that the baby would cause much harm if I saved it, but there was no upside for me if I did. And at some point, there was no point in finishing the job of killing it; the pool was probably already contaminated by the opossum releasing its bodily wastes in the throes of death. It was just easier to cancel my plans and wait for the inevitable approach of death.

Instead of acts, I believe that what really distinguish a sociopath conceptually from everyone else are our compulsions, our motivations, and the narratives we tell ourselves about our inner lives. Sociopaths don't include elements of guilt or moral responsibility in their mental stories, only self-interest and self-preservation. I don't assign moral values to my choices, just cost-benefit. And indeed, sociopaths are without exception obsessed with power, playing and winning games, appeasing their boredom, and seeking pleasure. My story lines focus on how smart I am or how well I play a situation.

Similarly, I like to imagine that I have "ruined people" or seduced someone to the point of being irreparably mine. The stories I tell myself to explain my actions are self-aggrandizing. I spend a lot of time spinning reality in my head to make me seem more clever and powerful than reality would suggest. (Sociopaths are highly immune to depression, and this ability to tell ourselves wonderful stories about how attractive, smart, and wily we are, and to believe them, surely helps.) The only situation in which I may feel shame or embarrassment is when I have been outplayed. I am never embarrassed that someone may be thinking something bad about me, as long as I have conceived of some gambit in which I have fooled or outmaneuvered them.

Normal people feel emotions that I simply don't. For them, emotions like guilt serve as convenient shortcuts, telling people when they're crossing societal or moral boundaries that they're better off observing. But guilt is not absolutely necessary to live within social acceptability. And it certainly isn't the only thing that prevents people from murdering, stealing, and lying. Indeed, guilt is often unsuccessful at preventing these actions. It follows, then, that the lack of guilt does not make sociopaths criminals. We have alternative means of keeping ourselves in line. In fact, because guilt does not drive our decision-making, we experience fewer emotional prejudices and more freedom of thought and action. For instance, I felt no need to insert myself and exercise my own moral judgment regarding the old lady who may or may not have survived the internment camps. I would like to think I was better able to help her in her unique situation because of my emotional distance. Recent research suggests that emotions and gut reactions play a dominant role in forming moral judgments and that rationalization of those emotions only follows. The human brain is a belief factory, and part of its job is to rationally justify moral feelings. Rational decision-making is not fail-proof, but neither is guilt and remorse. Neither sociopaths nor the empathic—"empaths"—have a monopoly on bad behavior.

There seems to me to be something wrong with requiring people to pretend to feel remorse. Is it any wonder then that sociopaths are known as being liars? There is really no other option for them, when to show their true feelings (or lack thereof) or to express their true thoughts would get them extra jail time, cause them to be branded as an antisocial, or any number of other negative consequences, simply because they do not share the same worldview as the majority.

Living in a world of empaths makes me vividly aware of how I am different. In John Steinbeck's novel *East of Eden,* he describes a sociopathic character, Cathy:

Even as a child she had some quality that made people look at her, then look away, then look back at her, troubled at something foreign. Something looked out of her eyes, and was never there when one looked again. She moved quietly and talked little, but she could enter no room without causing everyone to turn toward her.

Like Cathy, there has always been something foreign seeming about me. As a sociopath friend of mine put it: "People, no matter how stupid, can't put their finger on it, but somehow know I'm not quite right."

Sometimes it feels like I am in the movie *Invasion of the Body Snatchers* and any slipup or indication that I am different will draw suspicion. I mimic the way other people interact with others, not to trick them, but so I can hide among them. I hide because I fear that if I am discovered there will be unpredictable negative consequences as part of being affiliated with a disorder plagued by pejorative connotations. I don't want to end up fired from my job or kept away from children or institutionalized just because other people can't understand me. I hide because society has made it almost impossible to do otherwise.

Have I earned your hostility?

I'm not necessarily a sadist. I intentionally hurt people sometimes, but don't we all? It seems like the greatest harm is often inflicted through passion—the angry ex-husband who won't let anyone have his wife if he can't, the armed zealot willing to die and kill for his cause, the father who loves his daughter just a little too much. There's no danger of this kind of explosive excess of ardor from me.

Even so, I often try to soften my edges around people with whom I share the closest relationships. I actively shield them from realizing that I am meticulously calibrating their value to me at all times, because I know that they are hurt by such things. The consequences of their hurt often result in discomfort to me in the form of withheld privileges or retracted social favors—friends and even family are only so forgiving of bad behavior before they start to withdraw—so I have trained myself to behave with "sensitivity" to their feelings like most of you do, by holding my tongue or indulging their harebrained ideas about themselves and the world. Of course I am ruthless with my enemies, but that is also a very common human quality.

A few years ago, I suffered a series of setbacks. It was a time of loss and introspection, and it was then that I realized that the "sociopath" label explained the pattern of thought that was at the root of many of my problems. A friend had casually diagnosed me years earlier but I hadn't thought about it since. This time I took it seriously. I started looking for answers and browsing the basic information that was available on the Internet and in popular science magazines. I was appalled that all of it reeked of a particular bias. There were some amusing blogs written by victims of con artists, but there weren't any sociopaths writing about their perspectives online. I saw an opportunity for offering a different perspective that coincided with my own interests at the time. I figured that if I existed, there must be others like me—other sociopaths who didn't make their impact in a world of crime but out in the business and professional world. I wanted to shape the dialogue to reflect my point of view. I wanted to expand the discussion of sociopaths beyond the traditional study of incarcerated criminals. The entrepreneur in me also thought there could be some benefit from being the first to do it and doing it well, so in 2008 I started writing a blog called SociopathWorld.com, which I intended as an online community for people who identify as sociopaths, as well as people who love and hate them.

At the time of this writing, thousands visit the site a day; since the blog's inception, there have been more than a million discrete visitors from all over the world. An active online community of aggressive narcissists, violent sociopaths, and morbid empaths comments daily—some are sensitive and thoughtful, while others are crude and sophomoric. To my occasional amusement, their discussions often divert wildly off topic—they engage in bullying and peer pressure, express territoriality, shame and tease—setting up a complicated social dynamic I had not imagined. Some lay out the facts of their lives, as if confession would offer absolution, or at least a modicum of self-acceptance, which I can understand. Still others quietly skulk on the site—perhaps trying to glean what they can from it to gain some mastery of their own lives, or simply to feel closer to a largely anonymous group of deviants of which they feel they are a part.

My favorite part about running the blog has been encountering scores of other sociopaths. I managed to tap into a hidden community, populated by complex characters and rich with histories. Despite these differences, I recognize myself in them and they in me. I am different than a killer or rapist or serial-embezzler sociopath who has no check on her behavior, but we all cross Hare's threshold line into the category of sociopath. We share a kind of capital that we have each been cultivating largely in isolation, learning in our own private ways how to be. Maybe the world hates us, and maybe we do not know or even like each other, but at least we can understand one another, in our way, and know that there is a precedent for people like ourselves. Via my exposure to the myriad variety of sociopaths and other personality types that I've run into on the blog and in real life, I have also been able to eliminate many misconceptions I myself had about sociopathy—for instance, that all criminal sociopaths are overly impulsive and low-functioning. I've also reaffirmed to myself that sociopaths really are different from the average person, often in very dangerous or scary ways. Once they've targeted someone, I've seen sociopaths on my blog fixate on that individual like the proverbial pit bull, slowly eliciting information from them until they've acquired enough leverage to out them to their friends and family, and marriages are disrupted and homes are broken, all for the sport of it. Sociopaths have both the power and inclination to ruin lives, and this is just what they do to strangers on the Internet.

I don't ever mean to give the impression that no one should worry about sociopaths because I am not so bad. Just because I'm smart, high-functioning, and nonviolent doesn't mean there aren't a lot of stupid, uninhibited, or dangerous sociopaths out there who genuinely should be avoided. I try to avoid people like that; after all, it's not like sociopaths all give each other hall passes to avoid harassment. And the really extreme ones probably aren't commenting on my blog from their isolation cells, so who knows in what ways they would be similar to or different from the sociopath next door. We share many things in common, but we differ in how those traits manifest themselves in our behavior.

In my experience, sociopathy exists on a spectrum of severity, from the death row inmate to the ruthless venture capitalist to the calculating cheerleader mom. Consider, as an example, someone with Down syndrome. I have two relatives that have Down's—one blood and the other adopted. The blood relative does sort of look like the rest of his family, his siblings, and his parents, but he also looks unmistakably like his adoptive sister who also has Down syndrome. In fact, most people would probably say he looks more like his adoptive sister than his blood siblings—unless the observer was intentionally trying to look past some of the more obvious Down's markers, such as the distinctive broad, flat face, creased eyelid, short stature, and so on.

Down's is an interesting condition. Throw an extra chromosome in there, and it affects the way seemingly every other gene is expressed. It's almost as if you take the individual's raw genetic material and put a very distinctive mask over it.

I think that sociopathy is something like this. My personality resembles my siblings' quite a bit. And it resembles the personalities of many people around me, my colleagues and friends, people whom I have chosen to surround myself with due to our mutual or complementary views of the world. But my personality also resembles those of other sociopaths a great deal, sometimes in ways more conspicuous because of our relative rarity in the general populace. It's amazing to me how much of my habits of mind and proclivities of action I can share in common with strangers—with people who are of different genders, ethnicities, races, nationalities, backgrounds, ages. But I am not just like every other sociopath. From what I have seen of us we are all very different. But there is no mistaking a certain family resemblance.

When I first started my blog, I struggled in writing my posts with this issue of what it means, day to day, to be a sociopath. On the one hand, if I talked openly about the limited role sociopathy played in my life, I ran the risk of not seeming sociopathic enough. But I also wanted to present myself as a real person, not a caricature you'd expect to see on television. I've decided to lean more on the side of authenticity and less on the side of titillation. I have a similar goal for this book. I know I will live for a long time. I have managed to remain undetected so far, but there's no telling how long that will last. Will I end up being shipped off to a sociopaths-only gulag? Perhaps if I'm lucky. Many visitors to my blog have called for much worse, including our total extermination. I'm hoping that once you get to know one sociopath, you'll show even this cold heart some compassion when the cattle cars come to ship me off somewhere.

And hopefully you'll gain something too—awareness and understanding of a type of person that you probably see and interact with daily. I don't think that I'm the prototypical sociopath. Not everything I do in my life is straight out of a sociopath handbook. A lot of readers question whether I am a sociopath at all. Certainly not everything I do falls in line with all the diagnostic criteria psychologists have developed for sociopathic behavior. I think this surprises people, particularly those whose only idea of a sociopath comes from the psycho killers they see in movies. But to the extent that we share these things in common, particularly a common mind-set, I understand other sociopaths in a way that is often eerie. I want to reveal my internal dialogue and motivations, because I believe that to learn to understand the mind-set of one sociopath is to get an uncommon insight into the minds of all other sociopaths. You might even find that the way I think is not that different from your own.

Archaeologist Klaus Schmidt has opined that the presence of monsters and hybrid creatures in modern human culture, unknown to Neolithic man, indicates a high degree of development. The idea is that the further a society is from nature and, inevitably, a healthy fear of it, the more it finds itself inventing things of which to be afraid.

There is a romantic poem believed to have been written by Chrétien de Troyes in the twelfth century called *Yvain, le Chevalier au Lion.* In search of chivalric adventure, Yvain comes across a monster in a clearing—"so passing ugly was the creature that no word of mouth could do him justice." I imagine the creature as a young girl. She is lying in the bedroom she shares with her sister in her parents' large house, dark tendrils of hair touching her eyelashes ever so slightly. She daydreams of throats split open in effusions of brilliant red.

In order to ascertain whether a fight is in store for him, Yvain engages the monster in conversation:

> *"Come, let me know whether thou art a creature of good or not."*
>> *And the creature replied: "I am a man."*
>> *"What kind of a man art thou?"*
>> *"Such as thou seest me to be: I am by no means otherwise."*

People are interested in the mind of a sociopath, and understandably so, but I suspect for the wrong reasons. This book is sure to disappoint if you are looking for graphic tales of violence. They don't exist, and in any case absolutely anyone could be a gruesome killer if put in the right situation. I don't think there's anything very interesting about that, or at least I don't have anything to add to that particular fact about humanity.

I think it's more interesting why I chose to buy a house for my closest friend, or gave my brother $10,000 the other day, just because. I recently got an e-mail from a friend with terminal cancer, saying I give the most thoughtful and useful gifts and how she is so grateful to know me. I am considered a very helpful and considerate professor and am consistently rated one of the best in the school. I am devoutly religious. I am functionally a good person and yet I am not motivated or constrained by the same things that most good people are. Am I a monster? I prefer to believe that you and I simply occupy different points on the spectrum of humanity.

Chapter 2

DIAGNOSIS: SOCIOPATH

How did I eventually come to think I was a sociopath? With all of the benefits of hindsight I can see that there were plenty of signs. But it took a professional and personal collapse in my late twenties to make me care enough to investigate.

My family likes to joke about my inability to stick to one thing for longer than a few years. High school was a little bit of a farce but I tested well enough to become a National Merit Scholar. In college I majored in music on a whim. I chose percussion because the core requirements were split to cover four instruments, and I didn't have the attention span to focus on just one. I chose to go to law school because it was one of the few graduate programs without prerequisites and I needed something to do. I tested well on the LSAT and got into a top law school, despite having the GPA of someone who, though clearly intelligent, is easily bored.

After law school I was hired as an attorney at a self-described "elite" law firm. All of my colleagues were recruited from the top of their classes at their top ten schools. I barely made the firm's grade cutoffs, and I had graduated with honors. We were supposed to be the best of the best, and the firm charged a premium. Just two years out of law school, my base salary was $170,000 with a double bonus totaling $90,000 and I was in a lockstep pattern of significant raises every year I stayed. But I was a terrible employee.

I have never been able to work well unless it directly benefited my mind or my résumé, no matter how lucrative the work was. I spent most of my effort in dodging projects and scheduling my day around lunch appointments and coffee breaks. Still, when I got my first bad review I was surprised. I was even more surprised when I eventually got called into my supervising partner's office and told to shape up or ship out.

I didn't shape up. I interviewed with other firms and got an offer from a similarly prestigious firm that paid more, but I wasn't interested in continuing to be a well-paid paper pusher. I was meant for greater things than being a junior legal associate; I was sure of it. A couple months later I was out on the street with a banker's box of personal belongings, waiting for a friend to pick me up.

Around this same time, a close friend's father was diagnosed with cancer. Whereas she had once been a pleasure to be around—intelligent, wise, independent, and insightful—she was suddenly emotionally fragile and beset by family obligations. I was exhausted by trying to accommodate her, and I felt that I was suddenly putting more effort into the relationship than I was getting out of it. I decided to cut off all contact with her. At first all I felt was relief. Eventually I missed her, but I had expected that, and I tried not to let it bother me too much.

I spent the next couple of years receiving unemployment insurance checks. My family was worried for me. They wondered what I was planning on doing with my life. But I never had those sorts of existential crises. I always live in two-year increments. I figure anything beyond that is just so uncertain that it can basically be disregarded as a possibility.

This compounding of losses was unusual for me, though— even my two-year plan seemed bleak. I found myself at loose ends, directionless and, I had to admit, fairly mindless. I had squandered a prestigious and lucrative job in my chosen field. I considered going to business school, but for what? To repeat a cycle of success and devastation for the duration of my life? I had heartlessly put aside a friend in her time of need. How many more relationships did I have to destroy? I knew these were not the actions of a normal person, and I began to admit that my life was not sustainable. If I wasn't normal, what was I?

With a ruthlessness I usually reserved for other people, I stripped away my own artifices to discover who I really was. I realized that all my life I had been trying to be like the chameleons I had learned about as a child in my big book of small reptiles. The social part of me had evaporated, making it apparent that all of my efforts to entertain were designed to sit on the very outer surfaces of me, separate and apart from what existed inside. And those insides—they were impenetrable. I had never liked people to look at me; I wanted to be the only one doing the looking. But now I realized that I never bothered to look closely at myself.

I had grown accustomed to believing my own lies. I would fixate on moments that made me feel normal. A monster would not cry at a sad movie. Her heart would not break from a lover's departure. So my tears were proof that I was normal, as was the pain in my chest, about which so many songs have been written. How could my heart be broken if there was no heart to break? It had been easy to convince myself that I was not the one with the problem.

It is one thing to lie to others, but I had been lying to my-self for years. I had become reliant on self-deception and for-gotten who I was. And now I didn't really understand myself at all. I wanted to stop being a stranger to myself; for the first time in my life, that bothered me enough to want to do some-thing about it.

Though it would prove to be a turning point, this was not my first period of deep introspection. During college, I got myself into an awkward social mess (I'll relate the details in chapter 5), and my life went completely to hell. I didn't have any label to identify with, but after a long period of unflinch-ing honesty and self-analysis I recognized that I was a very manipulative, cunning person who was unable to connect to anyone on more than a superficial level, obsessed with power, and willing to do anything to get ahead, among other things. To the extent that those things were negatively impacting my life, I tried to tame and control them—or to at least divert them to situations where the stakes were lowest.

I didn't know then what a "sociopath" was nor did I have any inkling that I might be one until a few years later during law school, when a coworker raised the possibility. We were working together as summer interns, largely busywork that didn't matter. I was bored, so when I learned that she was an openly gay woman who had been adopted as a child, I started to pry into her personal life, hunting for insecurities. Slightly overweight, cheerful, and gregarious, she appeared to be a treasure trove of plush emotional vulnerabilities. It turned out that she was much more than that—she was intellectu-ally curious and wide open to the possibilities of how to live in the world. We shared offices and spent hours talking about politics, religion, philosophy, fashion, or anything else that would distract us from the drudge work. From the very beginning, she felt compelled to mother me, giving me advice on how to dress appropriately at work and feeding me quinoa salads she had prepared for me to keep me from dining on cheeseburgers every day. I noticed and began to analyze how she made everyone feel comfortable around her. I hoped to replicate little nuggets of her charm, and I told her so. Whereas I viewed the world through the lens of bloodless rationality, she could not have been more touchy-feely; though she was an intelligent woman who valued rationality, she made a deliberate choice to abandon it occasionally in favor of soft intangibles like "compassion" and "mercy." Even though I don't naturally value those things, I respect that they are legitimate interests that people have, the same way that I acknowledge that not everyone will have my exact taste in, say, music or automobiles.

She had a master's degree in theology, and I loved to probe her beliefs, first about whether God made her gay, but later about anything that seemed important to her. I remember specifically questioning her about altruism, with which I had little personal experience. I explained to her that, to my mind, to have the ability to measure with such stark precision the utility of a person—just as any other thing—made it senseless to regard that person in any other way. At that time, I had yet to abandon my friend whose dad had cancer, but there were plenty of other ruined relationships that I could have been referencing—I routinely disposed of people once their burden to me exceeded their utility. I told my coworker that one of these disposed-of people had accused me of lacking altruism. Perhaps, I had conceded. But perhaps this thing that I allegedly lacked—altruism—was nothing more than garbled thinking that did no more than freeze people in a moment of indecision, whereas I was free to cut off entanglements at will. My co-worker nodded sympathetically.

One day, not long after our altruism conversation, we were discussing how to behave appropriately in situations in which I was expected to comfort anguished loved ones. Perhaps she could see that I seemed clueless, because she asked me then if I thought I might be a sociopath. I remember not knowing how to answer and having to look the word up, not sure exactly what a sociopath was or why she would think I was one. *Socio-* for *social* or *society*, *-pathy* for a morbid affliction or disease: a disorder of social conscience. That did sound familiar.

I was not offended. I was already well accustomed to the idea that there was something pointedly different about me that could not be altered. I realized early on that other people did not treat their lives as if it were a complicated game in which all events, things, and people could be measured with mathematical precision toward achieving their own personal satisfaction and pleasure. Somewhat more recently, I also noticed that other people felt *guilt,* a special kind of regret that did not arise from negative consequences but from some amorphous moral dictate that had taken root in them from consciousness. They felt bad in a way that I never felt when they hurt others, as if the hurt they had caused was so cosmically connected to the goodness of the universe as to reverberate back to them. These things I had pretended to feel for many years, had attempted assiduously to mimic the manifestations of, but had never actually felt in my life. I was more curious than anything. If there was a label for who I was, then maybe I could learn something more about myself. In fact, I had no trouble recognizing myself in the descriptions I found in my research.

It turned out that my officemate had been acquainted

with a man she discovered was a sociopath. Rather than live out the sob story of the con artist's innocent victim, she had maintained a deep and enduring friendship with him. In retrospect, her willingness to regard me as a human being despite her firm belief that I was a sociopath offered me the possibility that I could be understood and accepted as I was. She was proof that not all people with consciences and empathy were appalled by the existence of people like me.

I was actually glad that there was a word for it, that I wasn't the only one like this. It must be a similar feeling to that of people who discover for themselves that they are gay or transgendered: in their bones, they'd known it all along.

Years had passed from that tentative self-diagnosis to my period of introspection after being fired. Once the word *sociopath* had entered my consciousness and my initial satisfaction with finding a label had faded, I had treated it as an unimportant oddity, like an interesting but irrelevant quirk, until eventually I forgot it. But as my life crumbled around me, I knew that I couldn't keep living like I had been before, acknowledging that I was different but ignoring the differences. I was so desperate for answers that I had begun seeing a therapist, but she was nothing more than a thing for me to toy with, and even then, she was too expensive for the limited satisfaction our sessions gave me. But through those therapy sessions, I had remembered that summer internship and that casual diagnosis of "sociopath." I sensed there were answers about myself there, so I started reading a book that just happened to be available in its entirety online, written by the father of the modern concept of psychopathy, Dr. Hervey Cleckley.

Cleckley, in his groundbreaking book *The Mask of Sanity*, first published in 1941, presented the profile of the personality he called the psychopath, but which we now commonly refer to as the sociopath. Cleckley explained that a psychopath was extremely difficult to diagnose, because his mental faculties were fully intact, as was his ability to function in society as a seemingly normal human being, even a particularly successful one. Cleckley wrote:

> *Not only is the psychopath rational and his thinking free of delusions, but he also appears to react with normal emotions. His ambitions are discussed with what appears to be healthy enthusiasm. His convictions impress even the skeptical observer as firm and binding. He seems to respond with adequate feelings to another's interest in him and, as he discusses his wife, his children, or his parents, he is likely to be judged a man of warm human responses, capable of full devotion and loyalty.*

According to Cleckley, psychopaths are antisocials who excel at seeming social—seeming to feel, desire, hope, and love like everyone else. They exist virtually indistinguishable among society. In fact, the psychopath excels in many ways that others do not. Cleckley's psychopath is uncommonly charming and witty. He is unflappable and eloquent, keeping his cool under pressure. Under this "mask of sanity," however, is a liar, a manipulator, a person who disregards his obligations with little to no sense of responsibility. He is exciting because he is impulsive, whimsical, and prone to making the same mistake multiple times. His narcissism keeps him from forming any real emotional bonds, and he tends to be promiscuous. His own emotional world is mostly a poor imitation of natural emotions. Cleckley acknowledged that this unique suite of personality traits could suit the psychopath equally well to a career in business as to one in crime.

Nowhere else have I recognized the sociopath inside me more than in Cleckley's clinical profiles, more than half a century old. From his observations of hundreds of patients, Cleckley distilled what he believed to be sixteen key behavioral characteristics that defined psychopathy. Most of these factors are still used today to diagnose sociopaths/psychopaths and others with antisocial disorders. They include the following:

* Superficial charm and good intelligence
* Absence of delusions and other signs of irrational thinking
* Absence of nervousness or psychoneurotic manifestations
* Unreliability
* Untruthfulness and insincerity
* Lack of remorse and shame
* Inadequately motivated antisocial behavior
* Poor judgment and failure to learn by experience
* Pathologic egocentricity and incapacity for love
* General poverty in major affective reactions
* Specific loss of insight
* Unresponsiveness in general interpersonal relations
* Fantastic and uninviting behavior with drink and sometimes without
* Suicide threats rarely carried out
* Sex life impersonal, trivial, and poorly integrated
* Failure to follow any life plan

If you've ever recognized yourself in a horoscope and thought, "Hey, maybe there is something to this astrology business," then you understand my encounter with Cleckley's book. Not everything is quite right, but many things are spot-on, and in general, it's frighteningly accurate. My lack of life direction, my cold treatment of friends, my inability to focus on my job—the psychological pattern underpinning many of my problems was laid bare. I was particularly amazed by his descriptions of his patients, some of whom I shared so much in common with that I felt he could have been writing about me. There was one woman in particular, Anna, whose description seemed like a fictionalized version of myself:

> *There was nothing spectacular about her, but when she came into the office you felt that she merited the attention she at once obtained. She was, you could say without straining a point, rather good-looking, but she was not nearly so good-looking as most women would have to be to make a comparable impression. She spoke in the crisp, fluttery cadence of the British, consistently sounding her "r's" and "ing's" and regularly saying "been" as they do in London. For a girl born and raised in Georgia, such speaking could suggest affectation. Yet it was the very opposite of this quality that contributed a great deal to the pleasing effect she invariably produced on those who met her. Naive has so many inapplicable connotations it is hardly the word to use in reference to this urbane and gracious presence, yet it is difficult to think of our first meeting without that very word coming to mind, with its overtones of freshness, artlessness, and candor.*

It's clear that Cleckley was taken by her. I love the way he describes her idiosyncrasies: the accent, her artlessness, her eternal youthfulness, her attractiveness that seems to be something more than mere beauty, her intelligence, and her charm. These describe me as well. She loves *The Brothers Karamazov,* but Cleckley later discusses how Anna does not have the highbrow tastes and prejudices that accompany the typical "intellectual" of her education and breeding, treating gossip magazines with the same interest as the music of Russian composers. Again, he could have been writing about me. Cleckley goes on to tell about how Anna quite sincerely taught Sunday school, volunteered for the Red Cross, and engaged in haphazard same-sex liaisons, one time with a nurse after being universally adored during a hospital stay. There were incredible parallels to my own life, from such seemingly insignificant ones like teaching Sunday school or being a model hospital patient to relatively more prominent ones like fluid sexuality. I was floored.

Cleckley does clearly lay out why he believes that Anna fits his criteria, primarily because of her lack of remorse about her lascivious lifestyle, but it's clear that she is not just a sum of points on a checklist to him. She is a person. And it wasn't the checklist that I identified so strongly with upon reading Cleckley's book; it was the people. Even Cleckley acknowledged that the checklist was just a gross generalization of why these people seemed so similar to each other—despite their vast differences in education, background, socioeconomic status, criminal history, etc.—and yet so different from the rest of the world. I could quibble with whether or not I met a criterion like "unreliability," but I could not deny the remarkable similarities that I shared with Cleckley's patients.

Cleckley's book was widely popular, circulating beyond a purely academic or medical audience. He edited the volume several times, making efforts to create as exhaustive a profile as possible of the modern-day psychopath. Cleckley

understood that psychopaths and sociopaths, while sometimes or even often engaged in extremely antisocial acts,
could also live lives completely undetected, adapting to their
surroundings well enough to pass as normal, even to become
contributing members of society.

Because Cleckley realized that there were sociopaths in
the world who either do not engage in criminal behavior or are
too clever to ever get caught, what began as a study of solely
male patients in mental institutions became a much larger
volume that included women, adolescents, and people who
had never been institutionalized. Many of his later subjects,
like Anna, had learned to live relatively normal lives within the
general populace. From my own experience, I was sure that,
had Cleckley peered into the classrooms of today's law schools
and offices of mega law firms, he would have found plenty of
viable test subjects.

Now that I knew that I was not alone, that there were people out there much like me, I wanted to find out more about us.

*He gazed upon the mirth around him, as if he could not
participate therein. Apparently, the light laughter of the
fair only attracted his attention, that he might by a look
quell it, and throw fear into those breasts where thought-
lessness reigned. Those who felt this sensation of awe,
could not explain whence it arose: some attributed it to
the dead grey eye, which, fixing upon the object's face,
did not seem to penetrate, and at one glance to pierce
through to the inward workings of the heart; but fell
upon the cheek with a leaden ray that weighed upon
the skin it could not pass. His peculiarities caused him
to be invited to every house; all wished to see him, and
those who had been accustomed to violent excitement,*

and now felt the weight of ennui, were pleased at having something in their presence capable of engaging their attention.

—JOHN WILLIAM POLIDORI, *The Vampyre*

In 1819, John William Polidori wrote a novella called *The Vampyre,* inspired by a fragment by Lord Byron, which would spark a vampire craze across nineteenth-century Europe and influence Bram Stoker and the modern vampire genre. The title character of Polidori's novella was based on the wayward Byron himself. The vampire enters London high society and beguiles all who cross his path with his mysterious and contrary manners. Accompanying a young gentleman companion southward through Rome and Greece, he seduces and murders young women, unbeknownst to his companion, only to die himself from an apparent murder. A year later, however, the vampire reappears in London, where he seduces and marries his companion's sister, leaving her drained of blood on her wedding bed.

At once beautiful and treacherous, the vampire occupies the unique position of the appealing monster. He is far from deranged or wild and, in fact, his manners are superior to those of the people he meets. His demeanor is uncanny and yet beguiling, his eyes hollow but intoxicating. His apparent deficits attract his victims and his peculiarities engage them, while he views them as nothing more than objects. The vampire does not seek his lonely existence; he merely lives it out to its fullest measure, unable to function any other way. He drinks blood because it fulfills him; he toys with people because it amuses him. His soul cannot rest.

The gothic vampire is the sociopath writ large, charismatic and sophisticated, a predator walking among us undetected. His myth dates back to the medieval period and is rooted in Slavic spirituality, based on a clear distinction between the body and the soul. An unclean soul gave rise to the vampire, whose continuing existence was both unnatural and interminable.

Sociopaths have been around for a long time, always at the margins. We exist in every culture. According to a 1976 anthropological study by Jane Murphy, members of the Yoruba tribe in Africa called cold souls *arankan*, "which means a person who always goes his own way regardless of others, who is uncooperative, full of malice, and bullheaded." The Yupik-speaking Inuit knew antisocial members of their tribe as *kunlangeta*, of whom it was said "his mind knows what to do but he does not do it"; he is someone who "repeatedly lies and cheats and steals things and ... takes sexual advantage of many women—someone who does not pay attention to reprimands and who is always being brought to the elders for punishment." This concept of an individual who has the mental capacity to understand social norms but refuses to follow them is the key to the clinical diagnosis for modern-day sociopathy.

So, while it's clear that people like me have existed throughout the many cultures of the world, our modern society likes to apply clear labels to people: Are you a sociopath, or something else? In the science fiction film *Blade Runner*, the sociopath analogues are the replicants, organic androids who have escaped to Earth and are hunted by Harrison Ford in his nuclear-dusty postapocalyptic world. So human-seeming are the replicants that they can be detected only through a set of emotionally provocative questions. In the movie, Harrison Ford can't resist the charms of Sean Young's porcelain skin and perfectly heart-shaped lips, even knowing she is a manufactured thing—that she can feel no empathy despite what he can see in her big, soulful eyes.

I remember watching the movie as a young girl, captivated by Sean Young's quivering poise and futuristic office attire. Even then I felt sure I could survive pretty well in their harsh world, that all the scattered neon and miscellaneous steam would make it a hard enough place to live that all the weaklings would be relegated to subsistence living, and the strong ones like me would thrive. I imagined wheeling and dealing in pidgin Chinese, darting through alleyways in my dinged-up hovercraft. The irony, of course, is that in my adulthood I would willingly subject myself to very similar diagnostic questions—that I too would be clinically outed by tests designed to measure my lack of humanity.

The *Blade Runner* example is an interesting comparator because the emphasis is on identification, not diagnosis. The replicants are truly "other" and presumed to be subhuman; therefore there are no ethical constraints on what becomes of them, despite evidence that their internal worlds may have been just as rich as those of the humans. Similarly, even health professionals like Martha Stout, Harvard Medical School faculty member and author of *The Sociopath Next Door,* speak in terms of "identifying" sociopaths, as opposed to diagnosing. The message seems clear: These people *are* sociopaths, they aren't people who have sociopathy. Diagnosis is for people for whom there is a treatment. Because there is no known effective treatment for sociopaths, there is just the question of what to do with the sociopath problem. In *Blade Runner,* society had come to a definitive decision of what fate would befall its empathy-free creations.

The sociopath problem for our society is, how do we keep sociopaths from acting in antisocial ways? Before society can even begin to discuss solutions to that problem, they need a reliable way to identify sociopaths. Before psychologists can identify them, however, they must be able to understand them. And to be able to understand them, they must be able to identify them. One psychologist has illustrated the tautology in the following way: "Why has this man done these terrible things? Because he is a psychopath. And how do you know that he is a psychopath? Because he has done these terrible things."

It's a classic chicken-and-egg dilemma that has prompted countless criticisms of the most popular diagnostic criteria. All diagnostic tools are based on the observable traits of people who have been diagnosed as sociopaths, which, apart from being rather circular, introduces the risk of biases that might skew which traits get included or not included. Of course there must be some starting place. Cleckley and others observed that some traits occurred more commonly in his patients than in the general populace. Once that recurring group of traits had a name, researchers could try to figure out if they all had a common cause, if they were related to other identifiable groups of traits, how many people had that group of traits, and what kinds of things those people got up to compared to the larger population. But Cleckley was well aware that his checklist was just his own poor approximation of the essence of sociopathy, and consequently was not infallible or even all-inclusive—a humility that I sometimes feel is lacking with researchers of sociopathy.

The current primary tool for identifying psychopaths (and, by association, sociopaths) is the PCL-R (Psychopathy Checklist–Revised), developed by Dr. Robert D. Hare, professor emeritus of forensic psychology at the University of British Columbia and generally considered the primary authority on criminal psychopathy. "Science cannot progress without reliable and accurate measurement of what it is you are trying to study," Hare explains. With a research assistant he compiled a list of twenty traits that he noticed recurring among the prison population he was studying: lack of empathy and remorse, megalomania, manipulation, charm, self-interestedness, impulsivity, proficiency at lying, along with criminal-specific traits such as juvenile delinquency, revocation of conditional release, and criminal versatility. He instructed other psychologists giving the assessment to award two points if a trait was present, one if they were unsure or it applied somewhat, and zero if it wasn't. The test was reliable, in that repeat assessments resulted in approximately the same score, but its validity has been heavily criticized.

Validity is a measure of how well a diagnostic tests what it is meant to test—in this situation, how accurately the PCL-R identifies psychopaths. The PCL-R has been criticized for being exclusively based on the prison population. Hare himself has admitted that it was done solely for convenience: "Prisoners are easy. They like meeting researchers. It breaks up the monotony of their day. But CEOs, politicians . . ." In a widely publicized scandal, Hare threatened to sue two psychologists who warned in a paper that the checklist was increasingly being mistaken for a complete definition of psychopathy, which is a broader personality construct that includes deceitfulness, impulsivity, and recklessness, but not necessarily physical aggression or illegal acts. The authors contended that Dr. Hare's checklist warps that concept by overemphasizing criminal behavior. Their article reflects the growing consensus that sociopathy does not equate to criminality. Nor has Hare defended why each trait on the checklist is scored exactly the same. It's not immediately obvious why a trait like lack of empathy should earn exactly as many points as something seemingly less significant like superficial charm. There is also the question of what defines this (or any) personality disorder, a person's actions or her interior motivations. While a case history of bad decision-making is easy to evaluate, it's harder to truly understand another person's modes of thought.

There are significant differences of opinion among academics and clinicians about whether psychopathy and sociopathy are diagnosable conditions at all. The good folks at the American Psychiatric Association who put together the *DSM* have decided to exclude both terms, despite movements by researchers for revisions in favor of antisocial personality disorder, or ASPD, a diagnosis based on observed behavioral patterns. The World Health Organization's *International Statistical Classification of Diseases and Related Health Problems* describes a similar diagnosis it calls dissocial personality disorder but also does not include sociopathy. ASPD and sociopathy do not share all of the same characteristics; ASPD focuses primarily on the criminality of behavior, rather than the internal thought processes of a sociopath, since thought processes are difficult to ascertain, particularly with unwilling, institutionalized subjects. For instance, although I consider myself a high-functioning sociopath because of my weak sense of empathy, my failure to conform to social norms, and my predilection to manipulate others, I could not be legitimately diagnosed with ASPD.

Further confusing the diagnostic problem of sociopathy is the overlap in behavioral characteristics between sociopathy and other personality disorders such as narcissism, like enhanced self-regard and diminished empathy, as well as some social developmental disorders like Asperger's that are also seen on the autism spectrum.

In his book *Forensic Psychology: A Very Short Introduction,* David Canter, a psychology professor at the University of Huddersfield, warns that "we should not be seduced into thinking that these diagnoses are anything other than summary descriptions of the people in question" and echoes the concern that they are "actually moral judgments masquerading as medical explanations." The first line in the preface of Robert Hare's book reads: "Psychopaths are social predators who charm, manipulate, and ruthlessly plow their way through life, leaving a road trail of broken hearts, shattered expectations, and empty wallets." So you can imagine what side of the fence he's on. Still, these diagnoses are being used, and important decisions like whether or not to deny someone parole are made primarily on the basis of them.

Unlike the problematic definitions of psychological diagnoses, neuroscience may offer some more clarity. Recent brain scan research and other studies suggest a link between these characteristics and something more "definitive" and unique about a sociopath's brain. But it would be a mistake to conflate the list of characteristics of a sociopath with the definition of *sociopath,* just as it would be a mistake to assume that all Catholics would share the exact same traits—or that having a certain list of traits is what makes people Catholic. The diagnosis of sociopathy is useful, but only to the extent that people understand its limitations. The main limitation is that we cannot identify it by its root source; we know it only by its symptoms and characteristics. This is somewhat disappointing to people. It would be easy to think that I am bad because I was treated badly or raised badly, that I grew up in an environment devoid of love and filled with enmity. But I didn't suffer the kind of outrageous abuses that so many people do. Mine were of the ordinary variety, maybe some benign neglect. When people ask me whether I had a bad childhood, I tell them that it was relatively unremarkable. We know from twin studies that there is a strong genetic component to socio-pathic traits, and we also know that sociopaths have different brains from most people. But just because they have differ-ent brains does not mean that their unusual brains are what makes them act differently. The fact that they act differently could actually be affecting their brain circuitry. Similarly, just because a sociopath's brain is different does not mean that is what is causing the sociopathy—that could be, according to Hare, a "by-product of some other environmental or genetic factor commonly found among psychopaths."

We don't know the root cause, but we also know there isn't a cure for this disorder, not that we would necessarily want one, for reasons that I hope will be clear upon finishing this book. Dr. Cleckley observed and counseled sociopaths as a psychologist and professor at the Medical College of Georgia. He wrestled with how to treat sociopathic patients and crimi-nals, whom he believed to be deeply disturbed but essentially intractable. In the preface to his final revision of *The Mask of Sanity,* which he wrote at the very end of his life, Cleckley ex-plained that he had been unable to discover an effective treat-ment but was heartened by the belief that he had contributed to the understanding of sociopathy—and especially that the relatives and loved ones of sociopaths could have some expla-nation for the unusual behavior of their beloveds. Indeed, he cited at length instances of incurable patients—individuals who had all the resources and support in the world to get bet-ter but ended up maiming significant others and committing other manner of misdeeds. To him we were a lost cause.

Cleckley was not alone in this belief. Recent estimates of the criminal recidivism rate for sociopaths is approximately double that of nonsociopathic criminals, and it is triple for violent crimes. Even the Yoruba and the Inuit tribes believed that these antisocial individuals could not be changed. The only solution was to neutralize or marginalize them, or as one Inuit purportedly told Murphy, the anthropologist, "Somebody would have pushed him off the ice when nobody else was looking."

Today psychologists and criminologists are occupied with the same conundrum with which the Inuit and Yoruba dealt through discreet homicide—what to do with sociopaths who simply cannot be trusted and who do not belong. In Great Britain, authorities have given sociopathic criminals life sentences solely on the basis of their sociopathy. In America, diagnosed sociopaths have been committed indefinitely in psychiatric facilities with no hope of release, since their doctors assume they cannot be cured. Take the story of Robert Dixon, who received a fifteen-years-to-life sentence for accessory to murder as the getaway driver to an armed robbery gone wrong. Twenty-six years into his sentence, he was up for parole. As part of the assessment of whether he was likely to reoffend, he was given a test that indicated that he was a sociopath. "I remember reading the report and feeling heartbroken," Dixon's lawyer recalls, "because I knew no matter how hard I worked from that day forward, that when I brought him back to the board, we were going to get denied."

While in his first edition Cleckley asserted that sociopaths should be considered psychotics due to their deep inability to function in society, he revised his position in later editions when he realized that this characterization stood in the way of making them responsible for their criminal acts. He faced a crisis; he never believed that sociopaths were crazy, or "manic," in the sense that others of his patients were. But he felt that they were just as troubled, just as deficient or wrongly equipped to live, and so should be kept apart from everyone else. He was concerned that dangerous sociopaths were not committed in mental institutions often enough, because an overemphasis on verbal intelligence and rationality in determining whether a person was mentally competent for the purposes of confinement weighed in favor of sociopaths.

But depriving the sociopath of freedom purely on the basis of her psychiatric diagnosis is fraught with questions of moral significance. Social scientists worry about control and maintenance—how do we deal with these strange creatures, they ask themselves, in a manner that does not make monsters of the rest of us? Can a person's lack of conscience justify a deprivation of his freedom? Society commits the insane to confinement by reasoning that they present harm to themselves and others. I've heard the argument that sociopaths cannot function in the outside world, so there is nothing that society can do but take the drastic step of separating the sociopaths from the rest of the world. But sociopaths *can* function; we just function differently. It's not like we're biting off our own hands or jumping off of buildings in the belief that we can fly. We're not crazy. And the truth is that we are sometimes quite successful. It is just that we live, think, and make decisions in a way that some people find loathsome and most find disturbingly amoral. What do you do to people you simply don't like?

The role that a diagnosis of sociopathy should play in criminal sentencing is an admittedly thorny issue. The legal standard for an insanity plea is that the perpetrator must not be able to distinguish between right and wrong. Sociopaths actually know what society considers right and wrong most of the time, they just don't feel an emotional compulsion to conform their behavior to societal standards. The debate is whether this faulty wiring makes them more culpable, less culpable, or equally culpable compared to a similarly offending nonsociopath. Kent Kiehl, a prominent researcher who specializes in scanning the brains of sociopaths in prisons, suggested treating them the same as people with low IQs, who may know that their actions are wrong but lack sufficient "brakes" on their violent impulses.

Furthermore, there is the question of effectiveness of punishment. Cleckley asserted that treating sociopaths as ordinary criminals—and simply imprisoning them when they had committed a wrong—did not work, since punishment does little to deter them. Of course, the deterring effect of imprisonment on anyone is questionable. I doubt that empathetic people who commit crimes of passion are deterred by the thought of imprisonment, and I wonder how much it works on lifelong drug dealers born into gangs and poverty who thus have few alternatives. However, scientific research has been conducted to show that sociopaths are particularly nonresponsive to negative consequences, and I have found this to be true in my own life. The threat of punishment at home or school only served as a challenge to figure out how to circumvent the consequences when I did what I wanted to do anyway. I didn't fear the punishment, I just saw it as an inconvenience to work around.

Cleckley's intuition that sociopaths do not respond normally to negative consequences was validated by a famous study by Hare in which he administered mild electrical shocks to both psychopaths and a normal control group. A timer ticking down preceded the shock. Normal people would show signs of anxiety as the timer got closer to the shock, anticipating the slight pain. Psychopaths were remarkably unfazed by the shock and did not express a comparable increase in anxiety as the timer ticked down.

This blithe reaction to negative events may be due to the excessive dopamine that characterizes the sociopathic brain.

Vanderbilt University researchers have linked the excess dopamine in sociopaths to a hypersensitive reward system in the brain that releases as much as four times the normal amount of dopamine in response to either a perceived gain of money upon the successful completion of a task, or chemical stimulants. These researchers suggested that the overactive reward system is to blame for a sociopath's impulsive, risk-seeking behavior because "these individuals appear to have such a strong draw to reward—to the carrot—that it overwhelms the sense of risk or concern about the stick."

I have my own doubts about this hypothesis, though. A hypersensitive reward system could explain why sociopaths are allegedly sex fiends, at least compared to the rest of the population. It could also explain why you'll see them at the top of their field, professionally speaking. Sociopaths are probably contributing to society in all sorts of random ways in order to trigger an enormous amount of dopamine flooding through their brains. Risk takers, though? Maybe we are, but I don't think it's because of excess dopamine, particularly because an earlier study at Vanderbilt showed that *low* amounts of dopamine were highly correlated with risk taking and drug abuse. From personal experience, I feel like my risk-seeking behavior stems from a low fear response or a lack of natural anxiety in potentially dangerous, traumatic, or stressful situations.

I do all sorts of risky and often stupid activities, particularly when you consider that I am a financially secure white-collar professional with a brilliant IQ who was raised devoutly religious in a stable middle-class home. When I was young, I did the usual reckless teenage stuff: mosh pits, hitchhiking in developing countries, being towed in a shopping cart from the back of a truck, fistfights, etc. I might have grown out of some of the more childish thrill-seeking activities, but I never quite grew out of the inability to learn from experiences.

One summer I lost all of my savings trading high-risk options. Not only were the options risky, I took an incredibly risky approach to them—holding when I should have sold and putting all of my eggs in one basket. Even after many failed trades, I still took unnecessary gambles. I knew objectively that I was losing a lot of money, but I couldn't make myself feel the pain of it in a way that seemed to matter. Though it doesn't seem related, I don't use knives. The risk of injury never sinks in, even with such a mundane tool. I've cut myself many times, lopping off chunks of skin or cutting down to the bone and requiring stitches, but I can never force myself to be more careful, so now I just don't use them.

I've always loved to bike in cities, partly because it's so dangerous. If a car starts creeping into my lane, I will punch at it or use my portable tire pump to swing at it. If a car cuts me off, I will follow it until I catch up, then dart in front and come to a skidding halt, forcing them to slam on their brakes. I'm sure it's incredibly dangerous for me to do this, and really only for me, but it also freaks the hell out of them. And I don't really care for my safety enough to change my behavior. It's not that I'm being irrational. It's that suffering the consequences of something rarely involves actual "suffering." Maybe there is a small thrill in taunting drivers or risking my life savings, but mainly it's that I just don't feel sufficient anxiety in these situations warning me to be more careful.

I can't tell you how many times I have gotten food poisoning from eating rotten and questionable food, but I never seem to learn my lesson. A few years ago I woke up naked on the floor of a YMCA shower. I couldn't remember how I had gotten there, but I am sure it was something stupid. People who know their limits don't end up passed out naked in a YMCA. I don't have the off switch in my brain telling me when to stop—no natural sense of boundaries alerting me to when I am on the verge of taking something too far. When I do these things, it doesn't feel as if I'm so overwhelmed by the carrot; it's more like I am so unimpressed by the stick.

I have always lived in the worst neighborhoods. Rent is cheap and I figure there's no need for me to pay a safety premium if I have health insurance. It drives my friends and family crazy, but it makes me easy to shop for when it comes to birthdays and Christmas: pepper spray, dead bolts, automobile theft deterrents, etc. Just after college I lived next door to a drug-infested Chicago housing project, taking night jogs through the neighborhood with headphones blaring loud enough to cover the sounds of gunshots, which were pretty loud. Recently I walked in on my apartment getting burglarized for the second time—the first time was just a few days after I had moved in. When it's not getting burglarized, I get visitors banging on my door at all hours of the night. (I think one of my neighbors might be a drug dealer and these people are mistaking my apartment for his. Just idle conjecture.)

Perhaps my risk taking can be best seen in terms of my affection for and mishaps with motor vehicles. I love cars. I feel invincible behind the wheel, and I often put myself and others at risk because I didn't think through the consequences of my decisions. Once when my brakes started going out, I opted to drive the car into the mechanic's rather than pay for a tow, even though I had driven much too long on the brakes, until they were all but useless. It was rainy that day and I had to drive several miles on a steady decline. Making matters worse, when I got close to the shop, I saw that I would have to cross a bridge over train tracks, which rose and fell dramatically over the distance of about a block on a busy four-lane main thoroughfare. By the time I was at the bottom of the bridge without brakes, I was going at least forty-five miles an hour, much too fast for traffic that was slowing at a red stoplight up ahead. Making a split-section decision, I jerked the wheel to the left and power-slid across two lanes of opposing traffic, across both lanes of a parallel frontage road, and finally jolted to a stop when the right rear and then front wheel made contact with the curb on the far side of the street. I looked up at the addresses on the buildings and noticed that I was just south of the driveway to the mechanic's, so I crawled into the parking lot and used the parking brake to come to a full stop, all to the gaping stares of onlookers.

Of course I was pretty pleased with myself at the time. It's nice to have proof of your seeming invincibility. But if it had gone horribly wrong—had my car slid off the bridge and exploded on impact—I would have felt much the same about it. As long as I keep surviving, I seem okay. It's not that bad things don't happen to me; they do. But I just don't feel that bad about them. Maybe in the moment I feel some regret or anxiety, but it's quickly forgotten and the world seems ripe with promise again. I'm not superhuman, not entirely immune to sorrow or pain. I just have an extremely robust sense of optimism and self-worth that keeps me looking at the world through rose-colored glasses.

Although I am largely immune to misery, my siblings and friends aren't. They sometimes hate me for my recklessness and the third-party externalities it causes. I vividly remember trying to coax my frozen hands to operate a tire jack in a snowdrift on the side of the road, replacing the tire that I had "fixed" myself a couple days earlier while my oldest brother spat epithets in my direction. After one burglary too many, my friend begged me to move to a different neighborhood—for peace of mind. When I assured her I was not bothered by the experience, she pressed on, saying, "Peace of mind for your loved ones, then." It's hard to find any incentive to change, though. I have always managed to get out of scrapes, whether that meant begging for money from strangers, pleading for mercy from police, or spinning webs of lies to cover my tracks. Because I was always willing to go double or nothing and because my unlucky streaks never lasted for long, I always managed to come out okay. And precautions are expensive, either in terms of actual costs for safety or opportunity costs for risks that you could have taken but didn't. I understand that for a lot of people precautions are worth the money for, as my friend put it, "peace of mind." But my mind is almost always at peace no matter what I do. Which is why I never bothered to be more careful.

After a number of years of living as a self-diagnosed sociopath, even running a blog for sociopaths, I decided to get formally assessed. At first I wasn't inclined to seek a professional diagnosis. I had read all of the criticisms of the diagnostic criteria. I trusted my own self-assessment as much as I would anybody who happened to have a degree in psychology. However, eventually I decided that the lack of formal diagnosis might lead some readers to discount my point of view. Without a formal diagnosis, how could they know that I was an actual sociopath? I figured that if I was going to risk outing myself as a member of one of the most hated subclasses of humans, I might as well ensure that people believed me.

My diagnostician was Dr. John Edens, PhD, a professor at Texas A & M and a leading researcher in the field of sociopathy, whose opinions have recently been solicited for articles in the *New York Times* and on NPR, among other media outlets. Dr. Edens worried that the test he intended to give me was strongly wedded to Hare's criminal-oriented model of sociopathy. Given that I had no documented criminal record, Dr. Edens felt that the test score in my case might be somewhat questionable and might in fact understate my true level of sociopathic traits.

I underwent a form of the PCL-R, the PCL:SV (Psychopathy Checklist: Screening Version), among other tests. The PCL:SV, as the name implies, is a checklist of criteria historically associated with Hare's conceptualization of psychopathy. It was developed to assess for psychopathic features while relying less on the extensive file and criminal-history data required to complete the PCL-R. The PCL:SV is comprised of twelve individual criteria scored from 0 to 2 points, which are summed to form a total score from 0 to 24. The test is divided equally into two parts. Part 1 includes the personality traits typically associated with sociopathy, including lack of remorse and empathy for others, and interpersonal behaviors, including deceitfulness and grandiosity. Part 2 taps more socially deviant behaviors and activities, including irresponsibility, impulsivity, and adult antisocial behavior.

During the interview, I was asked about my significant history of impulsive, aggressive, and generally irresponsible conduct—things like fistfights and theft—that, while perhaps not having resulted in criminal charges, easily could have led to various encounters with the criminal justice system under different life circumstances. Dr. Edens noted in my report that these actions appear to have been almost entirely for thrill-seeking purposes rather than for any type of economic gain or other instrumental purpose. He noted: "Whether Ms. Thomas's lack of police contact has been due to her successfully manipulating her way out of 'jams,' various protective factors evident in her life (e.g., high intelligence and educational success, generally supportive family structure, and other socio-economic advantages), random luck, or some combination of all of the above is unclear at this time." I talked about my family, my reckless teenage years, my inability to stick with my jobs after law school, and my subsequent self-analysis that had led me to his office, telling Dr. Edens stories that I had all but forgotten.

I scored a total of 19 out of 24 on the PCL:SV. There are no sharp diagnostic cutoffs, but according to the manual, scores of 18 and higher "offer a strong indication of psychopathy." I got a 12 for part 1 (personality) and a 7 for part 2 (antisocial behavior). Dr. Edens remarked: "Notably, 12 is the maximum score one can obtain on Part 1 of this rating scale and indicates the presence of pronounced affective and interpersonal characteristics typically evidenced by highly psychopathic individuals."

This linear grading system is in line with recent evidence that, in Robert Hare's words, "psychopathy is dimensional (i.e., more or less), not categorical (i.e., either or)." Those with higher scores are more outwardly antisocial, but even those with lower scores "may present significant problems for those around them, just as those with blood pressure readings below an accepted threshold for hypertension may be at medical risk." So Dr. Edens also had me take several other personality tests designed to look for sociopathic personalities. The most specific to sociopathy was probably the Psychopathic Personality Inventory–Revised (PPI-R), a self-report questionnaire developed to tap various personality characteristics historically thought to be indicative of psychopathic personality. This scale provides both a total score indicative of a global index of psychopathic traits as well as eight subscales that assess more specific traits. Dr. Edens reported: "Perhaps more notably, Ms. Thomas's results were beyond the 99th percentile for any sub-sample within the PPI-R's normative database, regardless of age or gender. Needless to say, these findings are highly consistent with a psychopathic personality structure."

Other tests included the revised NEO Personality Inventory, also a self-report questionnaire, for which Dr. Edens noted that my profile mirrored that of "the prototypical psychopathic personality among females." Finally, I took the Personality Assessment Inventory, for which I scored very high for traits like egocentrism and sensation-seeking characteristics, interpersonal dominance, verbal aggression, and excessive self-esteem, as well as very low scores on measures tapping negative affective experiences (e.g., phobias, traumatic stressors, depressive symptoms), interpersonal nurturance, and stressful life events.

I liked Dr. Edens. He seemed like a reasonable person—a genuinely caring person. At one point during our interview I thought that he might cry, he seemed so distressed on my behalf. I don't remember what we were discussing, perhaps some story about my father beating me. I think if anything he was worried for me—worried about what a diagnosis like "sociopath" would mean for me in my life. Of course it's hard for me to worry about things like that. If I can't manage to care about my own health and safety, I'm not likely to care about the potential fallout in my professional and personal life from being officially diagnosed a sociopath. He must have realized that too. Maybe that's why he seemed troubled.

We talked about how none of the tests are designed for someone like me, who seeks the diagnosis of her own free will and choice. Criminals have an incentive in an institutional setting to lie and distort their self-assessments, particularly in situations like a parole hearing. The diagnostic tests were designed to be administered with a healthy dose of skepticism. But what to do with an individual who seems to have an incentive to be diagnosed a sociopath? Several times he noted how I could possibly be tricking him by lying to him to make myself seem more sociopathic than I was, but he had to admit that lying for the purpose of self-aggrandizement was also consistent with sociopathy. Still, I wasn't really tempted to lie. It would have seemed silly to lie. I was genuinely looking for answers and insight—as much as you can get from a three-hour appointment with a stranger.

Whenever suspected sociopaths write to me and ask whether they should get tested, I almost always tell them no. It's just too risky. Because there is no real treatment, the only upside to a formal diagnosis is peace of mind, that you know who you are. The downside is having a major blemish on your record that could affect every aspect of your life, should it fall into the wrong hands. Even Dr. Edens showed an overabundance of caution in sanitizing the e-mailed version of the report, lest the "Internet gremlins" intercept it.

At the end of our several hourlong sessions Dr. Edens asked me, "What would you think if I told you that you are not a sociopath?" It was a question I had asked myself many times before. What if I just stopped the blog? What if I stopped trying to find answers in new psychological research? "I don't know, I guess I would be annoyed that I spent all day traveling and talking to you for nothing?" I replied. He laughed. When it was time to leave he told me how much I owed him for his time. I had forgotten my checkbook. We both joked at how that was a likely story from a sociopath.

I left his office having no clue what he would put in the

report. But I knew we shared a perception that sociopathy was understudied, overvillainized, and an important issue to get right. When I got the report back a couple weeks later it confirmed what I had suspected for a while—both in terms of my own diagnosis and also understanding better the inconclusiveness and subjectivity of the modern psychiatric diagnostic process.

A final question regarding detection is, why do we need to detect sociopaths? When I was growing up, my grandfather raised chickens and other animals on his ranch. Each chicken laid approximately one egg a day, so if he had seven chickens at the time, we would expect to see seven eggs. My grandfather was always very careful to feed the chickens and collect the eggs every day and taught me to be equally diligent when I stayed with him. If not, he said, the chickens might turn to eating their own eggs, and once a chicken has a taste for egg, it will continue eating eggs and have to be killed. I don't know if it is really true that there is no cure for a cannibalistic chicken, but that is what he told me to scare me into feeding the chickens and collecting their eggs regularly. One time while I was gone, he got sick and couldn't visit the chicken coop every day to feed them and collect their eggs. When he finally did get out there, he saw broken eggshells everywhere, the evidence of egg eating. Ever after, there were always one or two eggs missing from or pecked over in the daily collections. At least one chicken had gotten a taste for egg and wasn't willing to give it up, even with the renewed ample food source.

"How are we going to find out which one of them it is?" I asked.

"What do you mean?"

"We need to kill the chicken that is eating the other eggs."

He just laughed.

"No, seriously, Grandpa. One of these chickens is eating our food, taking up room in our coop, and ruining our eggs. We have to find out which one it is and kill it, right?"

"I don't have time to sit watching chickens. Plus that chicken actually helps. It helps to remind me to stay vigilant about caring for the other chickens and collecting the eggs. It also reminds me that nature is cutthroat, and that human nature is just that."

I wasn't satisfied with my grandfather's reasoning. The next day I woke up early and kept watch over the chicken coop. I saw the chickens go into the nesting area and lay their eggs, one by one. I also saw one of the chickens begin toying with an egg with its claws and pecking at it with its beak. I thought about killing the chicken. I had learned how to slaughter a chicken by hanging it up by its feet, securing its head in my weak hand, and with my strong hand locating the jugular vein with a knife and slitting it open, spilling the blood on the ground while the chicken flapped itself to death. The whole process took no longer than five minutes. Instead I yelled at the chicken, causing it to scurry away. I gathered the remaining viable eggs and walked back into the house.

I wondered if the chickens knew which one was the egg eater, and if they didn't, what they would do if they found out.

Chapter 3

WE'RE CREEPY AND
WE'RE KOOKY

I grew up in a home with many siblings, but my favorite has always been my older brother Jim. When he was eighteen he snapped and became what he later called "the Lone Wolf." On a trip with some of his friends he got sick and soiled himself in the parking lot of Walmart. The embarrassment and anxiety from this incident seems to have triggered a fugue state; he didn't tell his friends or even have the common decency to go inside the store to clean up. Instead he stripped his underwear off and left it on the asphalt of the parking lot, and segregated himself from the rest of the group. After searching they found him wandering around a different section of the lot and with skill convinced him to return to the car. For the rest of the now-awkward trip he wore a single set of dirty clothes and refused to wash himself. For the most part, he couldn't speak in coherent sentences, or really do anything to function like a human being. After a few days, he became Jim again, but he couldn't answer questions about the Lone Wolf and still can't.

For lack of better words, I would describe the adult Jim as

fragile. He is very sensitive to stress, easily overwhelmed by the most insignificant things, and almost consistently nervous. He acts like an abused dog that has been kicked one too many times in the stomach to feel at ease around strangers. Despite intensive therapy, he still can't seem to keep it together and will lash out in passive-aggressive ways or retreat completely, leaving a shell of himself behind. When I look at him I sometimes wonder, is this what empath M.E. would have looked like? I could never imagine myself turning out like Jim, which makes me wonder—how did the same stimulation produce two opposite characters? I often think about Jim—my empathetic counterpart—when questions arise about whether I was born as a sociopath or made into this by the circumstances of my childhood. There is compelling scientific evidence to suggest that sociopathy has a strong genetic component. Studies also show that sociopathic traits are stable and consistent through an individual's lifetime. Identical twins who share 100 percent of their genes have been found far more likely to both exhibit sociopathic traits than fraternal twins, who share only 50 percent of their genes. The closest thing I have to a twin is my brother Jim. At a little more than a year apart in age, we were often mistaken for fraternal twins. Jim and I did everything together. It's safe to say that we had nearly identical upbringings and experiences, but we turned into starkly opposite adults.

I n a large park in the city where I grew up there was a giant concrete dinosaur, a brontosaurus. Most of him lay beneath the surface of the sandlot, his massive body never to be excavated. Only his long neck and purple tail stuck out into the world—perfect for us kids to climb and swing on. My brother Jim and I spent a lot of time with the brontosaurus in late afternoons and early evenings—sometimes many hours—when my mother was meant to pick us up after school. It was near to the school but remote enough that it was out of sight of the school monitors. No one would suspect we had been forgotten by our parent, and we had prepared stories for ourselves in case anyone approached us: "Our mom is at the principal's office discussing our progress," or "Our mom was just called away for an emergency. She is having a neighbor come get us right now." The truth is we had no idea why our mother never seemed to be able to pick us up on time, but we didn't want to deal with the hassle of concerned strangers, so we lied. The story always involved a responsible adult just footsteps away, even as the sunlight waned.

One sunny afternoon when I was around ten years old and my brother eleven, my parents took us down to the park. It must have been a primary school holiday, because I remember that our older brother still had high school, but there were no other kids around. They deposited us by the brontosaurus and went off to do their own thing while we played our warrior and submarine games with each other and our old, slightly decrepit dinosaur friend, flipping ourselves onto his neck, reaching our arms into the dark crevasse of his lazily half-open mouth. When we tired of him, we hiked into the bamboo-infested creek and pretended we were Vietcong soldiers padding soundlessly through the jungle.

After an hour or so of this, we headed back to the parked car just in time to see our parents get in. I remember seeing my father open the door for my mother and her taking her seat in the leisurely, elegant way that she often did. Since my parents appeared to be getting ready to leave, my brother and I picked up our speed and walked a little faster toward them. We were looking forward to going home and getting something to eat, as our soldiering play had worked up our appetites. We were about 150 yards away from them when we heard the car start, but we didn't begin sprinting until we saw the car's reverse lights flash on, indicating that they had shifted out of park. I am not sure when I realized that our parents were leaving us. Even as the car drove through the narrow park roads, and we ran as fast as we could and screamed at the top of our lungs, I didn't think that they would leave. I wonder if they saw their kids trailing them in their rearview mirror like a scene from a horror show, monsters from whom they were trying desperately to escape in a low-speed chase—the low rumbling of their car in contrast to our wild gasping and hoarse yelling, our animal footfalls haphazard against the pavement.

We followed my parents' car for a half mile or more, but we weren't quite able to keep up with them through the park roads. When they hit the main road, we couldn't keep up at all, and they were soon gone.

The moment when you stop running after your parents' car is the moment that you lose hope. *The gods are fallen and all safety is gone.* It is a physical realization, in which hope drains out of you in direct proportion to the dwindling adrenaline that propels your body forward. Hundreds of pounding heartbeats later, doubled over and gasping for breath in the middle of the road, we might have listened for the sound of brakes and a car turning around. If we did, we didn't share it with each other. Instead, we made suggestions as to why they would leave us. Maybe they forgot that we had come with them, or there really had been some kind of emergency, perhaps involving dismemberment or maiming. Maybe they had gotten into an argument. We attempted to find patterns in their behavior, any sort of predictability that we could rely on, but their actions were often unexplainable. We sensed, though, that they would not come back for us. Actually, we knew they wouldn't, and they didn't.

We could have taken our chances on the winding road up to our house, but we decided instead to strike out on our own. For my brother, it may have been an attempt to shame my parents out of their bad behavior, the way that small children frequently run away, hoping to prompt their parents to cry heavy tears of remorse. For me, I wanted to see if we really did need my mom and dad, or if having to be a part of their family was all a fiction we were taught by church and television to keep us doing Saturday chores.

We didn't really sit down to make a plan for our survival, but we knew we needed supplies, so we walked over to the nearby high school, where our older brother's car was parked. Jim forced open a window while I reached my skinny arm in to unlock it. Inside was a treasure trove of ski equipment from a not-too-recent ski trip. We collected all of the knitwear for warmth and protection for the days ahead, and since we didn't have anything to carry the stuff in, we wore all of the clothes in layers upon layers. Each of us put on several hats, pairs of gloves, and jackets, many of which were grossly oversized. We looked ridiculously overdressed for a Southern California late afternoon, piled up with knit caps and gloves, but our minds were on surviving through the coming months.

We were very hungry. The obvious solution was to beg, and we were conveniently dressed for the occasion. We tried to find a piece of cardboard and a marker to make a sign but we only found some college-ruled lined paper and ballpoint pens. (Now when I see a beggar on the street, I often wonder at his resourcefulness in finding a thick permanent marker, a piece of cardboard, and scissors or a knife to cut it into an adequately sized rectangle.) But the street was in a forested, residential area and there was no traffic to which we could appeal. We just hung out, sweating in our homeless-style knitwear and kicking dirt. I'm not sure how long we stood there before we got bored and hungry and decided to give in.

I never resented my parents for leaving us that day. I don't know why they left. Maybe they just willed us to disappear from their minds for a little while. If they thought about it at all, I think they believed that the only realistic consequence was that we might have suffered a bit having to make that precarious walk home. If I resented them for anything it was for making us believe that they wouldn't leave. They bought into the "fiction" that we were a conventional family, the kind that looked out for each other, and that they were conventional parents. It wasn't that they didn't love us—I know they did in their own way—but at the same time it's not like it mattered; their love served no purpose to me. Their good intentions did not make my life any better, rather they seemed only to insulate them from the truth, allowing them to live in a dark world of collusion through which reason and objective facts could not penetrate. Anything that didn't leave permanent physical scars requiring explanation to their friends and neighbors went unnoticed.

I was raised as the middle child in a *Royal Tenenbaums*-ish family with a violent and shaming father and an indifferent, sometimes hysterical mother. I had a group of four siblings that banded together as if we were a small but well-trained militia. Growing up we had the distinct impression we were better than everyone else, and that the only people who could understand and appreciate us were the other members of our family.

My parents married young, my mom at twenty and my dad twenty-three. My mother had been coerced by her own dysfunctional family into dropping out of college. Once back home, she dated aggressively, trying out men who could save her. I am not sure why she chose my dad, but she did it quickly, pinning him down and asking if he was going to propose only a few months after meeting him. She gave birth to my oldest brother in the first year of their marriage and continued steadily to have babies after that.

My father was a lawyer. When he and my mother were dating, he worked for a big law firm, but after that job fell apart he began his own small-time legal practice. He liked to think of himself as a modern-day Atticus Finch, sometimes accepting baked goods as payment from his clients. He was phenomenally unreliable as a breadwinner, and we often came home from a day at the amusement park to find that the power had been shut off, because we were months behind in paying for our electricity. He spent thousands of dollars on expensive hobbies, while we were bringing a handful of oranges from our backyard to school for lunch. The year I was twelve he didn't file a tax return. He owned his business, hadn't paid or withheld any taxes all year, and then just didn't feel like paying them when April 15 rolled around. Of course he got audited and whatever remained of our financial security evaporated.

Much more serious than any financial hardships I experienced, however, my father's emotional and moral hypocrisy taught me not to trust emotions or anything else that couldn't be backed up with hard, indisputable fact. If my heart turned hard, I believe it was in response to his maudlin displays of feelings and insincere appeals to virtue.

I am not sure how other people perceived my father, but I know that he tried very hard to present himself as a good man and a good parent—to the world, to himself, and to us. He liked to think of himself as an admirable person, and almost everything he did was in service to this desire. He had a habit of listing his achievements, as if he carried his own mental dossier in his head for the purpose of recitation: his bar association, his service to clients, his standing in the church, and most important, his philanthropic ventures. He needed the world to know that he was a giving, generous person.

My parents were involved in some of our school activities, particularly the musical ones. Sometimes my dad ran lights for my high school band performances while my mother accompanied the choir members. I think they must have been pillars of our provincial little society. Once we were running late when, in the car on the way to a concert, I realized I had forgotten to bring my instrument. We did not risk their missing their engagements by turning back; instead, I stood in the wings while my mother sang and my father ran the house lights, finding nothing unusual about my parents participating in my school event while I was excluded.

Whenever my father behaved badly, I think he felt more disappointment in betraying that image of himself than for damaging us. It didn't matter whether he really was this ideal person; it only mattered that he looked that way, even to himself. I could not respect how easily he could deceive himself. We would watch sad movies together as a family, and he would turn to my mother with tears in his eyes, holding out his forearm and exclaiming: "Look! Goose bumps!" He wanted desperately for us to witness evidence of his ability to feel, to be human, and he needed our affirmation of this fact more than anything else.

One day when I was around eight years old I was watching a news special with my father when I made a callous remark about a disabled child. He asked in horror, "Have you no empathy?" I had to ask him what he meant. I just didn't know the word, but he acted like I was a monster. The message was clear: His feelings and sense of self-righteousness made him a paradigm of humanity; my lack of feelings made me a blemish on his good name.

It's hard to overstate how much I loathed him for these very simple things. The very first recurring dream that I can remember was about killing him with my bare hands. There was something thrilling about the violence of it, smashing a door into his head repeatedly, smirking as he fell motionless to the floor, no longer able to parade around the globe in his imagined greatness. It was reassuring to know that I could do it if I needed to, and my dreams were a place where I could practice and plan for it—working out and relishing every detail of quieting him from our lives.

My mother is beautiful. Throughout my childhood, people regularly stopped her in the street and told her so. When she was young, she was very musically talented, or at least we thought so. She taught piano lessons to neighborhood kids, and sometimes it seemed like our family was living off the forty dollars a month she made off each student. For three hours every day after school, kids would rotate through the house, banging on the keys of the family piano, while we would watch television or do our homework. I remember waiting on the staircase for whatever kid to finish, judging his performance and resenting him for making me wait for my mother's attention. At the end-of-year recitals, I suspected her obvious pleasure had less to do with each child's individual accomplishments and more to do with her own achievement of coaxing beautiful or semicoherent music out of such unformed things.

My mother loved the spotlight, and it suited her. After my youngest sister was born, my mother got serious about her actress/singer ambitions. She auditioned for and got a supporting role in a professional dinner theater production, and she'd come home glowing from each performance, on a high from the applause and adulation. She appeared in several musicals and concerts after that and became a staple in community productions.

My father especially enjoyed the concerts that involved our church choir, which our friends and neighbors would be guaranteed to attend. However, when my mother's career took her too far away and therefore had no directly positive impact on his reputation, he would berate her for needing attention and admiration from outside of the family, meaning anyone other than him.

It is true that she did need the attention and admiration from outside of our house. I think it filled in the empty spaces in her, built up a temporary infrastructure to maintain her as a going concern, a functional adult and parent. By the time she pursued her acting dreams, she had already put away her hopes of my father's becoming a wealthy, successful attorney. Her kids kept multiplying and gaining more volume and mobility, filling her house with chores and responsibilities that further constricted any space available for her own breathing and dreaming. Fictional characters allowed her to take refuge from us and her life, to escape into dialogues and story lines that did not involve scraped knees and stuffy noses. She needed to enjoy the freedom of being a different person for a few nights a week, of being appreciated for aesthetics rather than domestic utility.

Whenever one of us would get sick or hurt, my mother would throw up her arms and cry, "Oh great! Well now what am

I supposed to do?" And you could see all the ruined plans and missed opportunities for the day flash across her face like ripples in a pond. Every cup of tea she would prepare for you would be accompanied with sighs. Every "Are you feeling better?" was loaded with accusatory urgency, as if your failure to get better was a direct assault on her ability to live freely and well.

When the seasons or plays inevitably ended, she would become deeply depressed—to the point of becoming physically ill. She totaled several cars. I imagine her mind involuntarily searching out happier memories of being onstage or laughing with friends, undeterred by red lights or road signs. Perhaps they were not memories at all that had distracted her, but fantasies of another life she could have had if she had made only slightly different choices.

Her car accidents were like little earthquakes in our lives, reminders of our mortality, and consequently that we (and she) were alive. I respected her little rebellions, even if they meant that I would go hungry for a few evenings or my brother's head would get split from the impact of the car windshield. I don't remember ever being angry with her for these things; she was just trying to live, and it is true that our existences, over which she had little control, had interfered with her happiness in countless ways. My dad, of course, would point with recrimination to my brother's wounded forehead after the accidents. But no one really cared about my brother's forehead—least of all my dad—and life went on as it always did.

But she did get us soup when we were sick. She fed us and clothed us, as did my father. She put her hand on our foreheads with looks of concern that made wrinkles in her own forehead. She kissed us at bedtime; he did too. And even though I did not, my mother would cry when my father beat me with his belt, for what I can't remember. And when I graduated from law school, my father genuinely rejoiced—never had I seen him so happy as that day. I never doubted their love for me, but their love was inconstant. It was sometimes very ugly. It didn't prevent me from harm; rather, it often caused me harm. The more they felt secure in their love for me, the less they seemed prompted actually to look after my well-being.

I learned a lot from my parents. I learned to limit the emotional effect that other people could have on me. I learned to be self-sufficient. They taught me that love is exceedingly unreliable, and so I have never relied on it.

The question of nature versus nurture for sociopaths is controversial. Arguing "nature" seems to give sociopaths a free pass—being "born with it" somehow makes them more pitiable and acceptable by society. Whereas arguing "nurture" suggests that sociopaths can one day reverse their condition through hard work and therapy, or alternatively recruit more of their kind by abusing children. The answer is more complicated than that, however. Psychologists and scientists believe sociopathy, like almost everything about us, is some combination of genes and environment. While there is a clear heritable link, environment also plays a huge role in triggering those genes and how a particular sociopath develops. According to psychologist and author of *Social Intelligence* Daniel Goleman, if a gene never gets expressed, "we may as well not possess that gene at all," which raises an interesting question—are you a sociopath if it is coded in your genes but it's not expressed in your behavior? Sometimes there is no clear answer to how or why a person's sociopath genes get triggered. As for myself, I have always felt like I am precariously balanced, neither on the right side nor the wrong side of life but ready at every moment to tip completely to one side or another. I often wonder how different my life would have been if my upbringing were any better or worse than it was.

Some of the most formative environmental factors for sociopaths may have happened before the sociopath's earliest memory. Although the brain doesn't reach maturity until twenty, according to Dr. Goleman, the first twenty-four months of a human being's life are most central to her development, as it is the period of greatest growth. For mice, the corollary period is the first twelve hours after birth. Baby mice who are licked and thus nurtured more by their mothers during these hours thrive better and are more clever and self-assured; those babies that are less licked become slower learners, easily overwhelmed, and anxious. Scientists have hypothesized that for humans the equivalent might be empathy, attunement, and touch. Dr. Goleman's research accords with the infant attachment theory first developed by psychiatrist and psychoanalyst John Bowlby, who conducted research on orphans after World War II. He and other scientists found that children who had not been regularly touched in their infancy failed to thrive, did not grow, and even sometimes died. According to attachment theory, infants who receive insufficient or no responses from their parents during distress grow to be rebellious, independent, and detached children, failing to prefer their parents over strangers. As adults they have trouble making lasting, meaningful relationships.

When I was an infant I had a particularly bad case of colic, a poorly understood condition affecting infants whose main symptom is frequent, inconsolable crying. My parents complain about it even now, what a difficult child I was, especially because I came so soon after my brother Jim, who was needy in his way.

My parents have very vivid memories of taking me to functions with my extended family during which I would wail the entire time. Each aunt, uncle, or grandparent would think they had the solution, and each would eventually give up in desperation. When my parents recount the stories now, they express a hint of vindication that no one else could console me. It seems to reflect a happy truth for them—that there was nothing wrong with them as parents, only something wrong with me. My father openly acknowledges that he would frequently just leave me in a room to cry myself to exhaustion. At the age of six weeks I was finally taken to my pediatrician—I had ruptured my navel due to excessive crying. I'm sure my parents did as well as they could, but it no doubt must have been difficult to tolerate such a child, much less nurture it.

Long after my colic days were done, my mother says that I was a remarkably independent child. When I was left in the church's nursery for the first time, I was the only baby who didn't cry or ask for my parents, playing quietly and happily with the unfamiliar toys of the schoolroom until I was picked up. It was as if it made no difference to me where I was or who was looking after me. Maybe I missed a window of opportunity, like those less-licked baby mice.

The brain learns different skills at different stages that are tied to neural development and growth. If a child misses the correct developmental window to learn a particular skill or concept, for example empathy, that child's brain may never be able to catch up or become normal. The most extreme examples are of children who grow up in isolation or in the wild, sometimes known as feral children. The *Tampa Bay Times* reported the story of Danielle Crockett, who was rescued by police from her mother's trash- and vermin-filled home in July 2005. Upon discovering Danielle locked in a closet and living in her own filth, one of the officers, a rookie, staggered out the front door to vomit. A veteran investigator of the Florida Department of Children and Families was spotted hunched over the steering wheel of her parked car, sobbing. "Unbelievable," she described it. "The worst I've ever seen." Danielle was six years old at the time but looked more like a four-year-old. She wore diapers, was nonverbal, and was unable to walk or feed herself. As the police officer flung her over his shoulder, her diaper leaking down his uniform, her mother shrieked at him, "Don't take my baby!"

Danielle had a "normal" brain, with no sign of genetic mental retardation, but she behaved as if she were severely mentally handicapped. One doctor called it "environmental autism," although as she put it, "even a child with the most severe autism responds to [hugs and affection]." Danielle did not react to people in any way. "In the first five years of life, 85 percent of the brain is developed," she said. "Those early relationships, more than anything else, help wire the brain and provide children with the experience to trust, to develop language, to communicate. They need that system to relate to the world."

Danielle will never be normal. After several years she was able to be potty trained and taught how to feed herself, though she still does not speak. When she was taken in by an adoptive family, the *Miami Herald* asked, "Will their love be enough?" The short answer is no. Her brain had missed too many windows of opportunity—too many neural connections were never made.

Sometimes I hear people say that they were "born this way," whatever way that happens to be. To say you are born a sociopath is like saying you were born smart or born tall. Yes, you may have the genetic predisposition for intelligence or height, or indeed to speak or walk upright, but the existence of feral children is an important reminder that no one is destined for any outcome at birth, that we rely on the most basic daily interactions, nutrition, culture, education, experiences, and myriad other influences in our development to become who we become.

Was I born to charm? Born to harm? If we can't say for sure, then how did I get here? Given that a propensity for emotional problems runs in my family, I think my genetic predisposition to sociopathy was triggered largely because I never learned how to trust. In particular, my parents' erratic emotional lives taught me that I couldn't depend on anyone to protect me. Rather than looking to other people for stability, I learned to depend on myself. Because interaction with other people is inevitable, I inevitability learned manipulation, particularly how to direct and misdirect people's attention to achieve my desired outcomes. For instance, my experiences taught me that it was useless to appeal to people's love or sense of duty, so I appealed to other, more salient emotions like fear or people's own desperate desire to be loved. I viewed everyone as objects, pieces in my chess game. I had no awareness of their own internal worlds and no understanding of their emotional palette because their bright hues were so different from my own drab shades of gray. Perhaps because I never thought of people as being distinct individuals with their own senses of self and manifest destiny, I never learned to think of myself that way either. I had no definite sense of self to adhere to or otherwise be invested in. Largely without structure, my life became an endless series of reactions to contingencies, impulsive decision-making driving me from one day to the next. Unlike people without my genetic predispositions who might have come out of these experiences desperately searching for love to fill the void, I felt largely indifferent.

After my brother Jim and I walked home from the park that day, our parents' car was parked outside in the driveway, just like it always was. Inside, they didn't ask us any questions. In general, they didn't worry about our suffering. I think our suffering did not register with them because they could feel no consequences resulting from it. And because we were the kind of children that accepted silence as explanation, they never experienced recrimination. It was as if it had never happened. They went to bed that night satisfied that their children were safe and warm like anyone else's.

Now that I am grown and can see my family dynamics with better perspective, I am more convinced than ever that the environment in which I was raised had a significant role to play in my development into a sociopath. Lots of children live in families with unreliable parents, physical discipline, and financial instability—these things aren't uncommon. But I can see how the antisocial behaviors and mental posturing that now define me were incentivized when I was growing up— how my own emotional world was stifled and how understanding and respect for the emotional world of others died away. But there's a chicken-and-egg problem here: it's hard to know whether my distrust of my dad's overt displays of compassion caused me to downplay my own sense of morality, or whether I never really had much of a conscience to begin with, and that is why my dad always seemed so ridiculous to me.

I don't ever remember thinking differently than I do now, but I do have a sensation or memory of an early cognitive fork where I chose to think more proactively. I must have been somewhere between ages four and six. Here's an example to illustrate what I mean: Have you ever been a pedestrian at a traffic light? There's always a moment of hesitation when you arrive at your corner and see the red hand telling you it's not safe to walk. You could follow what it says and just wait your turn. Or you could make your own assessment of whether it is safe to cross by looking at the cars and studying the traffic light patterns. There are advantages to both approaches. The one is safe and doesn't require mental effort. The other one is risky and possibly will only shave a few seconds off your commute at best and land you in the hospital at worst. But if you get good at it, those few seconds could multiply by the thousands over years of commuting. And there's something demoralizing about standing on a corner while a host of braver souls plows into the intersection, eager to get on with their lives.

I could sense this was true about life, even at the age of four or so. I could choose to take charge of my life, to leverage my time, talents, and health, and to potentially profit or die trying. Or I could contentedly get in line and wait my turn. It was not a difficult choice to make, but rather a decision made in direct response to my environment and how I could best survive and even thrive in that environment. My way seemed to offer a competitive advantage. I chose to eschew relying on instinct and instead to rely on rigid mental analysis and hyperawareness of all of my thoughts, actions, and decisions.

Years later I questioned whether I had made a mistake—and whether it was possible for me somehow to still be normal. Maybe there were legitimate reasons why everyone else thought the way they did about life. Maybe crying really is the best response to being hurt instead of vengeance. Maybe love is more valuable than power in relationships. But by then it was too late. The windows had closed.

Growing up, everyone in the family was inclined to interpret things that I did as normal. There were other words for what I was, words other than "sociopath." "Tomboy" explained why I was reckless all of the time. Did you know that drowning deaths for boys are four times what they are for girls? No one really has a good explanation other than that boys tend to be more reckless, less judicious, and more impulsive. So when I was a child jumping off ocean jetties into heavy surf, no one thought I was a sociopath—they thought I was a tomboy.

"Precocious" explained my fixation on the power structures of the adult world. Most children are content to live in their own child worlds. I found my peers, particularly my non-siblings, to be unbearably simpleminded. Unlike them, I was obsessed with learning everything there was to learn about how the world worked, on both micro and macro levels. I would hear something in school or in casual adult conversation like *Vietnam* or *atomic bomb* and then spend a week or two obsessed with learning everything I could about this new thing, this thing that seemed to matter so much to other people. I remember the first time I heard about AIDS. I must have been seven or eight years old. My aunt was babysitting me. She was a childlike woman and I could tell from her interactions with my parents that she had no power or influence in the outside world (there were plenty of those people, I had already noticed). She doted on us because she had no children of her own (there were many of those people as well, easy marks for a child's manipulation). We heard *AIDS* on the news. My aunt got upset and started crying. I didn't know at the time but found out soon that her uncle, my great-uncle, was sick, and gay, and that was one of the reasons why AIDS seemed so fraught for her and others. I asked her what AIDS was. She gave me a child's understanding of the disease that should have satisfied me, but it didn't. My need to know the whys and hows of the world was not easily sated. I continued to ask other adults (the only people who seemed interested in the things I was interested in were adults) and they laughed at my interest, calling me precocious. They didn't call me a sociopath. They never wondered why I wanted to know. They assumed that I wanted to know for the same reason that they wanted to know—fear. And that was partly true, but I was not afraid of AIDS. I only wanted to understand completely why AIDS made everyone else afraid. So it never mattered much what I did because they would readily excuse my behavior in whatever way was convenient or simply ignore it.

As a child, my outsize inner life seeped out onto the surface in all sorts of messy ways that my family pretended not to see. I talked to myself all the time, repeating everything I said sotto voce as if I were acting in a dress rehearsal. My parents ignored my blatant and awkward attempts to manipulate, deceive, and inveigle adults. They neglected to notice the odd way that I associated with my childhood acquaintances without really forming connections, never seeing them as anything more than moving objects—instruments in my games. I lied all the time. I stole things, but more often than not, I would just trick kids into giving them to me. I snuck into people's homes and rearranged their belongings. I broke things, burned things, and bruised people.

And I played my part beautifully. I never failed to up the ante in our neighborhood games. If we were jumping off the diving board into the pool, I asked how much more fun it would be to jump off the roof into the pool. If we were dressing up in paramilitary garb, I suggested that we might as well kidnap our neighbor's lawn ornaments and make elaborate ransom notes for them. We cut out letters from magazines and made a "proof of life" video. Because the neighbors were so good-spirited and we had taken such pains in accomplishing our absurd adventures, we got away with smiles all around.

That was the thing with me. I made people smile so much

that it was easy to laugh off anything I did as harmless and silly rather than dangerous or reckless. I was a natural clown, an entertainer. I danced with gusto. I yelled and told stories. If there had been YouTube back then, I would have gone viral. My family could often ignore my other quirks because I was so charming and kooky. They could imagine they were just living inside a Saturday-morning television show involving a high-spirited kid and her colorful high jinks. At the end of each episode, they would smile, shrug their shoulders, and shake their heads.

But my lack of inhibition also meant that it all came out unfiltered, the charm interspersed with the awkward and disturbing. When I was *on,* I could delight everyone. But sometimes I could be too much. I would demand too much attention, pushing past cuteness to an uncomfortable grotesque. Other times, I would turn *off,* withdrawing completely into myself as if no one else was around me. I felt like I could turn invisible.

I was a perceptive child, but I couldn't relate to people beyond amusing them, which was just another way for me to make them do or behave how I wanted them to. I didn't like to be touched and rejected affection. The only physical contact I wanted entailed violence, and *that* I craved. The father of one of my best friends in grade school had to pull me aside and sternly ask me to stop beating his daughter. She was this skinny, stringy thing, all bony and with no muscle, with this goofy laugh; it was like she was asking to be slapped. I didn't know that what I was doing was bad. It didn't even occur to me that it would hurt her or that she might not like it.

I was not a typical child. That was obvious to everyone. I knew I was different, but there were no real indications to me of how or why I was different. Children are all selfish things, but maybe I was a little more self-interested than most. Or maybe I was simply more adept at accomplishing my self-serving ends than others, unfettered by conscience or guilt as I was. It was not clear. Young and powerless, I developed my own forms of power by convincing people that pleasing me was in their own best interest. Like many children, I objectified everyone around me. I envisioned the people in my life as two-dimensional robots that turned off when I wasn't directly interacting with them. I loved getting high marks in my classes; it meant I could get away with things other students couldn't because I was one of the smart kids. I made sure to stay within the realm of socially acceptable childish behavior—or at least to have a sympathetic narrative prepared in case I was caught. Other than being adept at childish manipulation, I never seemed different from my peers, at least not in a way that could not be explained by my exceptional intelligence.

Everything I learned about power—how great it feels to have it and how terrible it feels to be without it—I learned from my dad. Our relationship for the most part constituted a quiet wrestle for power—he demanded dominion over me as part of his home and family, while I enjoyed undermining what I believed to be his undeserved authority. When I misbehaved I would sometimes get beaten black and blue by my father, but I never reacted. If anything, what bothered me about the beatings was that he thought he was winning our power struggle, but I knew it wouldn't last. If someone who loves you is hitting you that hard, you have more power than he does. You've provoked a reaction in him that he cannot control, and if you are like me, you will use this incident however it suits you for as long as you are associated with him. For my image-obsessed father, the threat of my disclosing these beatings was enough to torture him. Perhaps at a church social gathering I might wince as I lowered myself gingerly into a chair, making meaningful eye contact with my father when well-meaning third parties asked if I was okay, a look of terror flashing over his features as he anticipated my response. Strategically speaking, the beatings were the best thing to happen to me. His guilt and self-hatred were more potent than any other weapon in my little child arsenal and more enduring than any bruises that I may have suffered.

My father often made ridiculous demands of his children. He would tape lists of demands like "build a fence" and "fix the sink" to the doors of our bedrooms so we would see them when we woke up. I had gotten used to attempting the impossible when my father requested it. The way he asked me always made it seem like a dare, questioning whether I had the smarts or the courage to make things happen. Because that's what I prided myself on, getting stuff done. Unlike my father, whom I considered to be largely inefficient, I was great at taking care of business. That was my role in the family.

His narcissism made him love me for my accomplishments because they reflected well on him, but it also made him hate me because I never bought into his self-image, which was all he ever really cared about. His dossier of civic duty and success meant nothing to me, because I knew better, and mine was and would be far greater than his. I think I did a lot of the same things he did—played baseball, joined a band, attended law school—so that he would know that I was better. I lived my life so that I had no reason to respect him.

One night in my early teens, driving home from the movies with my parents, I got into an argument with my father about the movie's ending, which he thought was about overcoming obstacles and, of course, I thought was about meaninglessness, as I did about most everything those days. I was full of a teenager's petulance and contrariness mixed with a little more intelligence and cruelty than the average kid.

I didn't mind arguing with him. I in fact made it a point not to back down from any of our arguments, particularly if they presented an opportunity to challenge some part of his provincial worldview, which I had already concluded was distorted in self-serving ways. We were still arguing by the time we pulled into the driveway of our house, and I could tell that he wasn't going to let it go. I told him, "You believe what you want," and went into the house. My impassivity often provoked his worst behavior.

I should have known that he wasn't going to let me get away that easily, or maybe I knew but didn't care. He followed me up the stairs, because it bothered him that his daughter—who was just a child—refused to agree with him, didn't care if he disagreed with her, and thought nothing of casually dismissing him.

At the time, my parents were going through one of their rough patches. My father would bully my mother and she would have momentary breakdowns in which she would lie on the bathroom floor and respond to us by rhyming whatever it was we said to her:

"Mom, are you okay?"

"What did you say?"

"Do you need help? Are you well?"

"No, I'm feeling swell."

Sometimes when my parents fought, she would try to assert herself using whatever she had learned from the self-help books that lined the headboard of their bed. One of her favorite lines was "I'm rolling up my window on you." It meant that she was refusing to let him affect how she felt, which drove him mad. In retrospect I wonder who it was that wrote that self-help book and how many of its readers ended up with swollen lips and bruised eyes. The idea that my father couldn't make an impact on a person was enraging to him. Had my mother actually rolled up a car window on him he would have smashed the glass.

That night as my father became increasingly hostile about our argument over the movie, I told him, "I'm rolling up my window on you," and then I slipped into the bathroom at the top of the stairs, shutting and locking the door.

I knew there would be consequences. I knew he hated that phrase, and that my repetition of it presented the specter of another generation of women in his house who refused to respect or appreciate him, and instead despised him. I also knew that he hated locked doors. I knew these things would damage him, which is what I wanted. And in any case, I needed to pee.

It was only a moment before he was pounding on the door. I imagined his face on the other side, getting redder and redder, contorted in an ugly display of anger. I remember wondering detachedly how long I would have to wait for him to go away. He began to shout.

"Open up!"

"Open up!"

"Open up!"

Each time he said it was louder than the last, swelling with impending violence. There was a pregnant pause, then the first big punch into the door, and then a crack. I wondered, curiously, about the door's sturdiness, about whether its designer contemplated this kind of domestic disturbance to its integrity. I thought about how many blows it would take for my father to get through the door, and I wondered, curiously, how much danger I was really in. What did he imagine he would do when he got through the door? Would he drag me out of the bathroom by my hair, kicking me in the soft of my stomach, screaming at me to agree with him about the ending of the movie? It seemed absurd.

I sat down on the tub to wait it out. The loud noises triggered a rush of adrenaline in the form of increased heart rate, heightened sensitivity to sounds, decreased peripheral vision; I observed these facts to myself calmly. I passively ignored their invitation to feel a sense of urgency as being counterproductive. Despite my body's involuntary physical reactions, there was no emotional panic. I don't know what it feels like to panic in a situation like this. What would a panicked person even do? There are so few options in such tight quarters. If anything, I was intrigued, curious to see how events would unravel.

By now the punches had knocked a hole in the door, and I could see through the hole that his hand was bloody and swollen. I wasn't concerned about his hand, although it occurs to me that another daughter might have been. I wasn't glad that he was hurt either, because I knew that it gave him satisfaction to be stricken by such passion that he could disregard his own pain and suffering. The bathroom door was not the only door that would be damaged by my father's fists. The bedroom door at the end of the hall accumulated several indentations throughout my childhood (it opened to my oldest brother's bedroom), as did the door to the master bedroom (resulting from fights with Mom). Walls were occasionally dented from having been punched near the heads of his family members.

He kept working at the jagged, splintered hole until it was big enough for him to stick his face through it, which meant that it was of considerable size. I remember achieving confirmation of his ugliness, seeing his face glisten with sweat under the harsh bathroom light. But he wasn't grimacing in anger as I had imagined; instead, he was smiling widely so that his teeth showed. He asked me with a wild gleefulness, "*You* are going to roll up your window on *me?*"

By then I must have seemed startled enough to satisfy him.

He withdrew his face, and through the hole in the door, I could see that he had lost his propelling anger. Any power I had gained by walking away from him and locking that door was stolen back from me the moment he saw the distress in my eyes, even if it was only slight.

He walked over to the closet to take out some gauze and other medical supplies to tend to his hand. In his youth he had worked as an EMT and was very proud of his first aid skills, so I knew that he would be meticulous with his self-ministering, as a point of pride. When I was certain that he was fully engrossed in his task, I slipped out of the bathroom, down the stairs, and outside, where I hid in the dark.

I stayed out there for a while, breathing deeply and contemplating my next move. I was not scared per se, but more aware of the way my world had changed in the past fifteen minutes. I was suddenly less concerned about my math homework and more concerned about preparing for a physical assault. Before hiding in the trees, I grabbed a hammer from the shed and held it up with the claw end out. For a few seconds, I would have killed anyone who came near me.

A little while later I heard my oldest brother yelling my name. I didn't answer, waiting. I heard him go back inside. A few more minutes, and then he came back out.

"It's okay. People are here."

"Good," I thought. "Witnesses." But I knew that my dad was over it already. He had gotten the satisfaction of inflicting injury on himself, fear on me, and physical destruction where his loved ones could see it. He had everything he wanted, and was therefore done for the night.

My mother had called a church official to help calm my father, in front of whom we all knew he wouldn't lay a hand on me. For the remainder of the night, he wouldn't do anything but express contrition. Even this would be delicious for him, a crucial element of the dramatic narrative that he and I had set into motion. I dropped the hammer and snuck back inside.

That bathroom door didn't get fixed for months. When he finally got around to replacing it, my dad threw the old one out around the side of the house, as the yard was our family's repository for broken things. My brother Jim found it there and told me to come down to see it, but when I got out there he was gone.

I stood and stared at it a little before he showed up with a pickax and a sledgehammer in his hands. Jim let me take the first swing, and after that we took turns smashing it to splinters. I felt the breathless exhilaration of destruction, obliterating from existence this object that had contributed to invoking anxiety in me, that had dispelled any false sense of safety I may have felt within my own home. The impact of metal on wood, the aching in my arms—it all felt wonderful, powerful.

I don't know where Jim was when my dad was punching through that door. If he was around, he certainly didn't do anything to stop it. I couldn't count on him to do things like that for me. He just wasn't strong enough, and I could never really fault him for that. In truth I could take better care of myself that way than he ever could.

I could, however, count on Jim to maintain a deep and abiding hatred of my father on my behalf, which was actually the worst revenge I could get on my dad. Children can be so cruel that way—loving each other so much more than they could love a parent despite the affection that is heaped upon them.

Family folklore holds that I was not the most brilliant of my siblings, but I was decidedly the most accomplished, unhindered as I was by emotional and moral constraints. And with my obsession with power structures and the way things work, I was naturally the heart of the operation, the central command in which all resources were inventoried and tactically dispatched. More than being the typical "peacemaker" middle child, I was a powerbroker, negotiating deals and functioning as a clearinghouse between warring factions. Because I was relatively passionless, I was neutral (and rich) Switzerland.

My siblings and I were extremely insular and tight-knit—not because we are particularly affectionate, but rather from a common desire to optimize our group success. Wordlessly, we all seemed to acknowledge that our collective survival was paramount at the cost of all else, except that to me the whole point of the exercise was to ensure *my own* survival. Switzerland is a neutral banking powerhouse not to benefit all of Europe, but to benefit itself. I would have sacrificed any of my family members for myself in a heartbeat, if not for the fact that their presence in my life was—to varying degrees—essential to my happiness. This was made clear to me by the time Jim and I took sledgehammers to that bathroom door, if not sooner. We were like sticks: apart we were easily broken, but together we were strong. To say that I love them is insufficient or beside the point. I liked to have them around.

In some ways, my family might have appeared to be an ideal American family, an army of fresh- (but blank-) faced children with very few concerns outside the narrow world in which we lived. We regarded each other and our parents as immutable facts of life. We played games and read books, ran around in the backyard building things and breaking things, made expeditions into the woods and always got out alive.

We trauma bonded. And even though my siblings reacted to those traumas each in his or her own individual way, there is a strand of stupid toughness that runs through all of them, not unlike my great-grandparents who survived the Depression. The toughest of us—besides me—is my sister Kathleen. Her husband thinks that she is more of a sociopath than I am, and I can see what he means. She can be very callous and calculating. Her children have a healthy fear of her, and failure is not really an option for them. Her first child was born a little over a year after she got married. After previously not wanting children at any point in her life, she could think of nothing else but creating the perfect genetic amalgamation of her and her husband in as short a time as possible. When her baby was born, she took to the task of rearing her child with a military efficiency in accordance with the baby guides she had read in advance of his arrival. It was as if she wanted a do-over, replacing the family with which she had grown up with a new one that she could create and shape into something much better.

Kathleen resented our parents, I realized, for all the things that she felt she deserved from them and never got. They never attended her dance recitals, for instance, never volunteered for the school play she was in. It took me a long time to understand that these things constituted a measure of her perceived value in the world, and my parents' failures were directly correlated in her mind to her diminished worth as a human being. For this measure, and almost everything else in life, she had a fixed standard—an immovable notion of what was good or bad, sufficient or insufficient, moral or immoral. Indeed, Kathleen put the *imperative* in *moral imperative.*

And that is where she and I departed. She put all her manipulative energies into what she believed was good and right, as opposed to me, who simply invested in whatever benefited me most at the moment. While I targeted people based solely on who caught my interest, she would target only bad apples in order to see them ruined and the good (embodied by her) prevail. While my self-image was that of a pagan god, hers was of an avenging angel. With her sword unsheathed (a little too eagerly, if you ask me), she was constantly alert to fight for the righteous cause, defying authority whenever it was exercised unjustly. I enjoyed this about her. Sometimes it felt like we were an invincible sibling team, alternately invoking fear and inspiring admiration in the hearts of our peers. She was easy to get riled up and enlisted in any of my "causes," simply by making them sound like causes, like the time she was scheduled to give the valedictory speech and I convinced her to turn it into an elaborate prank as an act of defiance to a school administration that "mistreated" students. By the time my youngest sister, Susie, got to high school, there were few teachers left unscathed from the devastation left by Kathleen and me—Kathleen because she was compelled to right the wrongs of public school, and I because I had to win at all costs, sometimes allowing the costs to flow unchecked just to see the volume of my power.

But Jim was always my partner in crime. He was older, but growing up it often felt like I was his big sister. He was easy to manipulate, so sweet. I never had to try hard with him. His default was to give me what I wanted, and so we were best friends. Being attached to Jim was a problem, though. I was used to things not lasting. My parents were unpredictable, so

I had gotten used to relying on myself. When things got rough at home, I found great comfort in thinking that there was nothing really keeping me there—except Jim.

I used to wonder what life would be like without him. It bothered me to think that what we had would end, and so I used my analytical mind to plan the prevention of this possibility. He and I would spend hours talking about what our lives would look like together into adulthood. We planned where we would live, how we would support ourselves, what activities would fill our days. At some point our dream was to own a model train store together. Together we would build miniature cities around which our engines would run, their chains of red and yellow and blue cars trailing in loops without end. Later it was to play music together. It didn't matter what kind.

He was the one assurance in my child life. I could always count on him to provide for all my needs as best he could, and so I was extraordinarily selfish with him. I made him pay me money to play the games he wanted to play, which he would sometimes resist, but he always relented in the end. And I knew he would, because he wanted so much to play with me, and he didn't mind being exploited enough to make a fuss. He never disagreed with me with any conviction. He never defended himself. I demanded things of him all the time with the knowledge that he would inevitably cave.

He was so concerned about upsetting me, and I never thought once about whether what I did would hurt his feelings. I was just happy that I could do what I wanted, and I had this tagalong older brother with me to bail me out when stuff got bad. He wasn't always particularly useful. He was softhearted, sensitive, mostly passive, but my enemies were his enemies and he would oppose them with whatever tools he had.

Although my oldest brother, Scott, bullied everyone, including his siblings, Jim bore the brunt of it. Scott was a thug. We called him the stupid brother, because all he had was brute strength, which he used to achieve his will. It was instinctual for him to target Jim, whose weakness seeped out from his bones. Scott was the muscle, the soldier—emotionally blind. He brutalized people without noticing the impact on them, and for a long time, he did things to Jim without it ever occurring to him that they might have some negative effect on Jim. In this way Scott and I were very similar.

Even though I didn't like Scott, he had his value to me. He taught me how physical strength could be used for psychological intimidation and how to channel my love of beating people into games and sports. We would box each other with ski gloves or pretend that we were wrestlers in the WWF. I held my own against him by being shorter and faster, and it was fun for me. I liked that he treated me as his equal and not a weaker, younger thing, that he didn't even think to do so. We would egg each other on and dream up more violent games to play.

But Jim had no natural inclination to fight either of us, and he ended up absorbing all of the blows. He would just lie on the floor with his arms in front of his face. I couldn't tell if he just didn't think he had any other choice, or if he thought he did have a choice and that this was what he was choosing. I knew I didn't want to live like him, that I couldn't. To me, Jim's choices were emotional ones, and they were bad. His actions seemed irrational and therefore beyond my understanding. Watching him, my respect for his emotional world diminished, as did any regard for my own emotions or those of others.

I am not sure when it happened, but eventually my oldest brother and I realized that we shouldn't hit Jim anymore—that he was too delicate for it. We realized that we had to protect him or he wouldn't survive life's blows. We were the strong ones, the ones who could take care of business. At first we started pulling punches against him, and then we stopped throwing them at all. Soon we started blocking other people's punches. We say now that we have spent our lives coddling him, which means that from his early teens to now we have been putting ourselves out for him, buying him cars and houses, cosigning loans with him on which he will inevitably default. We are worried that if we do not, he'll snap.

Jim was so different from me. Being so close, it often felt like we were confronted with the same challenges and chose opposite ways of dealing with them. But the antisocial behaviors that now characterize me constituted the best choices for me when I was growing up, and I made them consciously. I followed so closely behind Jim in age that it was easy to see what worked or didn't work for him and then avoid his same mistakes. I equated his emotional sensitivity with his frailty. Where I forged ahead, he bent. Where I demanded things, he gave. Where I fought with all my might, he elected passive resistance or simply succumbed to whatever fate someone else had chosen for him. Who would want to live that way? I would think to myself. Because he was so concerned about my feelings, or my dad's, he had to deprioritize his own emotional well-being in favor of ours.

I often think it would be interesting to do a controlled experiment on identical twins with sociopathic genes, putting one of them in a "bad" environment and another in a "good" environment. Then we might get some real answers about what role genetics plays. I once read about a doctor who had a mad-scientist dream of determining what role genetics plays in the development of gender. One day he got his chance. A botched circumcision had left one boy in a pair of identical twins with a horribly mutilated penis. The doctor convinced the parents that it was much better for them to remove the entire penis and raise the boy as a girl. They agreed. S/he struggled with feelings of ambiguous gender until finally s/he confronted the parents, who confessed. After he started living life as a man, how did he feel when he looked at his identical twin? Did he see in his twin "what could have been"? Sometimes I wonder if my brother looks at me and asks himself the same. But because he is an empath, I think it is much more likely that he pities me.

My siblings are brutally honest with each other, because it is our nature to be brutal, but also because we assume that if we don't tell each other the ugly truths about ourselves, no one else will. We are competitive. If asked for a complete ranking of the family members based on any given trait—attractiveness, intelligence, agility, or depravity, for instance—we could give you a list without having to take a second to think about it. Not everyone in the family is a sociopath; I am the only one who has been diagnosed as one. But we grew up sharing a perspective of blunt practicality and disdain for moral sentiment, having tacitly agreed to a collective rejection of the outside world.

Sometimes there weren't a lot of incentives to make friends outside of the family. When strangers came to the house—friends or future spouses—we ignored them. Once when my father had invited over a young man for dinner, we ate silently and neglected to address him. After dinner we all went into another room and played computer games. When we failed to invite the young man to join us, my father complained, to which I responded matter-of-factly that we simply wanted him to leave. My father describes us as "vicious," which to me inaccurately implies that we go out of our way to hurt people. We don't go to that kind of trouble; it is that we rarely give anyone a second thought. For whatever reason, we do care about each other, however. Perhaps it is an evolutionary imperative to preserve our genes that makes us want to keep each other alive and relatively well. Or perhaps it is an alliance that we long ago worked out among ourselves to ensure each person's individual survival. I can't say. Whatever our differences, we stuck together, and for the most part benefited from doing so.

We have grown into adults who are all likely to survive an apocalypse, which, being Mormon, we were taught to take seriously. It doesn't matter if it comes in a gradually encroaching ice age or a sudden storm of nuclear fire; we'll band together to survive and we won't suffer any survivor guilt. We each have our roles in the family based on our perceived usefulness and are expected to dispatch these duties proficiently and efficiently. Collectively, we can remodel houses, build traps, make butter, shoot guns, put out fires, destroy reputations, sew clothes, and navigate bureaucracies. Most of us can defend ourselves relatively proficiently with guns, bows, knives, sticks, spears, or our fists. When one of us fails, we demand that he suffer the consequences. But we're not savages, either. We love art. There was always music in our house—my brother on the piano or my sister dancing on the stairs. It seemed that whatever ugliness was upon us, some species of happiness was only a few notes away.

And there wasn't a lack of love in my family. It was an unspoken deal we made to care about each other, if necessary to the exclusion of all others. Though they accept me and never questioned my behavior as a child, I know they've been tempted to blame themselves for the way I turned out, wondering about little things that they did or didn't do that could have pushed me here.

For my parents, their denial that anything might be wrong with me came from a deep insecurity that they had irrevocably damaged me. They had viewed me as troubled from birth, and everything they did after that seemed to make me worse. My tomboyishness made them worried that I would become a lesbian. My proclivity for violence, stealing, and arson made them anxious that I would become a criminal. I imagine that my colic as a baby must have set the tone for my parents in their relationship with me. There was nothing that could be done for me; my high-pitched complaints indicated to my parents that I had already decided they were inadequate. Even as a baby, I didn't tire; I was relentless, unreasonable, and immoderate. They must have approached me with such consternation, as there were mysteries in me that simply could not be solved.

If I had grown up today, some elementary school teacher would probably have had a serious conversation with my parents and asked them to get me psychological testing. As it was, I wasn't sent to a therapist until I was sixteen. By that time my mother had emotionally emancipated herself from my father's dictatorial rule. She was keen to also get us the "emotional help" we needed, but I was the only one she deemed so damaged as to warrant professional help. By then she had noticed that I was not just fiercely independent and reckless, but also emotionally apathetic. And it didn't seem like I was going to grow out of it. It was too late, though; I was already too smart for the therapist. Or maybe I was never amenable to therapy. Either way, I wasn't going to change. I had already chosen to view the world as a set of opportunities at winning or losing in a zero-sum game, and I used every encounter to gain information to my advantage.

Everything I learned about people's motivations, their expectations, desires, and emotional responses, was cataloged in

my mind for later use. Therapy was a treasure trove in this respect. It taught me about what was expected of me as a normal
person and therefore made me better able to disguise myself,
to scheme my manipulations with greater precision. In particular, it crystallized a valuable piece of data that I had already
internalized—that frailty could excuse anything. I learned to
capitalize on my vulnerabilities, real or imagined. Therapists
helped me find them, as their job was to look for them, coming up with reasons for my deficits and digging for trauma
wherever they could find it. So many valuable tactics for seduction and exploitation were uncovered in my teenage therapy
sessions. And school was the society in which I could exercise
those tactics.

Chapter 4

LITTLE SOCIOPATH IN
THE BIG WORLD

When people on the blog and elsewhere ask me how they can know if they are sociopaths, I often ask them about their childhoods: If you were always on the outside looking in, separated from the other kids and maybe even from your family by a wall of emotions that they seemed to feel effortlessly while you did not; if you could instinctively get a sense of how power flowed between various cliques, between the students and the staff, and within your family; if belonging never meant anything to you yet you found you could easily enter and then manipulate any group at will; then maybe, just maybe, you were a tiny wolf in lamb's wool, a young sociopath without knowing it.

My childhood was unusual only in that it never had a start and never had an end. From a very young age, I filled my life with minutiae and little conquests. While others were learning to play kickball, I learned to play people. I was not subtle. I used friends as pawns purely for access to their toys or whatever else they could offer me. I generally didn't need to play out elaborate ruses of the kind I'd spin a few years later;

I simply did the minimum necessary to insinuate myself into their good graces so I could get what I needed: food at lunch when my family's pantry was empty, rides home or to activities when my parents were MIA, invitations to birthday parties at fun venues that I was otherwise priced out of, and the thing that I craved more than anything else—the fear of others that let me know that I was the one in power, I was the one in control. I think it unnerved people how little I cared about things that other people cared about, like the well-being of others or my own physical safety. When one of my classmates cried about having a split lip from my punching him, I just stood there, watching, and left when I got bored with the blood and drama of it. I liked toys and candy like every other kid, but I couldn't be blackmailed or manipulated with them, refusing to be tricked into sharing or playing nice like the other kids were.

Other children weren't my only targets. Adults tend to believe children, especially when they make their faces seem so expressively open with emotion, especially when the child seems to be the victim of adult overreaching or abuse. I knew what that looked like in other children, the face of the victimized. They would widen their eyes quizzically, pause, then slowly reflect on the reality of their situation (was that man with the van and free candy really being nice, or was there something more insidious going on?) with the wheels turning in their tiny little heads and their mouths half-open. Looks of consternation would manifest on their chubby, soft faces, and then a sad realization would slowly spread across them, their faces falling—they have been victimized and you, adult, are the only one who can help them. Sometimes I would watch myself in the mirror, seeing if my face could also make those faces.

I was better at manipulating adults than I was at manipulating other children, which is why I often wonder about child sociopaths who can't manage to remain undetected. Adults do not inspect children's behavior closely. It's been so long since they saw the world through child eyes that they don't really remember what is normal behavior for children. There are times when they do not understand children, but they also have vague memories of being misunderstood as a child. Careful not to make that same mistake, adults tend to have a much greater tolerance or margin of error when it comes to unusual childish behavior. They're much more willing to write off a child obsessed with collecting worms during recess as being a simple variation of the eccentricities of childhood, whereas the child's peers would more readily classify that child as an anomalous freak.

Children sociopaths are not obvious to adults, which is perhaps why people debate their very existence. It's rare to hear stories of child sociopaths that seem ripped from the pages of *The Bad Seed*. In a *New York Times Magazine* article titled "Can You Call a 9-Year-Old a Psychopath?" the author told the story of Michael, a boy who had been terrorizing his parents since soon after his baby brother was born. Michael would fly into a rage at the slightest interruption to his life, like being asked to put on his shoes, punching and kicking walls while screaming at his parents. When his mother tried to reason with him with reminders about how they had talked about his behavior and that she had hoped they had gotten past it, he stopped cold in his tantrum and replied, "Well you didn't think that through very clearly, did you?" Other horror stories included another nine-year-old boy who pushed a toddler into the swimming pool of a motel, then pulled up a chair to watch it drown. When asked why he did those things he replied, curiosity. Unfazed by the threat of punishment, he seemed to welcome being the focus of attention.

This sort of behavior is by far the exception. At least to adult eyes, the behavior of a typical child sociopath is much more subtle. Paul Frick, a child psychologist with the University of New Orleans, explains that more common behavior might be the lack of remorse shown when caught. For instance, normal children tend to feel conflicted about getting caught with their hand in the cookie jar. On the one hand, they wanted that cookie. On the other hand, they feel like there is something morally wrong about stealing. A child sociopath would not show this same type of remorse. The only thing the child sociopath would regret is getting caught. Even the *New York Times* journalist who interviewed Michael was surprised at how normal he seemed: "When I entered the house, of course, I was thinking of adult psychopaths who have led criminal lives for decades, which is normally how they come to our attention. I was maybe expecting a child version of that, but of course that's kind of ridiculous. Even among adult psychopaths, that would be a small minority."

No, fooling adults was never my problem; it was always my peers who were more sensitive and exacting in the homogeneity of "normal" behavior that they required. I'm good, but I'm not flawless, and they required near perfection. Let me give an example of what I mean. If a person were to go to a Mormon church for the first time, there would be many things that might give them away as a non-Mormon—perhaps the newcomer would be wearing jeans, or would be a woman wearing slacks instead of a dress or a skirt, or even a woman wearing a skirt cut above her knees. There is an extremely high degree of homogeneity in Mormon culture, and in ways that may not be immediately obvious to the uninitiated. It is not just a pressure to conform that makes everyone so uniform; it actually reflects a shared underlying belief system and similar experiences.

You can try to imitate the physical trappings of Mormonism all you want, but unless you've studied and practiced Mormon culture extensively, you will never be confused for a cultural Mormon. Similarly, since I did not share the same worldview and underlying beliefs and experiences as my childhood peers, I could pretend and imitate all I wanted, but there would still be small discrepancies that would give me away, or at the very least make me seem quirky to my peers.

I usually had friends despite my perceived oddness, but I experienced periods in which I was avoided or even ostracized by everyone. I could overwhelm people, put them off. I was too aggressive for them, or they could see how deceptive, un-trustworthy, and scheming I was. Sometimes my considerable charisma could outweigh the off-putting aspects of my personality, but sometimes it went the other way. My ability to under-stand my occasional status as a social pariah was spotty; I was good at observing the way other kids reacted to me, but I didn't always care enough to do anything about it. I was too impul-sive, too willing to sacrifice several months of social capital in exchange for a moment's indiscretion.

Of course I was never bullied or picked on. If anything, my peers were afraid of me. And I usually had enough sense to be selective about whom I targeted—no one too likable. Kids love vigilantism, so I frequently went after bullies. I re-member this one set of white trash twins. One of the kids had something wrong with his legs, so he would show up to school with braces or special shoes. He far exceeded children's toler-ance for diversity. Perhaps because they were identical and to distance himself from the less fortunate twin, the other one became a big bully. He was little but scrappy, and since he couldn't really pick on the true alphas, he would pick on everyone else, hoping merely to establish his dominance as a beta. Everyone hated him, but no one wanted to provoke his wrath. I didn't care either way about him. I think maybe I scared him. But one time he was basically forced to confront me during an undersupervised game of capture the flag. I had cheated somehow and his team goaded him into calling me on it. Words turned into shoves and pretty soon I had him pinned to the ground and I beat the crap out of him. Not too long, lest we draw attention. Just enough that he didn't get up for several minutes. The other kids loved me for that for at least several months. I was happy to do it. To me, stopping a bully was like helping put out a fire. It may not have reached my house yet, but fires are unpredictable and they spook the surrounding wildlife into behaving unpredictably. The probability that it will somehow affect me is high enough that any preventative measures on my part are often warranted. And beating on a bully makes you a hero in people's eyes. I guess that's why Batman does it.

I often wonder how my life would be different if I had been educated outside the public school system (or even outside the U.S.). Maybe I would pretend less or be less good at it? As it was, trying to blend in with the other children required me to learn the skills of an anthropologist. As an outsider trying to fit in, I had to learn about people through observation and the recognition of patterns. I became very perceptive. I also became good at acting. I could see that other kids thought and behaved differently from me, often reacting emotionally whereas I stayed calm, and so I began to mimic them. I think my first attempts at imitating normal behavior were honest attempts to actually be normal, in the same way that an infant imitates the speech patterns of its parents not to try to trick, but in an honest attempt to communicate. I didn't realize it at the time, but I would never be normal. Maybe it was the cognitive fork in the road when I was four years old. Maybe it was the code written in my DNA. Either way, it was too late by that time to turn back—if I ever indeed could have. I was irrevocably different from other people, in ways that I had yet to fully understand. I wasn't able to articulate that then of course, but I knew it in my bones.

In the years when I played observer, I'd watch with contempt as the kids who weren't popular fawned all over the kids who were. I'd see them for the weaklings they were and wonder why they thought belonging mattered so much that they were willing to debase themselves. I couldn't even conceive of the idea that anyone or any group was important enough for me to humiliate myself. After I had observed long enough and learned what I needed to know, I easily became one of the popular kids. But even when I was schmoozing with the jocks and the cheerleaders and the class clowns whom everybody loved, even when kids from lower grades wanted my attention, I knew I was not one of them. I'd known that I would never really belong no matter how many people claimed to love hanging out with me, because the person they thought they knew was not the real me.

I did however enjoy playing my games with them. With my friends, I'd usually find little ways to prey on their insecurities. Have you ever picked a scab? Or poked at a tender tooth? Probed a sore muscle? There's something exploratory about it, and I was this way with my friends' insecurities. They fascinated me. I have never had an insecurity. I know it sounds absurd. It's not like I think that I am the best at everything. I am well aware of my many failings. I guess it's just that they don't bother me, and I certainly don't identify with them in this bizarre, fixated way that I often see people do.

Often my lack of insecurities would trigger them in my

own friends. For instance, a girl I was friends with in high school was shy around boys. She worried that she was undesirable. I happened to be surrounded by boys all of the time: I was a drummer, a surfer, and an extreme-sports enthusiast, all male-dominated fields. Almost all of my friends were male and I never once lost any sleep over whether they found me attractive or not, which I think was actually what made me attractive to them. I knew that she wished she could be more like me in this way. I knew that part of her hated me for it. I knew that more than anything, she wanted to prove one day that she was more desirable than I was. So I set up a little game for us to play.

There was a boy who had a crush on me. We'll call him Dave. I knew he had a crush on me because he was very open about it but was torn because he was very Christian and I was Mormon. This made him the perfect companion for absolutely everything. I loved teasing him with his attraction to me, particularly knowing that he would never act on it because he equated it with rebellion against God (or something). Frequently I would hang out with Dave with my insecure friend— we'll call her Sarah—because I knew she had a bit of a crush on him and was oblivious enough not to notice that he was interested in me. Or was she? I wasn't really sure, but I loved the awkward dynamic that it set up in all our interactions.

One Saturday we were out and about and decided to go together to a party later that evening. We stopped by Dave's house so he could pick up a change of clothes. While we were waiting for him, Sarah and I got to talking, or more accurately, I got her talking. I could tell that she was thinking that tonight was her chance to prove that somebody liked her better than me. Maybe because Dave had been flirting with her all day in an attempt to give me some of my own medicine? In any case, she wore on her face confidence and a premature sense of victory.

"Why are you smiling?" I asked.

"No reason." She giggled.

"No, seriously, you can tell me. What is it?"

"It's nothing. It's stupid."

"You want to make a bet to see who can kiss Dave first?"

"How'd you know?!"

"Ha, I didn't until just now. But we can, you know. Do you want to?"

Of course she wanted to. She thought she was going to win. She wanted to see me humiliated for once. We invented elaborate rules and came up with some reward (I knew the more complicated the "rules" seemed, the more it would seem like a legitimate and fair endeavor when really it was just me setting her up for embarrassment and feeding her insecurities). Of course I won, but only after dragging it out as long as possible, and only after she had thrown herself at him and had been soundly rejected. It was doubly delicious knowing that not only had I crushed Sarah's newfound confidence, but Dave had given up his religious beliefs for me only to be spurned the next day.

Despite my bad intentions, for the most part everything I did was relatively tame, at least when you consider that there are children shooting up schools. I never thought of myself as a predator because I never raped or killed anyone. But looking back, I wonder if my essential understanding of my outsider status, combined with the instinctive sense that I had to carefully observe other people in order to both survive and thrive, is how the human predator thinks.

If I'm a predator, do I prey for sport or to survive? I learned how to be this way to survive, but it's also true that I do it when it's not necessary. Many predators engage in similar behavior, so-called "surplus killing," or attacking prey without an immediate need or use for the animal. Have you seen videos of killer whales batting around their prey only to kill and abandon them? Scientists assure us that they aren't actually killing for the fun of it (how would they know?), but rather that surplus killing is a survival mechanism—those who engage in surplus killing are the most aggressive, and the most aggressive predators are the ones who survive and procreate.

Predators who engage in surplus killing are constantly at the ready, always willing to make the kill. Similarly, I am always ready to play to win, no matter whom I am playing against or how innocent or nonthreatening they are to me in that moment. It makes sense. If I were only ruthless when I needed to be or only toward particular types of people who "deserved" it, I don't think I could be as effective. I would be constantly questioning myself—is this person worth it? Do I really need to be going after them in this particular way? Instead, my natural inclination is to be aggressive to everyone. Nowadays I put a lot of effort into suppressing this urge. I've allowed myself to be tamed by people in order to have longer-lasting relationships, but the animalistic urge to destroy is always bubbling underneath the surface. For many I'm a beautiful and exotic pet but inherently dangerous—like a white tiger to my family and friends' Siegfried and Roy.

This natural aggression was always the biggest obstacle preventing me from having a normal social life. All through growing up, I could try everything to hide my true nature, but it would always find ways to seep onto the surface in the form of unveiled aggression. When someone invoked my wrath—a tattling schoolmate or an insipid teacher—my eyes turned into dark simmering pools, the roiling of revenge plots apparent just below the surface. I tilted my head forward, my hands curled into fists and my eyes narrowed, as if to focus all my malignant energy on my antagonist for optimum destruction. I glowered like villains do in the movies, shattering the illusion of normalcy I tried so hard to project. Often it felt as if, at least socially, it was always one step forward, two steps back.

It was in my preteen years that I realized how crucial it was to actively cultivate attractive personality traits. I would study my peers to discover what made them seem likable to each other, and I became all of those things. That's when I picked up surfing, played in rock bands, and became a social climber. In addition to getting good grades, I started watching indie films and listening to underground music, did alternative sports like BMX biking and street luging and wore thrift-store clothes. I became so uniquely accomplished, talented, and charming that I was naturally included on everyone's list of people to know and like (or fear). Not only could I wear any number of masks to suit any situation, I had learned how to wear them with consistency.

I didn't stop behaving outrageously, but I made it a point to perform well in school so that any slipups would be overlooked as quirks. My mother's love of music—her view of it as her salvation—was passed on to me. I played the drums in the school band and in rock bands with other kids. When I was in junior high and high school, music masked a lot of my antisocial behaviors. Musicians are expected to be narcissistic and outrageous; it would be disappointing if they behaved normally. So the things I did seemed appropriate in the context of my rock star ambitions. When you're holding a guitar or banging on drums, you're supposed to scream and dance wildly, to be aggressive, to bully crowds into going crazy in mosh pits, to elicit the love and attention that they are all too willing to give.

I was fortunate that Jim continued to include me in his social life, even though I was his kid sister. In high school, all of his friends were older—not exactly edgy, but energetic and committed to ska music. They dressed in vintage suits and skinny ties. Every weekend they went to clubs and house parties to hear their favorite bands play, and my brother and I would go with them. It was my introduction to mosh pits and crowd surfing, knives, broken bottles, and crowd fights where people got dragged off in stretchers and cop cars. It was thrilling.

In high school I would get into elaborate feuds with people. Once I fought with one of my teachers over who should be in charge of the class—I thought I should be; for some reason he thought he should be. I bought yards of black fabric and cut out armbands, eventually getting half of the school involved in the "protest" against him. (Teenagers are eager to rebel against any sort of authority, which I was only too willing to exploit.) Another time I wanted to start a competitive drum line that would compete in shows around Southern California. We needed instruments, so, figuring it was better to ask forgiveness than to ask permission, I forged the entrance forms and took the school's gear on the weekends, when I was sure no one would notice. I picked fights with people much bigger and stronger than I was, but mostly they were at rock concerts as part of a mosh pit, where the violence was tolerated. Cunning and calculating even then, I managed to stay out of serious trouble to preserve my freedom.

In order to avoid complaints and simply because I liked to, I mostly played with the boys as a child. They rarely tattled about injuries. I liked running around and jostling with them, coming in with a thin coat of sweat and grime from my time in the yard. When I was very young, I refused to wear a shirt so that I could be just like the boys. I didn't understand why anyone would choose to hold baby dolls rather than make war with army soldiers.

I loved contact sports, everything about them. Touch football was classic that way. Especially after it rained and the fields were muddy, it was natural for tackling and black eyes to happen. Or playing tag on the playground equipment, we would fling ourselves off platforms and whip around corners, our bodies colliding in clumsy ballets. It was such a rush to smash my body into someone else's, such satisfaction when one of my playmates got sent off to the nurse's office with a bloody nose! In high school softball, I wasn't the best player, but I'm sure I collided with other players more than anyone else. I stole bases with relish. Even if the ball had been thrown to the baseman by the time I got there, my unmitigated determination in running straight for her often freaked her out enough that she would leap to one side. One time as I was stealing home, I spooked the catcher so much that she clotheslined me though she didn't even have the ball yet. It's true that sometimes people are alarmed by my enthusiasm, but usually, I consider it their problem.

Risk taking, aggression, and a lack of concern for your own health or that of others are all symptoms of sociopathy, and my childhood is rife with evidence of them. I think that narrow escapes from death are probably better experienced young than old. They imprint in your mind a healthy sense of your mortality for later use. When I was eight, I almost drowned while swimming in the ocean. I can't recall the experience in great detail but I do remember the force of the ocean overcoming me, water as invisible as air swallowing me alive. My mother tells me that when the lifeguard fished me out of the water and breathed life into me, my first signs of life were gasps of laughter. It was perfect timing. I learned that death could come at any moment but was not so bad, really. I never developed a fear of it. At times I have flirted with it, even longed for it, but never actively sought it.

One Sunday I got very sick. It was a couple months before my sixteenth birthday. I usually kept these things to myself. Even then, I didn't like involving other people in my personal issues, because it presented an invitation to interfere with the activities of my life. But that day, I relented and told my mother about the sharp pain directly below my sternum. After she expressed her usual exasperation, she gave me some kind of quack herbal medicine and told me to rest. Now I felt pain plus nausea.

The next day I stayed home from school, which did nothing but make me feel behind in all of my activities. It took all my challenging classes, music and sports groups, and other extra-curriculars, plus toying with the interior lives of my friends, acquaintances, and authority figures, to keep my mind and body occupied. Boredom was my enemy, and thus, so too was illness. The next day, despite still being sick, I went back to school; that week I played softball and hit a double.

Every day my parents would suggest another new remedy. I carried a little bag of medicine with me wherever I went: Tums, Advil, ibuprofen, and various homeopathic cure-alls. I knew that there was pain, but I could not gauge its severity or analyze its meaning. It was an obstacle, like missing a player on the field or being farsighted. I had to play harder, strain my eyes—to contend with this thing growing in my insides, pulsing for attention, and blanketing my body with a reluctance to function.

All the energy that I usually used in social situations to blend in and charm others was redirected into controlling and ignoring the pain. A few days into it, I began to snarl at people, to glower. I ceased engaging in flattery or even polite pleasantries. I stopped reacting to people with nods or concerned facial expressions; instead, I stared at them with the dead eyes I had previously reserved for when I was alone and unseen. I couldn't be bothered to smile. There was no filter between my secret thoughts and my mouth, so I ended up telling my friends how ugly they were or why they deserved the bad things that came to them. I didn't have the intellectual ability to properly regulate my emotions or to turn on the charm. Without the mental stamina to constantly calibrate my effect on people, I embraced the raw flavor of my meanness, the mélange of dull sadism and sharp disregard.

I didn't even know I was doing it, as I hadn't realized how much brainpower it had taken me simply to maintain my personal relationships, how much was required of me to restrain my natural impulses. Only later when none of my friends stuck around did I realize what had happened. They can only make exceptions for you for so long. I behaved with sufficient meanness that my vile behavior justified many of my friends' abandonment of me. It was like I had spent my adolescence wearing medieval chain mail under my clothes only to suddenly lose it unawares. Unrestricted by its weight, my movements were outsize and bizarre.

Mornings, afternoons, and evenings passed this way, in silent, growling submission to pain. My abdominal pains migrated to my back at the level of my kidneys. I grew sweatier, clammier, and greener. My dad suggested I had muscle strain. I went back to school and had to go to a band festival about forty miles away. On the bus I was feverish and lay down on the floor on the ride home. All weekend I stayed in bed. Tuesday, I went back to school but was too sick to stay in class, so I spent the afternoon sleeping in my brother's car. I don't remember the season, but the afternoons were sunny, and the warm, undifferentiated sunlight streamed in from the windows, turning the car into a greenhouse, an incubator. Curled up in the backseat, I felt the delicious warmth blocking out the mixture of throbbing, sharp, and dull pains now populating every wide expanse and narrow corner of my body. At home I disappeared into bed. When my mother came to wake me for dinner, she unraveled a shivering, hot, wet child from the covers. When my dad got home he stared at me for a while and contemplated his next move. He looked at my torso, saw that something was very wrong, and relented: "We'll go to the doctor tomorrow."

The next day, everyone at the doctor's office was very solicitous, calm, and soothing. They did some tests, and after the results came back, everything changed into rushing and accusations. The doctor said something in outraged tones about my white cell count. I could sense my mother receding into quiet, semicatatonic disavowal, the state she retreated to when my father punched things or screamed at her. The doctor was all questions—if I had felt pain, what I had been doing for the last ten days, and why I hadn't spoken up sooner—the kind that suggested I had done something wrong, and I stopped answering them. I was bored and restless. I didn't want to be there anymore. I wanted to be free to do my own thing instead of being a passive victim at the mercy of the well-intentioned. Someone asked me if I wanted to lie down; I politely declined and then passed out. When I came to, I heard shouting and my father convincing the medical staff not to order an ambulance. Even in my delirium I could sense their mistrust of him.

My dad would have done anything to get away from the reproachful stares. Behind my own fluttering, half-closed eyelids, I could see the wild panic in his eyes. It wasn't panic about his daughter dying. Or rather, it was. But it was the moral judgment of his friends and neighbors upon my dying rather than the loss of me that terrified him. That he would allow his daughter to die from neglect. That he and my mother had let me suffer in excruciating pain for more than a week without seeking any medical attention, because—as I discovered later—he had allowed our family's medical insurance to lapse. To think of it now, I am surprised that he didn't leave my mother and me there to sort it out ourselves. In a way, my mother was luckier than my father. Her oppression allowed her to escape responsibility; her powerlessness absolved her guilt.

When I woke up following surgery, I saw my dad standing over me with tired anger. He gave me the rundown: The appendix had perforated, spewing toxins into my guts. My insides had become septic with infection, and the muscles in my back had become gangrenous. The surgeons had to cut out chunks of rotted flesh, and a plastic tube was inserted in the wound to drain the pus out. There should be no lasting damage.

"You could have died. The doctors are very angry." At me, his tone implied. It was as if I should have apologized to everyone.

Hospitals are, of course, dehumanizing places. The worst time of day is predawn, when the floors are especially cold and the daylight peeking through the blinds feels like a reckoning. The night nurses get replaced by the day nurses, fresh in their cheerful cartoon scrubs and eager to inflict their cruel practicalities. The gaggles of interns and doctors make their rounds, pulling curtains to examine and catalog flaccid, damaged flesh connected to tubes and machines—cyborgs in clinical phantasmagoria.

Stripped of your armor, you can embrace the savage that the hospital makes of you, or you can grasp desperately for the human. For me, it was an easy choice. I was well acquainted with the savage in me—the animal that knew no other thing than its will to survive and thrive. I had no trouble turning off my sense of dignity or my need for connection, because I knew that to do so was the most efficient means of getting through the days ahead. There was also a sense of relief that I didn't have to put on a mask for anyone. It saved me a lot of mental energy. Life was whittled down to the essentials—sleeping, eating, and defecating—interrupted by frequent physical violations that could be predicted and planned for. In this, I was a model patient. I did as I was told, dutifully doing my breathing exercises and taking my laps around the floor, hospital gown flapping open behind me. One nurse thought I was "brave." I think she was talking about my steely-eyed, grin-and-bear-it kind of attitude. There were no tears, no complaints from me—a total lack of affect. In a victim, it is courage and thus admirable; in a predator, it is a lack of humanity and instills fear.

After about a week, I was scheduled to leave, as long as I maintained my upward wellness trajectory. The nurse told me that my final barrier to departure was the morning breakfast. Too nauseated to eat, I tried nibbling the foods with the highest volume-to-density ratio so it would look like I had downed more than I had, but it still appeared as if I hadn't touched anything. In this instance, my dad saved me. He showed up an hour before he was due at a meeting, cramming pancakes into his mouth with one hand and flushing scrambled eggs down the toilet with the other.

On the way home, and with minutes to spare before my dad's meeting, we swung by the music store to pick up a compact disc I had wanted. It was closed, but he pounded on the door until he got the attention of an employee, gestured toward me with hurried explanations, and came back to the car with what I had asked for. People can surprise you.

I do not know how the family survived my hospital bills, but I am sure the same skills my dad used to get me my CD helped in getting out from under our enormous debt. When we got home, he walked me up the stairs and helped me into my bed, assuring me that someone would do something about my soaked bandages. He often said things like that, which were incredibly unlikely to actually happen.

My parents generally weren't much more attentive to personal safety than I was. My family got into a surprising number of car accidents. When we were kids, we had a very serious accident on a dangerous mountain highway while on our way to visit my cousins. We got rear-ended (by someone who later appeared to be intoxicated), and the force propelled our car across several lanes of traffic until we collided with a concrete wall. Partly because us kids were all crammed into the back of the car, we all got pretty banged up, but for some reason, we didn't turn back home and instead drove the rest of the ten hours that it took for us to get to our relatives' house. I suspect we lived on the insurance proceeds from that accident for several years. Even now my first instinct upon being involved in an auto accident (usually not my fault; I'm a great driver) is to take a copious number of photos and solicit incriminating statements from the other driver.

I had been climbing on moving vehicles since I was little. I would climb onto moving vehicles, climb around already moving vehicles, and even once tried climbing under a moving vehicle. I loved to ride in the backs of trucks, dangling off.

When I was ten years old, a family friend asked my older brother Jim and me to operate an eight-passenger, gas-powered golf cart to shuttle guests to and from a Halloween party hosted about a half mile away from the parking area. We were polite and safe when taking passengers up to the house but performed increasingly risky acts on the way back down. On one trip, I was attempting to climb along the roof from the back of the golf cart to the front. My brother wasn't paying attention and when he didn't see me, he assumed that he had left me back at the house. He made a sharp U-turn and I went flying off the roof, barrel-rolling for several seconds along the pavement. I lost consciousness and woke up on my back, red taillights rapidly coming my direction. My brother (still unaware of what had happened) was backing up as part of a three-point turn and I just missed being run over by rolling out of the way.

"Where'd you go?" my brother asked, surprised, when I climbed back into the cart.

"I don't know. Nowhere," I replied.

Driving my own motor vehicle wasn't any less hazardous. One afternoon my mother introduced me to what would become, $1,200 later, my first car. The car was a beautiful disaster—a 1972 Pontiac "Luxury" LeMans, V-8 engine with dual mufflers coming out the back. The car was viscerally appealing, a sister of the GTO with a nearly identical body. It was the last year that the Pontiac maintained its curvy form, mimicking the musculature of the animals that cars of that era were frequently named after (Mustang, Charger, Cougar). The Pontiac's dual round headlights stared back at you; its grill and bumper sneered. Its fenders were rusted out by the wheel wells and the only thing saving the roof from rust was the white vinyl top. The best feature in my mother's eyes, though, was the Detroit steel. She believed that in an accident the other person would feel the hurt, not me. I proved this intuition to be accurate many times in my first few years with it.

The engine to my car was so simple that I did my own small

repairs and tweaks. I wanted to understand how it worked. I wanted to control it, not the other way around. When the starter went out one year while I was at college, I enlisted my boyfriend to help me replace it where it was stalled in a friend's apartment complex parking lot. I had no idea how to do it and neither did he, but I was always willing to try new things no matter how ill advised. Everything was going well until we began to disconnect the starter from the car before detaching the battery. Sparks started flying, catching the undercarriage on fire. We both quickly got out from under the car and I had to throw snow on the flames to put them out.

I got a lot of attention in that car, some of it lewd, but I never felt vulnerable in it—I always felt invincible. I learned how to handle its power, how to accelerate into turns, how to launch it off the line while drag-racing it with friends, and how to fishtail it in California rainstorms, which, due to their rarity, made roads especially slick from accumulated gas and oil.

I loved the confidence and power I felt with that car, because it was such a contrast to the dissonance of being female, teenage, and powerless. My brothers were closer to my daredevil personality than my sisters, with their mild games of dolls and house. They would go off to their church Boy Scout groups and shoot arrows and skulk around the woods with knives, and my equivalent Mormon female activities were cross-stitching homilies for pillowcases, baking snickerdoodles, and anything that involved the use of a glue gun. In general, the women in my life seemed like they were never acting, always being acted upon.

When I was in my tween years, men started telling me how much I looked like my mother. I correctly interpreted that to mean that I had started to become an object of sexual desire. By the time I was ten, I had already developed full plump breasts and my hips had the contours of a Greek vase. Men openly leered, their aggression palpable. The adult women in the world treated me like I was a slut, even though I had no idea why. And so my new body was primarily a liability at first. If I wasn't careful, it functioned like a suicide bomb, with collateral damage in the form of judgment from women and harassment from men.

I understand that all teenage girls experience some variation of this awkward transition between child and sex object. Even so, I think in a lot of ways it's much worse for someone like me—a budding sociopath. All I wanted was power and control. If I were a boy, I thought, I would be big and muscled. I would cut an imposing presence. I was always athletic, always aggressive for a girl. Even in male-dominated physical activities like mosh pits, I held my own through sheer antagonism. But I was also five foot three and 125 pounds. I wanted fear and respect but what I typically ended up with were unwanted advances from inebriated guys twice my size. I did not look like a predator, I looked like an attractive target for unsolicited and aggressive forms of attention. I was a strong, tough girl, but men were generally stronger and tougher. I was extraordinarily smart and conniving, but it was oftentimes not enough to vanquish the authority of adults half as smart and not nearly as conniving as me. It's not that I did not feel female so much as I did not feel as weak as I looked.

I have never identified very much with my gender, or at least, I have been extraordinarily ambivalent. But a lot of girls go through similar phases of rejection of and rebellion from gender stereotypes. When you grow up as a girl, it is like there are faint chalk lines traced approximately three inches around your entire body at all times, drawn by society and often religion and family and particularly other women, who somehow feel invested in how you behave, as if your actions reflect directly on all womanhood. These chalk lines circumscribe the manner in which you interact with the world, are the source of the implicit "for a girl" that seems to trail every compliment ("tough, for a girl"). You want to wave your arms around as hard as you can to wipe them away and scatter them to dust, but the chalk lines just follow you around, always keeping you inside that constant three inches of space. I felt that the label of *girl* was too limiting to contain my own grandiose conception of myself, and so I mostly ignored it.

There were obviously good things about my gender. My mother was largely passive with my father, but if she ever wanted something, all it took was a simple touch, a half promise of physical pleasure, to get him to do almost anything she wanted. In those hundreds of times when men told me my mother was beautiful, I eventually saw not just objectification but the power of dearly hoped-for pleasures. I have sometimes heard men lament that women have all of the power because they are the ones who say yes or no to sex. But I wasn't yet ready to deploy that kind of power. In my high school years, while other girls were learning about and experimenting with their sexuality, I was largely asexual. I didn't understand then that sex could be something that could give me pleasure. And I didn't understand it as a way of connecting to people, and therefore gaining a form of power over them. I didn't know that sex was a means to love, and that people will do anything for love.

I did, however, use my gender to great effect with many of my disgusting, perverted teachers. One of them I hated in particular. My high school English teacher had given me a failing grade on one of my assignments because my mother had turned it in for me on a day I'd been away at a softball tournament or drum competition. He ridiculed me in front of the class for having my "mommy bring it," trying to make an example of me. This teacher was old and vindictively petty. I never liked him. I had seen him ruthlessly attack other students in my class, so I never gave him any reason to target me. Still, there was something about my silent defiance that must have gotten under his skin, because he finally made up something plausible to attack me on.

"Thomas! You may have noticed that you received an F. I didn't even look at your paper, so next time you can save your mommy some time and either come in and turn in your work yourself or don't bother turning it in at all." I was instantly angry, but it quickly chilled.

"Screw you, fat man," I calmly retorted, and minutes later was waiting my turn in the principal's office.

From that time on we'd engaged in a low-grade power struggle. I wanted to take him down, and since he had such a bad reputation, the easiest way was just to create a paper trail of his inappropriate behavior. I started taking detailed notes of things he said and did in class that were even remotely questionable. I made friends with girls in my class, planting in their heads the total inappropriateness of even some of his more innocuous behavior. He wasn't that bad a guy, really. He was just old and a bit of a natural chauvinist in the way that men born before 1950 typically are. When we would take quizzes, he would project them up on the board and have everyone move forward, ostensibly so people in the back could see better. He always had the first row move their seats all the way up to touch his desk, and in that row just happened to be a girl who frequently wore the revealing spandex of a dancer. I started a rumor that he had us move like this to get a better view of her ample cleavage. It was a very plausible story, particularly with the way his face frequently contorted into what looked like a leer. It may have actually been true. In any case, it made good gossip and was accepted as truth shortly after it got started.

That rumor itself was not enough. Nor was it enough when I finally goaded him into making a lewd and demeaning comment about my breasts. The class was talking about a recent music department production.

"How did you like my solo?" I sneered after listening to him go on about everyone else in the class.

"Thomas! You have no class! Up there onstage, flopping all around, letting it all hang out. Not like these other girls," he said, gesturing to the dancer in front of him. I think he was trying to turn the class against me, but unfortunately for him I had gotten to them first. He didn't hurt my feelings; he had finally, unequivocally, overstepped the student-teacher boundary in front of witnesses.

After class I asked the dancer if she felt uncomfortable about his thinly veiled harassment. I was the picture of worried concern. She was touched by my sincerity. Yes, she had heard the rumor I started about her and this teacher (unaware that I was the one who started it). Yes, it did bother her. I was the sympathetic ear. She confessed all of her discomfort and I not only listened, I validated and fed the flame of her distress.

I used his behavior that day to paint him as out of control. I needed her to be afraid of him. I needed her to be one of the other voices raised in condemnation against him. I told her that we had to stop him before it got any worse. I told her that I was thinking of filing an official complaint against him for sexual harassment and asked if she would be willing to verify my story if necessary. I made it seem as if her participation would probably not be necessary, based on numerous contingencies, so she agreed. She would soon find out that she would be my star witness.

When I got home I told my mother about what had happened in class—strictly the facts, nothing about our power struggle or my preparations to get him fired. I told her about how "violated" I felt and about how I was not the only girl toward whom he had behaved in this way. I knew my mother felt bad about all of the times growing up that she had failed me, so she'd be inclined to help here. I told her I had found out that you make sexual harassment claims against teachers directly with the school district. Would she like to come with me to the district office the next morning to start the paperwork? My father was completely opposed to the idea, which I think made it all the more appealing to my mother.

I gave my statement and enlisted a small cadre of loyalists to paint him in as bad a light as they could. He was supervised for several weeks. There was always someone else with him whenever he was on campus, I noticed with delight. Officially he received a "strike," an official censure; unofficially I believe he was forced into early retirement and had to give up his position as head of the English department, which to me was success. I was never one to be greedy or get caught up in the "principle of the thing." I wasn't trying to get him fired to protect future generations of vulnerable young girls. I was trying to get him fired to show him that he was vulnerable, and to me, a helpless little girl.

Still, it was a good lesson in the limits of the formal justice system, one that I would face again shortly in law school. This was not the only time I tangled with a teacher, but no matter what I did and to whom I reported them, none were ever fired or even removed from their positions. And while I gained the satisfaction of causing them pain, I garnered a reputation for making trouble. Maybe I lied, cheated, and bullied in order to achieve their destruction, but it was nonetheless true that they were bad teachers who should not have been allowed around kids. One teacher was an idiot who favored the popular kids over the unpopular ones, ignoring their talent in order to bask in the social acceptance that he never received when he was a student in high school himself. Another was sexually obsessed with his students and paid special lascivious attention to the ones with large breasts (including me) and low self-esteem (not including me). I wasn't doing a public service in trying to ruin them. I just couldn't stand that such unfit people could have authority over me. And that was the double injustice of being a young sociopath and a girl, too.

Chapter 5

I'm a Child of God

I was raised in the Church of Jesus Christ of Latter-Day Saints. I attended church from infancy with my family, and I continue to be a practicing Mormon. Some people will find this hypocritical or will assume that my religious community will shun me if I am discovered to be a sociopath. They cannot fathom how I can negotiate my faith being who I am. But these people misunderstand the essential nature of Mormon beliefs, which is that we are all sons and daughters of a loving God who only wants our eternal progression and happiness. Mormons believe that everyone has the potential to be godlike, to be a creator of worlds. (This makes the LDS church a sociopath's dream; it's a belief that's well suited to my own megalomaniacal sense of divine destiny.) I believe that "everyone" includes me. And because every being is capable of salvation, I can only conclude that my actions are what matter—not my emotional deficits, not my ruthless thoughts, and not my nefarious motivations. My own adherence to the standards of the church, despite their frequent conflict with my nature, is proof that the teachings of the gospel are for everyone—every nation, kindred, tongue, and people. I like the idea that there is a creator of all things, including sociopaths. I like having a check on my behavior, a reason for being a good sociopath. And I like the reward for good behavior—the feeling of elation and otherworldliness inherent in prayer, song, and religious devotion.

The church is especially well suited to me, because its rules and standards are very explicit. Throughout my child-hood, I was able to make up for my inability to intuit social norms by following the church's clear set of expectations and guidelines—from detailed lessons on chastity to small pamphlets with handy bullet-pointed rules about what to wear, whom and how to date, what not to watch or listen to, and how much money to give to the church. I liked that these things were written down. I don't mean to imply that the Mormon church was actually okay with whatever I did as long as I didn't drink Coke, was abstinent, and tithed. I'm sure the church meant these things merely as guidelines and not as safe-harbor provisions, but having them stated so explicitly helped me to blend in with everyone else.

I was watching television recently, one of these mystery dramas in which the main story arc over the entire season involves people trying to figure out who killed the main character. After many episodes of intrigue and bad behavior, one of the characters remarks in exasperation, "I'm having a hard time figuring out who's evil and who's just naughty." Is there a distinction between being naughty and being evil? Who deserves mercy, and who is beyond hope?

I never felt like I was evil. I was taught in church that I am a child of God. I also read the Old Testament. There is a story in Kings where God has forty-two children dismembered by she-bears for insulting the prophet Elisha. It was not much of a stretch to believe that that God was my father.

And who doesn't have flaws? When it counts, most of us think we are basically good people. In Dan Ariely's book *The (Honest) Truth About Dishonesty,* he describes how the gift shop at the Kennedy Center for the Performing Arts was the victim of rampant embezzlement, mainly by elderly volunteers manning an unsecured cash drawer. Interestingly, there wasn't one person who was stealing tons, but many people stole just a little. Everybody cheats, and if you stay within the realm of what everybody does then you can (apparently) maintain the good image you have of yourself.

In our discussions on religion, my summer intern office mate who diagnosed me would argue that the Christian concept of sin is a state of being, not certain actions. We are all "sinners" and, simultaneously, we are all "saved." She thinks that evil, "if it has any meaning at all, means more than just 'I did this right today and I did that wrong today.'" According to her, evil doesn't lie in whether you drink caffeine or whether you do the right number of rosaries. It's different in quality from the notion of "transgressions."

Perhaps that is true, and perhaps that is why in the age of "reformed" religion, where the emphasis is more on "saved" than "sinners," none of those volunteering seniors saw their minor pilfering as evidence of their own inherently evil nature. Where those boundaries lie between being good, being good enough, and being bad is not clear. If modern Lady Justice is blind, it appears it is a selective blindness that is willing to overlook "normal" transgressions that normal people participate in and to readily condemn "abnormal" transgressions that people like me may be predisposed to commit.

I remember one of my first, formative experiences with justice. I have always loved to read. I could spend the entire day reading. When I was young, my parents were always giving us chores to keep us busy and away from the television, but if they saw that I was reading, they would just leave me alone. One summer—I must have been around seven or eight—I would go in the morning with my father to his office, then walk the few blocks to the local library and spend the day there tucked between the stacks.

It was amazing to me that you could check out books for free. It seemed like a scam, and even at that young age I was helplessly attracted to scams. I had gotten to know the librarians, and I tried to convince them that I was such an avid reader, they really should lift the ten-book restriction from my library card. When they told me they couldn't, I just stole my siblings' and parents' cards and loaded up on dozens of books, ostensibly for them. I was so pleased with how well my scheme was going, I lost focus on the reading and fixated on acquiring more and more books. I didn't want to return them. That would be completely counterproductive. Instead I hoarded them in my room. They were the spoils of my successful intrigue against the unsuspecting librarians, and now there was nothing they could do to stop me.

Maybe a month later, we got several envelopes in the mail from the library addressed to me, my siblings, and my parents. Everyone had overdue library books and the fines were quickly racking up. It didn't take long for my parents to identify me as the culprit. I hadn't understood that the library actually had an enforcement provision to get people to comply with their rules.

My parents weren't mad. I think they just chalked it up to my being so overeager about reading that I had bitten off more than I could chew. They made vague references to how I would have to do chores to earn the money. Doing the dishes one hundred times at fifty cents apiece didn't appeal to me, and it didn't seem really right that I should have to do that for what I felt was essentially an honest mistake (honest in the sense that I thought the rules of the game I was playing were one thing and they turned out to be another). I was sure this couldn't be the end of my scheme, so I tried one more thing.

"Can't you just write them a check?" I asked my father. I had seen him write checks for things before. I knew what money was, and checks seemed to be something that substituted for money when necessary—like this magical reprieve from having to use cash. My dad had to explain that it's still your money, but the bank simply keeps it for you. I was stuck. My seven-year-old brain couldn't think of any other ways to spin this, except maybe to ask for a dollar for every round of dishes. This was just how justice worked: there are rules and consequences, and if you break the rules you suffer the consequences.

When I say this was one of my first experiences with justice, I should explain. I had been punished before, but there was always an element of moral condemnation in punishments that didn't make sense to me, so I largely just ignored them as being an unpredictable cost of living life as a child. The library book situation was something new. My parents were not mad at me. There was no moral condemnation. And paying a fine seemed a reasonable consequence of not returning the library books on time. If I had to pay fines, everyone had to pay fines, which meant that books would circulate faster and I would have a better shot of checking out some of the more popular and desirable books. This sort of justice made sense to me in a way that moral judgments never did.

I was also fine with justice because I understood the flip

side: if you do particular good things, you get particular good rewards. Mormon doctrine has a scripture: "There is a law, irrevocably decreed in heaven before the foundations of this world, upon which all blessings are predicated—And when we obtain any blessing from God, it is by obedience to that law upon which it is predicated." Skeptics may question the objective truthfulness of this statement, but when your parents and everyone else around you believe it is true, it is easy to play the justice card to get justly rewarded for your good exploits.

The effect of this belief on my home life cannot be overstated. For the most part positive justice in my family operated as consistently as a gumball machine. If I put money in, I got a gumball. I would just find the highest reward-to-work ratio (to the point where it seemed like a scam) and engage in those activities over and over again, undeterred by boredom. Unlike my siblings, who seemed to have natural preferences for doing one thing over another, I just went where the money was, in a cold cost-benefit determination. For instance, my brother Jim hated to practice the piano, even though he was the most musically talented. To incentivize him, my mother offered to pay us five cents for every time we played through a particular song that we were learning. I had no natural love of music, but would sit at the piano for hours, my fingers mechanically pounding away at the keys while my mind imagined how I would spend the money.

Mormons are equally big on mercy. Every spring and fall we would gather around our television and watch a satellite broadcast of the semiannual General Conference of the Church of Jesus Christ of Latter-Day Saints, with speakers chosen from the general officers of the church. One of my favorite speakers was (now president of the church) Thomas Monson. He would always tell these entertaining stories about widows and orphans and the tender mercies of God. The message was clear—God loves widows and orphans, and he loves me just as much.

What about the sinners? In the Mormon world that isn't much of a problem. Everyone is a sinner. In fact people talk about it all of the time, in veiled references to "whatever trials and temptations we might have in this life." I remember looking side to side during church at those references, imagining double lives filled with sordid affairs and violence. I never felt that I was outside the norm for sinning. I still don't.

Everybody slips up because we're not perfect; that's what mercy is for. The problem is when you keep making the same mistakes, which I largely do not. One could say that by repeatedly manipulating, "ruining," and crushing people, I'm consistently violating the idea of doing unto others as I would have them do unto me. The thing is that I have no problem with others trying to ruin me back. In my mind, it's just business, not personal. We're all competing for power. Would I be upset if I had a sandwich shop and someone opened up a sandwich shop across the street? I might be annoyed, but I wouldn't take it personally. I don't have hate in my heart for these people. I may wish them ill, but it's not because I harbor ill will against them. They just happen to be players in my game and controlling others is how I validate my own sense of self-worth. Perhaps, one might argue, by trying to control other people I'm depriving them of their own power, dignity, and independence. I do not see this as a moral issue. People can still choose: either to submit to my control or to face whatever consequences there may be. Maybe God thinks this way too. Maybe this is why he sometimes kills children to make a point.

The biggest stumbling block I have faced with my Mormon faith is the idea of "godly sorrow." The Bible makes a distinction between godly sorrow and worldly sorrow. As a child I was taught that while worldly sorrow meant being sad you got caught, godly sorrow meant you were sorry you had strayed. Godly sorrow would change your future behavior: "that ye sorrowed after a godly sort, what carefulness it wrought in you." Godly sorrow is supposed to be a precursor to repentance, which of course is the key to invoking God's mercy. My problem is I don't think I have ever felt godly sorrow. When I do bad things, I can worry about the spiritual consequences and the possibility of a karmic backlash, the same way that I might worry when I am double-parked and concerned that I am about to get my car ticketed or towed. Is that enough, I wonder?

In many ways, my religion has been a handy tool in explaining my eccentricities, a good cover under which my sociopathic traits could be submerged. I've become accustomed to hiding in plain sight. I could say amoral things because my goodness was presumed. I could act in antisocial ways because my religious upbringing could be blamed for making me awkward around people outside of my community. Among Mormons, I took advantage of their innocence and mandated tolerance of the we're-all-God's-children variety:

> *We contemplate the human race, past, present and yet to come, as immortal beings, for whose salvation it is our mission to labor; and to this work, broad as eternity and deep as the love of God, we devote ourselves, now, and forever.*

There is a reason that Salt Lake City is the fraud capital

of the world: Mormons are unusually willing to see the best in everyone despite evidence to the contrary.

After high school, I attended Brigham Young University. Those students were even more trusting than the average Mormon and there were myriad opportunities for scamming. I started stealing from the lost and found. I would say I lost a common book like the freshman biology textbook, then take it upstairs to the bookstore to sell. Or I would see an unlocked bike that had been in the same place for a few days, figure it was unlikely to be missed, and take it. Finders keepers, right?

I didn't do these things to be antisocial—I don't even consider them to be antisocial. I did them because they helped me feel like the world still made sense. It bothered me how careful people were with one another in Utah. It was inefficient. Drivers would pull up to a four-way stop and become paralyzed with indecision. On the one hand, the rules of the road said that the first to pull up to the stop sign should go first. But people would not always follow this rule, instead treating it like it was some moral question that had to be contemplated anew every time. Sitting there frustrated while people kept waving their hands for other people to go first, I tried to imagine what must have been going through their heads. Perhaps something like: I may be first in time, but how do I know that they aren't first in need? And just because I have the right of way in this situation does not mean I should exercise it unrighteously. The result was snarled intersections, as predictability was sacrificed for godliness. People were trying to out-"good" each other to the point of absurdity. It was unnatural. And it's not godlike, I thought. A god would not give up an advantage for no reason. A god would cultivate his power, just like I do.

The whole thing made me feel off-kilter. On the one hand, they were some of the sweetest, most loving people I had ever encountered. One semester I took a New Testament class (every BYU student is required to take fourteen credits of religion to graduate). Out of the blue the professor asked, "What would you do if I came up and did this to you?" and then very violently nearly struck a student in the face. Unprompted and without thought, the student turned his face to the side, offering up his other cheek as well. I was shocked. I knew this was a literal interpretation of scripture, but was this taking things too far? It struck me suddenly that my targets might be the same people, that when I stole their books they turned the other cheek and let me steal their bikes too. Were they brainwashed victims? Was I evil? Or were we simply two opposing sides, each necessary to achieve a certain balance?

Mormon scripture teaches that there must be opposition in all things; if not there could be neither righteousness nor wickedness, holiness nor misery, neither good nor bad, and without it "there is no God." The biggest "opposition" in the Mormon faith is Lucifer, who became Satan, and who has a rather interesting and detailed backstory. Born a spirit child of God in the premortal world, he is our spiritual brother and was considered one of the brightest stars in heaven until he rebelled and became our necessary opposition. This was great for God, because his plan needed a villain: "man could not act for himself save it should be that he was enticed by the one or the other." And what about Lucifer? When I first heard this story in Sunday school I thought that Lucifer was almost a too-convenient patsy in God's plan. Did God trick Lucifer into rebelling? Maybe make some deal with him under the table? Or maybe God created Lucifer specifically for this purpose? Mormon scripture says "there is a God, and he hath created all things, both things to act and things to be acted upon." Was Lucifer created to act instead of be acted upon? Was I?

I started an elaborate shoplifting scheme from the BYU convenience stores. One of my friends told me about a sack lunch program that was woefully unsupervised. Over the course of a semester or two I took over a thousand dollars in merchandise. At first I consumed or hoarded the goods, like I did with the library books when I was young. Eventually I started giving the stuff away in fits of well-calculated generosity. I didn't do it for money (I was on a full scholarship) or even for the thrill of doing something sinful, because I didn't really see it as being sinful. It wasn't the thrill of being caught either, because I never considered that I might get caught. I didn't think at all about it at the time, but now, wondering why I did it, it was like all of the goodness of my fellow BYU students created this vacuum and I was sucked in. We were all part of a food chain and because they had already chosen their own roles at the bottom of the food chain—to be acted upon—the only spaces that were left were at the top, to act. I never questioned the rightness or wrongness of it, the same way a shark would never question the morality of hunting for its prey. I didn't create the food-chain power dynamic; God did. And I didn't ask to be at the top; it was as if I was made that way.

The reality is that I have nothing of what people refer to as a conscience or remorse. The concept of morality, when defined as an emotional understanding of right and wrong, goes right over my head like an inside joke of which I am not a part. Consequently, I have only the slightest interest in it and no special insight into evil, or no more than a certain level of self-awareness would reveal to any of us. Still, I often wonder what life would be like to feel that things were right or wrong, to have an internal compass to direct me to my moral north. I wonder what life would be like to always be "feeling" certain ways about things, to have conviction, which is apparently how many people experience the world.

Jean Decety, a neurobiologist at the University of Chicago who specializes in social cognition and empathy, has established that moral awareness is initially emotional. Young children in particular have a very strong negative emotional response to social situations that are unfair or hurtful, but the emotional moral judgment of the child evolves as an adult to be tempered by the "dorsolateral and ventromedial prefrontal cortex—areas of the brain that allow people to reflect on the values linked to outcomes and actions." So while children assume that every bad act is malicious, adults are able to apply moral reasoning, recognize and discount accidents, and find nuance in levels of maliciousness.

Decety is studying neurological mechanisms to determine why the brains of sociopaths and other people with antisocial personality disorders don't generate those negative feelings of discomfort or disgust when faced with immoral acts. It makes sense to me that sociopaths would have a comparatively blunted sense of morality if they either do not feel this emotional impetus or feel it less than empaths do, which is certainly the case with me—while I feel worry when I act badly, I have never felt anything as extreme as moral outrage. Evolution has shaped our emotional responses to reinforce activities that are to our advantage, like loving and caring for our children or fearing and fleeing from the sounds of a predator sneaking up on us. Having a gut instinct that told me how to be a moral person might be evolutionarily handy. On the other hand, emotional moral judgment also enables people to do really horrible things to each other, like lynching or "honor" killings, and justify them by calling them "moral."

Because sociopaths don't experience morality emotionally,

I would argue that we are freed to be more rational and more tolerant. There is something to be said for the impartiality of pure reason—religion-created mass hysteria among the supposedly mentally healthy populace has resulted in much worse damage and carnage in the world than anything sociopaths have caused. (Although I imagine that there may sometimes be sociopaths at the head of it all, whipping up the masses to do their bidding.) This idea is explored in Hannah Arendt's book *Eichmann in Jerusalem: A Report on the Banality of Evil,* a book suggesting that the bulk of the horrors of the early half of the twentieth century were done not by sociopaths like me, but by empaths who had allowed themselves to be manipulated by appeals to their emotion.

Similarly, the suggestion that we need to experience guilt in order to behave in a moral way is patently false and offensive in the same way that equating atheism with moral indifference is. Although hardwired emotional moral compasses typically help people to do what is good and avoid what is bad, there should be other reasons that people would do good things besides a sense of morality. It is rational for me to obey the law, because I do not want to go to jail; it is rational for me not to harm or injure other people, because a society in which everyone acted harmfully would inevitably cause me harm too. If there are legitimate, rational reasons for the moral choices we should make, we should be capable of choosing the right without relying purely on gut instinct. If there are not rational reasons for our moral choices, why should we continue to make them?

While I don't think sociopaths have any sort of moral urge to do good things, I think they can and do act morally in the context of pursuing their own advantage. A good analogy would be a corporation. There are a lot of corporations that do things that you like, maybe even good things, like produce vaccines or electric cars, although the primary motivation is to make a profit. But just because you are trying to make a profit doesn't mean you can't do it by doing things you like, or that you are good at, or that comport with the way you see the world, or want the world to see in you. In fact, behaving morally and well might smooth the path for you to pursue your own interest. Society functions better when we treat each other well, and you will personally do better if society is in good working order.

In criminal law, there are two concepts for wrongs that can be criminalized—*malum in se* and *malum prohibitum.* The former are wrongful acts that are wrong in and of themselves, and common examples are murder, theft, and rape. The latter are crimes that are not inherently wrongful, but are prohibited by societies in order to advance a social purpose, usually the optimal ordering or management of the public welfare; examples are driving on the wrong side of the road, breaking a curfew, or selling alcohol without a license. While laws governing *malum in se* are generally static, those regulating *malum prohibitum* are necessarily mutable, because they must be calibrated to the changing conditions.

Of course, the two categories are often difficult to distinguish. There is much debate about the illegal duplication of copyrighted digital media, for instance. Recording companies tend to characterize it as theft, a crime that is inherently bad, while teenagers and legal scholars suggest that it is criminal merely because it is prohibited by the state as an economic regulation.

In my personal universe, there is almost nothing that constitutes *malum in se.* I don't feel that anything is inherently wrongful. But, more important, I am never compelled to refrain from doing something merely because it is wrong—only because doing so would result in undesirable consequences. Thus, evil has no special meaning for me. There is no mystery in it. It is a word to describe a sense of wrongness that I do not feel.

I don't have any expectations of egalitarianism or righteousness, so I do not feel a similar sense of disappointment at the existence of evil or despair. I am not moved by signs of want, of beggars or poor starving orphans or slums or anything (although I often donate on little more than a whim). I am not outraged by inequity; in fact I embrace it as I do death. I don't feel the same sense of entitlement to beneficence that most people do. I do not expect things to go right in the world. I don't even believe in right. I believe that everything just is. And what *is* can be quite beautiful.

I suppose it's an odd distinction to make between being moved by perceived injustice but not inequity. I guess what I mean is that there is quite a deal of luck and context involved in every aspect of life, and that people cannot therefore expect the same outcomes from the same actions. In contrast, I perceive injustice as someone putting a thumb on the scale, artificially enabling one outcome over another—an intentional interference thwarting the natural course of things. I guess it's because I don't mind risk, it actually gives me a thrill, but I have no desire to play a rigged game. If I thought my life was rigged, I don't know what I'd do, maybe kill myself or others. It's only because I think I can (and most often do) play the game better than others that it keeps my interest enough to persist in playing it.

Sociopathy was first identified as an independent mental disorder more than two hundred years ago by the French humanitarian and father of modern psychiatry Philippe Pinel, in his 1806 work *A Treatise on Insanity: In Which Are Contained the Principles of a New and More Practical Nosology of Maniacal Disorders Than Has Yet Been Offered to the Public.* Pinel developed an interest in psychology after a friend became afflicted with mental illness that resulted in suicide. He was largely responsible for popularizing the "moral" treatment of patients with mental disorders based on prolonged observation and conversation.

In his treatise, Pinel set out three categories of mental derangement: (1) melancholia or delirium, (2) mania with delirium, and (3) mania without delirium, the last of which described individuals who were impulsive, amoral, violent, and destructive—while remaining competent and rational. Pinel theorized that the patients who suffered mania without delirium had only a certain part of their mental faculties distorted while the rest of their mind—principally, their intellect—remained intact. He wrote of this category of condition: "It may be either continued or intermittent. No sensible change in the functions of the understanding; but perversion of the active faculties, marked by abstract and sanguinary fury, with a blind propensity to acts of violence."

Pinel noted his surprise that maniacs could have entirely unaffected intellects. This was contrary to the generally accepted notion at the time that madness was caused by a deficit or derangement of mental reasoning faculties, as proposed by John Locke in his 1690 work *An Essay Concerning Human Understanding.* Because one could not think, Locke believed, one could not function in society—the key to sanity was rationality, and without it, a person was lost to insanity or mania. But Pinel found that there was a different kind of madness or mental deficit—a moral one.

In 1863, British psychologist James Cowles Prichard used the term "moral insanity" to describe people like me, a phrase that fills me with delight. In his work *A Treatise on Insanity and Other Disorders Affecting the Mind,* Prichard acknowledged Pinel's case studies and noted the existence of "many individuals living at large, and not entirely separated from society, who are affected in a certain degree with this modification of insanity. They are reputed persons of a singular, wayward, and eccentric character."

Prichard was a very religious man, and he struggled with the possibility that mental illness could be an affliction of not only the mind but also of the soul—that moral corruption was a sickness that could be medically categorized and clinically treated. While not the first, he was perhaps one of the most vehement critics of sociopaths. It offended him that a person in total control of his mental faculties could not or did not live rightly. Before, his assumption was that to be rational is to be moral. Like Pinel, Prichard was unsettled by the idea that delusion was not necessarily the root of bad behavior, and that doing evil could be—in some ways—perfectly rational.

Pinel was convinced that the emotional morality experienced by most people is inherently superior to the rational moral decision-making that sociopaths and others have to engage in. I disagree. Everyone uses shortcuts to make decisions; it would be impossible for us to make a fully informed, reasoned decision every time such a decision was necessary. For example, when you're in the middle of a bar fight, how do you decide whether or not to stab the guy who just punched you in the face? Empaths may use emotional shortcuts (in this case, either "This jerk deserves a shiv in the belly" or "I'd feel too awful if I actually killed the guy") to make quick decisions about how to act. Sociopaths don't or can't, so we come up with other shortcuts.

Many sociopaths use the shortcut of "anything goes," or "I am only in it for me." These sociopaths have decided that the rational way to increase their own benefits in life is to look out only for themselves and ignore the needs or demands of others. While some act entirely on selfish impulse, they are not always free to be out on the streets where you might meet them but are instead in prison. Apart from the most impulsive and violent sociopaths, there is a wide range of self-reflection and deliberation in decision-making. Some sociopaths are capable of reining in their impulses enough to decide that jail time is not to their advantage, so they choose to avoid major violations of the law (e.g., "The satisfaction of killing this jerk isn't worth the inconvenience of being locked up"). One sociopath from my blog, while realizing that most of what he does is dangerous, wrong, or both, still stated, "I have a line or two I won't cross for any reason." But that doesn't prevent him from committing with clear conscience many smaller infractions or injustices that empaths would find objectionable, for example accounting fraud or emotional abuse.

Other sociopaths, and I am one of these, have settled on a more "principled" approach to life and act according to religious or ethical beliefs, or, at the minimum, for their self-interest or preservation. We decide on standards of behavior or a code that we can refer to when faced with decisions ("I've decided not to kill people, so I won't stab this jerk"). As one sociopath reader of my blog put it, "To have morals is not important. Having ethics is what is important." My prosthetic moral compass generally functions well for me, and most of the time my method happens to track what the majority thinks is the moral thing to do. The one thing that sociopath "codes" tend to have in common, though, is that they don't fully map with prevailing social norms, those unspoken rules and customs that govern behavior in a group. For instance I know a sociopath who is a drug dealer but has his own standards of conduct when it comes to dealing with his wife (nicely) or his employees (not nicely). Similarly, I am typically not engaged in criminal behavior, but that doesn't mean I won't take whatever I need, from things as questionable and disgusting as your underwear to things as useful and valuable as a bike. I almost expect others to do the same. From my experiences and communications with other sociopaths, this rough blend of pure opportunism mixed with a more practical utilitarianism is not uncommon. One blog commenter put it this way:

> I'm an "intelligent" sociopath. I don't have problems with drugs, I don't commit crimes, I don't take pleasure in hurting people, and I don't typically have relationship problems. I do have a complete lack of empathy. But I consider that an advantage, most of the time. Do I know the difference between right and wrong, and do I want to be good? Sure. One catches more flies with honey than with vinegar. A peaceful and orderly world is a more comfortable world for me to live in. So do I avoid breaking the law because it's "right"? No, I avoid breaking the law because it makes sense. I suppose if I weren't gifted with the ability to make a lot of money in a profession doing what I like, I might try and profit by crime. But with my profession, I'd have to really hit the criminal jackpot to make it worth a life of crime. When you're bad to people, they're bad back to you. I'm no Christian, but

But sometimes efficiency does not perfectly align with what most people would consider morally right. One afternoon shortly after I got fired from my law firm job, I took my neighbor's bicycle so that I could bike to the beach with a friend who was visiting from out of town. The bike was sitting unlocked in the shared underground garage. There was a layer of dust on it and it needed a little air in the tires, but it was there and eminently convenient. I figured that it was unlikely that my neighbor, a stranger to me, would discover it missing. My efficiency-minded self imagined what the transaction would look like if I were to ask her for permission to use the bike: I would explain to her the situation and she would consent, provided I agreed to pay for any damage or loss. I would posit that the bike would be better for the ride because it would work grease through the moving parts. And bikes are meant to be ridden; it was socially wasteful to keep the bike in the garage, unused like that, when people needed bikes to ride. I would have been happy to pay her a rental fee if she wanted me to. This was the story I told myself.

I did not actually engage in this hypothetical transaction with my neighbor. I thought there was too great a risk that she would not see things my way. People can be very irrational, I reasoned to myself, and sometimes they cannot be trusted to make efficient decisions. She might say no because she has an irrational fear of strangers. There is an information asymmetry in our situation that could distort the way she sees this decision: In her mind, I am an unknown. But, truthfully, I had no intention of stealing the bike. I'd bring it back in just a few hours, better than I found it. But how could I credibly assure her of this? People are too distrusting nowadays.

Finally, she probably overestimates the value of the bicycle just because it happens to be hers. Maybe she bought it for $100, hoping to bike to the beach every week. In her mind the value of the bike would be emotionally rooted to that $100 sunk cost and her fantasies about a life of ease, even though the bike wouldn't sell for more than $10 at a garage sale. She and her husband were living a life beyond their means, I had often thought. They both drove Civics from the late 1980s but lived in a nice apartment building with young professionals. She might be upset about the thought of losing something as small as her beat-up old bike because she didn't have much to start with. It was easy to convince myself that I knew better than her what was best for the bike. Besides, what she didn't know would not hurt her, and I really didn't want to bother having the conversation with her.

In the evening, after I had returned the bike no worse for wear, I heard an angry knock on my door and was subjected to even angrier accusations. Apparently she had come home, shocked to find her bike gone. After looking for it for hours (looking for it? Where? And for hours?) she gave up, only to find it returned to its space in the garage. She had not failed to notice that her husband's bike remained there, and that my bike was also gone for the exact same period of time. It was clear that the jig was up, so I confessed that I had taken her bike.

She was taken aback by my untroubled admission. My money offers did nothing but offend her, and she even threatened to call the police, but I told her I thought it was unlikely they'd do much for her. I tried to explain that what I had done was technically not theft because I did not have the requisite mental state of intending to permanently deprive her of her property. At best what I had done was trespass to chattels, and good luck trying to prove actual damages. She stared at me in horror for a moment before threatening to tell the management. I figured that was an empty threat, though, and in any case had been planning on moving somewhere cheaper to live out my unemployment.

I didn't mind being caught. It was just a cost of doing business. Of course I wouldn't have remembered this incident if I had not been caught. Many other similar episodes have filled my life, too routine to recall. But I think it bothers people to see me this way—expressing no sign of remorse upon being caught. When I was a child and would get up to mischief with my siblings, my father used to beat us with a belt, lining us all up to take our turns, in equal parts emotional humiliation and physical intimidation. I never reacted—never cried and never apologized. I never felt the urge and, more important, I never saw the point. Part of it was because I knew he wanted to break me and I didn't want to give him the satisfaction. Part of it was that my tears were usually tools of manipulation and punisher-dad was not susceptible to manipulation. All I got was a cold sort of angry where most of my attention was focused on plotting payback. Although I had two older brothers who were much bigger than I was, I frequently got hit the hardest, leaving angry welts across my little buttocks and upper thighs. As an adult, I asked him why he did it. He said that he didn't remember details, but I must have been risking the lives of my siblings or something sufficiently horrible to warrant that kind of beating. Maybe. But maybe I just didn't seem affected by the punishments the way he had hoped I would be. My lack of reaction must have seemed like intransigence, which he hoped to break by beating me just a little bit harder.

My neighbor was similarly put out by my blank-faced

recitations of the legal elements of trespass to chattels in response to her obvious distress. It took everything I had learned about people to understand that she wanted apologies rather than remuneration, some compensation for the sense of personal violation that she experienced. It's difficult for me to comprehend these soft intangibles. It's not that I do not feel them; it's just hard for me to predict them in others. But even when I backpedaled and started apologizing, the neighbor was dissatisfied. Like my father, she seemed to sense that I wasn't sorry for what I did. I didn't feel any of that godly sorrow that precedes repentance, because I had not strayed, at least not according to my own reasoning. Taking the bike had been worth it.

This sort of behavior may seem uncouth, but is it really immoral? Prichard's disgust with sociopaths for being immoral seems largely unwarranted unless you ascribe to his particular brand of morality. Was I really in the wrong by temporarily taking my neighbor's bike? Only if you think that violation of the personal property of others is immoral. Even the law recognizes that this is not always the case: If you're stranded in a snowstorm, it would be permissible to break in to someone's ski cabin and spend the night, as long as you pay for any damage done to the cabin. The justification for this so-called necessity defense is that if you were able to find the owner of the cabin and ask them for permission, they would grant it to you. However, you can still use this defense even if you know for a fact that the owner would not grant you permission, for instance because you two are mortal enemies and the cabin owner has made it clear he would not piss on you if you were on fire. The cabin owner can take this position, but the law will not support it because it is unreasonable—and perhaps even immoral! When seen through this lens of reasoning (rather

than Prichard's religious one), perhaps my neighbor was acting improperly by being unreasonable in not allowing me to
borrow her unused bike. If I behaved improperly according to
societal standards, it was arguably only because I didn't show
the least bit of remorse.

In contract law, there is a concept called "efficient breach."
Most people assume that it is always "bad" to break a contract,
because it essentially constitutes breaking a promise. However, there are some ways in which doing so can be good, or
in the language of law and economics, efficient. This occurs
when complying with the terms of the contract would result
in greater economic loss than simply paying the other party's
damages that have resulted from your nonperformance. For
example, I commit to date someone exclusively. Maybe I even
marry him. If one of us later finds someone we prefer, it may
actually be better for both parties if one or both of us breaks
the agreement. If you believe in the value of efficient breaches
like I do, then you would never get upset if your partner
cheated on you.

In efficient breaches, it is often the immoral choice that
leaves everyone better off. I've lived my entire life this way,
since long before I ever learned the term in law school. My
child self understood the world in terms of choices and consequences, causes and effects. If I wanted to break a rule and
was willing to suffer the consequences, I should be allowed to
make that choice unhindered.

I engage in this kind of self-promoting calculus in almost
everything I do, often when the stakes are much higher. When
my good friend's father was diagnosed with cancer, I cut off
all contact with her. It sounds like a ruthless thing to do,
and it was. It wasn't that I didn't love her; in fact, I loved her
very much—perhaps too much. But I found I could no longer

enjoy any of the benefits she had provided to me—superior advice, interesting conversation—because she was horrible to be around most of the time. I had overinvested and was running many months into the red with no improvement. I found that I could not wear the mask of compassion or selflessness indefinitely without acting out in ways that were hurtful to us both.

And so I cut off all ties and walked away. There were damages on all sides, but I had no other means of mitigating them, so it was an efficient breach. I think she would agree with me, even when I include her hurt and suffering into the equation. That alone would typically make the end of a friendship in this way a net negative. In this situation, though, my abandonment of her was to her benefit, particularly considering that my behavior was only going to get worse—that I was already tapped out in terms of being able to be supportive. I didn't leave her because I stopped caring for her. I left her because I did care for her very much. It was efficient. Still, the first couple of months apart I was just so relieved. If I was reminded of my friend, it was with gratitude that I was no longer in that unsustainable situation. As the months went by, however, I began to feel the empty space in my life that she used occupy. It was unfortunate. But this too is part of the cost-benefit analysis, when I realize that situations can often turn regrettable even though I do not regret any particular decision.

Of course, there are negative real-world effects of making efficient breaches. In the marketplace, breaking promises decreases confidence and thereby discourages actors from engaging in future contracts. For instance, if you have been divorced too many times, people don't trust you, and so they don't want to play the game with you anymore. It's a problem. No matter how rational I may be in choosing when to follow rules and when to break obligations, it is often insufficient for the people I am dealing with. They want more: more feeling, more attachment, more commitment, more of what they're used to. At some point, I have to wonder if all of my rational decision-making can make up for my inability to empathize, and I conclude that it doesn't. People take for granted the empathy with which they were born, and the morality that they somehow internalize. Crying when someone you love cries— I was not born with this shortcut into the hearts of other people. Feeling guilt when you hurt someone you love is an internal safeguard to prevent you from losing them, but I have never been able to learn it. The work-arounds that I have devised for these things often fail me.

Fortunately, however, it is another of my sociopathic traits to persist with optimism and unflinching self-regard, and I've learned that few broken things cannot be mended. The angry neighbor never bothered me again. After my friend's father died, we reconnected and have become friends again. Friends and family have moved on from past hurts and forgiven me. The narrative of the sociopath has been told in the language of pathology, but sometimes I feel like Achilles. In exchange for superhuman might he had a single vulnerability. It was a fair exchange, I think—his demise was extremely improbable.

But I am not completely immune to feeling blue. Of the negative emotions I feel, regret is the saddest and strongest. I acknowledge that much of life is chance and all sorts of bad things might happen to me during life. I'm fine with that. The thing that haunts me more than anything else is the thought that I could unwittingly be the author of my own unhappiness—unhappiness so surprising that it never entered my mind that things could play out that way. It is the ultimate in powerlessness—not just the thought that nothing I do really matters, but that things I do could matter and actually make things worse.

Midway through college I met a girl in the music program who brought my true nature to the surface. We met at an audition for the same part, and even though she was the better musician, I won. She was one of those good-natured people whose infectious laugh rallied friends to her side. She was people-pleasing, serious, and friendly, uncomfortable enough in her own skin that people never envied her, but not so much that they were repulsed. They couldn't help but like her.

I had always stayed casually close to her so that my reputation would be aligned with hers; I capitalized on her easy likability, making certain that it would rub off on me rather than contrast with my affectations. But maybe this was where I failed. I tried too hard to understand her, as if her delicate balance of coquettishness and earthy charm was something that she had purposefully fabricated and that I could therefore dissect and re-create, but what she had was an accident, an empty convergence of quirks and unforeseen circumstances that she herself could barely describe or detect. She was who she was—it wasn't an act.

I know this because I secretly pored through her personal letters and journals, trying to understand—to eat up all the insecurities she seeped onto the pages. One day she caught me doing it. She avoided me completely after that, as did everyone else in the program.

No one really talked about it. But my ostracism was especially jarring because ignoring personal boundaries like this was the kind of thing I did all the time. Now they acted as if I was a monster. It was such a trivial, stupid transgression, something I imagine that most everyone has done or wanted to do but was somehow apparently so terrible that shaming me made everyone else a better person. I had violated a moral rule that I didn't fully understand, and no one wanted to be associated with me.

Without the benefit of social goodwill, I was forced to do everything the hard way, since the trust required for all my secret schemes had been destroyed. It was the best thing that could have happened to me. My actions had finally caught up with me in a way that I could not ignore. Faced with total social isolation, I had no choice but to try to be completely honest with myself.

I started to realize how little I knew about myself or why I did the things I did (and still do). I didn't like not knowing who I was, so I decided to develop a friendly curiosity about myself. I watched myself for about nine months without judgment or self-manipulation. I wasn't an ascetic, but I was intent on discovering my true self. My guiding principles during that time were unflinching honesty and acceptance. I thought that if I could garner enough self-knowledge, I could inch myself to happiness or whatever else it was I wanted in life, like a prisoner carving his way out of a concrete wall with a makeshift pick.

At the end of the nine months I had come to a few conclusions. First, I didn't really have a self at all. I was like an Etch A Sketch, constantly shaking myself up and starting over. And somewhere, somehow, in the last few years, I had come to believe certain things about myself that weren't really true. For instance, because I often am very charming and outwardly good-natured, I thought that I must be a warmhearted person. Pretending to conform to societal expectations had become so easy that I forgot I was pretending. I read all of these coming-of-age books about people growing up and growing out of childhood quirks and I felt like that is what had happened to me. In reality, I had just lost the self-awareness that I had as a child and even as a teenager. Several things that I had come to believe were mirages, and when I inspected them closer they disappeared, leaving absolutely nothing. I quickly realized that, almost without exception, this was true about everything in my life. All of the stories I had recently been spinning about my life were illusions—gaps occupied by part of my brain to fill in a hole, the same way our brain will sometimes fill in gaps in an optical illusion. I had told myself that I was normal, perhaps just a little too smart, but that my feelings were genuine and typical of a young woman my age. Now I felt like I had woken up from a dream. Without actively spinning stories, I had no self. If I had been Buddhist on my path to seeking Nirvana, this lack of self would have been a huge breakthrough, but I didn't feel a sense of accomplishment at having achieved that state. Instead I felt the only way anyone can ever feel without a sense of self—free.

Of course I knew that there were things that I did when I was "engaged." I laughed and plotted. I manipulated a lot, I realized. Manipulation was my default mode of relating with people. Every relationship felt like a dance of giving and taking that I was constantly trying to choreograph, gauging which dance partners would serve my interests best. I liked things like power and excitement. I had no real interest in the content of my activities, just the skill with which I did them. I loved to seduce, not just sexually, but to inhabit someone's mind so completely, and it was easy—easy to charm. I was a prolific liar, often for no real reason. I was a pleasure seeker, and although I had no real sense of what my self was, I still thought very well of myself. I didn't need a self to exist. I had a unique role in the world: I was like an enzyme among molecules, catalyzing reactions without being affected myself. Or a virus, looking for a host. I was different from normal people, but I knew that I existed. I acted and interacted. I was largely an illusion, but even an illusion is real in its own way—people experience it, and more important, people respond to it.

I believe that a lot of the sociopath's traits such as charm, manipulation, lying, promiscuity, chameleonism, mask wearing, and lack of empathy are largely attributable to a very weak sense of self. I believe that all personality disorders share a distorted or abnormal sense of self. The concept of a sociopath having an extremely flexible sense of self is not entirely original to me, but it is not often clearly stated in the scientific literature. I compiled my information from piecing together seemingly disparate elements of the literature on sociopaths in a way that conformed with my own personal experience. Psychologists look at the list of sociopathic traits and think they understand the "what," but they don't understand the "how." I believe the "how," the origin of many of our observed behaviors, is that we don't have a rigid sense of self. I believe that this is the predominant defining characteristic of a sociopath.

The person who has gotten closest to identifying this attribute of sociopaths is a professor at California State University–Northridge, Howard Kamler. He argues that "it is not just that [the sociopath] is lacking a strongly identified moral identity, he is likely lacking a strongly identified self identity almost altogether." When the sociopath feels no sense of remorse, it's due less to a lack of conscience and more to the fact that the sociopath does not feel that he has betrayed himself: "If a person has no strong sense of self in general, then of course he will probably have no strong sense of lost integrity when he violates life projects which for the rest of us would be central parts of our self identities." For example, I never get upset when I break up with someone, primarily because I never had any emotional attachment to my status as a "girl-friend." Similarly, I do not define myself as a successful professional of a certain intellectual or socioeconomic class, so it does not really bother me to be summarily discharged from prestigious positions and remain unemployed for long periods of time living on government payouts and the generosity of friends and family members. I know what I am capable of and that is enough. My particular status in any given moment is insignificant to me except to the degree that I am aware of its significance to others in the way they view me and treat me.

What is it like being self-aware without a self-construct? Much of my self-awareness is the result of indirect observation of the effects I have on people. I know I exist because I see people acknowledging my existence, just as we know that dark matter exists in the universe not because we can see or measure it directly, but because we can see its effects as its invisible gravity distorts the motion of objects around it. Sociopaths are like dark matter in that we typically keep our influence hidden, albeit in plain sight, but you can certainly see our effects. I watch for people's reactions to me so I am able to understand, "I make people feel scared when I stare at them this way." My awareness of self is made up of a million of these little observations to paint a picture of myself, like a pointillist portrait.

As a child, my self was easier to define and therefore to ignore: I was a part of my family, a student at my school, a member at my church. I didn't have to worry about betraying myself with bad behavior, only others; I was used to people looking over my shoulder all the time, so keeping my behavior in check was a constant concern. As an adult I don't have that same external structure. I make more of my own decisions as an adult, but my actions also have much more permanent and serious consequences. That is why my prosthetic moral compass has been so useful to me, in helping to define me and restrict my behavior; my personal code of efficiency and religion have, for the most part, kept me on the straight and narrow.

While I rarely break the rules, I tend to bend them. Mormons are well known for having dietary restrictions, most famously a prohibition on tobacco, alcohol, and caffeine. I drink green tea and Diet Coke, which seemingly puts me on the wrong side of the law, but I take an originalist interpretation of this provision. The actual language relating to caffeine prohibits "hot drinks," which presumably does not include ice-cold cola. At the time of the provision's inception, there was no green tea readily available, so it was unlikely to have been included in the prohibition. Consequently, I have a raging caffeine addiction.

The prohibition on sex before marriage has a much more considerable effect on church members, but it too contains some ambiguity. I'm told that in my grandparents' generation, the line was drawn at "sexual intercourse," and apparently people walked right up to that line. My dad once told me a story about how a church leader advised young men to "stay moral, go oral," although he now denies he ever said it. That loophole has since been tightened up, if not closed, with the prohibition on the potentially broader category of "sexual relations." With such vague terms, the church appears to be asking its members to interpret the complexity of sexual experience on their own terms. Don't mind if I do. I find richness in my sex life within the church's parameters, like a poet who chooses to write in sonnets over free verse.

Mormons are expected to pay a specific percentage of their "increase" to the church as a tithe, but that rule, like most everything, is subject to interpretation. I treat it like paying my taxes: I comply, but I maximize every possible deduction within the letter of the law. Indeed, I have never paid a tremendous amount of attention to the church's reasons for doing what it does or asserting what it asserts.

Rather than feeling a moral certainty about the rightness of the church and its articles of faith, my affiliation with the church makes sense to me in the language of efficiency. In fact, I have to acknowledge that there is no empirical certainty for the existence or nonexistence of a Creator in the cosmos. I simply proceed as if I could know, and believe. If the church's tenets by which I have lived are true, then I have invested wisely in my everlasting future. If they are untrue, then I have at least invested wisely in my present life by adhering to a reasonable moral code, with no measurable effect on my uncertain future. I understand my faith as a foundation for living—the infrastructure on which I create a life that provides me with immense pleasures and essential joy.

Even without a religious or ethical code, high-functioning sociopaths eventually learn that they can use their powers for good. Sociopaths cannot willfully blind themselves to exploitable weaknesses in others, but they can choose to use that special vision to be productive rather than destructive. Sometimes in choosing to manipulate or exploit weaknesses in others, you create vulnerabilities in yourself, for example by harming your reputation or feeding an addiction to increasingly outrageous antisocial behavior. Controlling our impulses also allows sociopaths to overcome our isolation by forming long-term, meaningful relationships. Sociopaths who truly seek to cultivate power realize that the greatest power they can acquire is power over themselves.

Chapter 6

SAINTS, SPIES, AND
SERIAL KILLERS

I recently visited New Zealand and learned that it has a very diverse ecosystem. Until the arrival of humans, it was populated almost entirely by birds. They occupied every niche in the food chain, from tiny flightless things to predators so enormous they could snatch a hundred-pound prey for dinner. For millions of years, birds dominated their man-less, mammal-less world, a universe of feathers, beaks, and talons, knowing of no other form of higher life. The birds acquired a host of abilities and natural defenses optimal for their environment.

But then in the thirteenth century, while the Europeans were still busy with their crusades, Polynesian explorers came, and with them came rats—with fur instead of feathers, teeth instead of beaks, and tiny paws instead of fearsome talons. The defense mechanisms that worked well against other birds failed against the rats. Small flightless birds who, when sensing danger, would remain perfectly still to avoid being spotted by predators flying overhead, would do the same when encountering a rat. Fighting for its life, in its passive way, the little bird focused its every effort on not moving a single muscle—only to be gobbled up where it stood.

The scientific term for animals like the little bird who had not encountered rats or humans is naïve. I find this charming, as if the little bird existed in a moral universe of which his New Zealand was a kind of Eden, its inhabitants living a peaceful existence disrupted only by the victimization of a cunning intruder, preying on their relative innocence.

I often think the people I encounter are naïve, but only because they may never have encountered someone quite like me. Sociopaths see things that no one else does because they have different expectations about the world and the people in it. While you and everyone else are doing emotional sleight of hand meant to distract the average observer from certain harsh truths, the sociopath remains undistracted. We are like rats on an island of birds.

I have never identified with the little bird, trapped by fear and an instinct for passivity, the wide-eyed victim of circumstance. I have never pined for an Eden of peace on earth and goodwill toward men. I am the rat, and I will take every advantage I can without apology or excuse. And there are others like me.

Some of the most amoral and manipulative people I met in my life I knew in law school—rats who gamed the system with little regard for others at a level of meticulousness baffling even to me. They calculated every event or encounter to optimize their advantage, even when the advantages were so trivial as to mean having a slightly better breakfast. Many of them seemed capable of committing massacre, grand theft, or real destruction, had a sufficient motivating desire struck them to do so. I don't know how many of them were diagnosable sociopaths, but clinical research and my own experience lead me to believe the rate was much higher than in the general population. Many, however, were the most interesting people I have known, and not so dangerous, really. Sociopaths are unlikely to be zealots; we can't be bothered to take up causes outside of ourselves.

The law school environment made everyone a little more sociopathic, since we were encouraged to view our successes in a zero-sum game measured by precise numbers. At the end of every semester in law schools across the nation, grades are collated and detailed rankings published. Rankings among my classmates had a direct relationship to our career prospects— it was as if everyone was walking around with a number above his head, and you could see it flittering there like a train station signboard, knowing that each adjustment around you reflected a change in the number above your own head.

Of course, I gamed the system perfectly. I had three years, two semesters a year, for a total of six semesters, each of which had a different impact on my résumé: possible first-year summer internships, whether I got on law review, the paid internship during our second summer, the last hope to improve my GPA before federal court judicial clerkship applications were due. I made Excel spreadsheets. I determined the odds. I chose classes and teachers on the basis of whether I knew I'd get an A. I used the school's generous policy of allowing law students to take undergraduate courses pass/fail to pad my class schedule with such fluff as Jazz Improvisation, Music Ethnology, and Introduction to Film. While some of my classmates were learning about the intricacies of federal jurisdiction, I was relaxing in a classroom while two try-hards were locked in a heated debate over whether Tuvan throat singers were misogynistic. And the best part about it was that there was nothing wrong with what I did. That's the beauty of numbers—there are no points awarded or taken away for being seen as either nice or ruthless, at least when grading is anonymous like ours was.

I look better on paper than I do in real life. On paper I have all the hallmarks of success. But in my real life, things have often come to me the hard way. I don't mean in the usual character-building way; I mean the untidy and indirect way that sometimes requires me to be extra resourceful and handily unabashed.

I am absolutely shameless when it comes to asking for, pushing for, and ultimately inducing people to give me what I want, whatever it takes. At BYU, I played in all of the top music ensembles and performed in the closing ceremonies for the winter Olympics. These bullet points on my résumé look impressive as long as you don't know that they were substantially the result of coercion. How? Through well-placed allegations of gender discrimination in my department with the university administration, an easy claim to make when all the music administrators were men. In law school I used the back door to get onto the prestigious editorial board of the student-edited law review, via a program designed to solicit more participation from women and minorities. From that subsidiary program, I campaigned vigorously and successfully to get elected to the editorial board, based again on the gender divide. To graduate with honors, I argued one of my professors into raising my grade. To get my first internship, I practically begged the interviewer during my sendoff handshake. I looked deeply into her eyes, beseechingly, earnestly, and said, "I *really* want this job."

I loved being perceived as smart and successful. And I didn't care if I had to do ugly things in front of a few people to get there. A few scattered looks of disgust and heads shaking in disappointment hardly mattered to me. It mattered much more that I had the right little asterisks and icons in graduation ceremony programs indicating my various honors. I am not ashamed to admit that seeing them still gives me pleasure.

When I graduated from law school, I landed a prestige-whore's job (and we lawyers are all prestige whores) with a fancy firm in Los Angeles, making ridiculous amounts of money. I pre-spent my first months' salary on a wardrobe that would make me look like a high-flying, style-conscious Los Angeleno, but once I was actually sitting behind my desk I just wasn't that interested in doing any of the work. I realize now that I was all about the form and disregarded the substance.

The thing that allowed me to survive this way as long as I did was that I didn't feel insecure about my backdoor methods. If anything, I was proud of them. I felt entitled to what I got. And why not? I had won every indicator of success in life through whatever means necessary—my test scores were consistently at the top of the charts, and my résumé was perfect. My career trajectory was astonishing, especially because it felt like a scam, and I loved to play that kind of game. When I was young, it was not enough for me to get A's on all my tests. That part was easy. What thrilled me was the risk of figuring out just how little I could study and still pull off the A. It was like this with being an attorney. I had no real desire to be one, only to playact as one. And really, to the extent that everything in the industry was a scam, I was just one pretender among many.

I loved the subtle and not-so-subtle power games that played out in my office. I became a connoisseur of insecurities and used that knowledge to manipulate junior associates and senior partners alike, in big and small ways. The insecurities of high-powered attorneys are especially delicious, acute, and ever-so-finely grained. They have the usual things, like penis size, body image, and age, but the other, more obscure things are far more interesting.

For instance, there was a partner in the office next to mine who was strangely insecure about the fact that he had six children. He wasn't motivated by a religious commandment to multiply, so he felt like he had to explain himself. He cornered me during the office Christmas party, drunk on appletinis, and all I had to do was grin and be gracious while he confessed his sin of having too many children among urban professionals. Then he suggested that I coauthor his latest treatise. I didn't take him up on the offer back in the office on Monday, but the feeling that he had revealed too much lingered.

Everyone has defenses to protect themselves from hurt, stratagems to disguise their weaknesses and to avoid potential exploitation. The girl who grew up in the trailer park wears only Christian Louboutin shoes and Hermès scarves. The Nazi's grandson works at the multicultural soup kitchen. The kid who grew up with learning disabilities spends his adulthood earning PhDs from the very best universities. The thing about these defenses, however, is that they work only if they are invisible. If they are somehow exposed, if another person can see them, then you might as well be naked, or standing stock-still waiting to be eaten. There is something so excruciating about being seen—really, truly seen—because people not only see the trailer trash in you, but they also see the striving heart that wishes it wasn't.

As in poker, many people have unconscious tells or little changes in behavior or demeanor that let me know the strength or weakness of the hand they've been dealt in life. Tells having to do with class usually work well. I don't believe I have ever encountered a person without some kind of readable insecurities about their class or socioeconomic status. And these self-doubts pervade every aspect of a person's life, from how to hold chopsticks in a sushi restaurant to whether to say hello to your mailman. In such circumstances, I can establish a favorable power dynamic by showing just the slightest disapproval couched in an easy, generous tolerance. It's a kind of gently condescending noblesse oblige.

I had been assigned to work for a senior associate named Jane in one of the firm's satellite offices, so I only saw her once every few weeks. In law firms, you are supposed to treat a person who is a couple years senior to you as if she is the ultimate authority in everything you do in your life, and Jane took this hierarchy pretty seriously. You could tell that she had never enjoyed such power in any other social sphere. Her pale white skin, mottled with age, poor diet, and middling hygiene, was evidence of a lifetime spent outside the social elite. But you could also tell she had tried to cultivate her own brand of brittle class privilege, albeit poorly. Jane had obtained—in answer to all of her dreams and as a result of her unimpeachable assiduousness—a modicum of power in her office, having satisfactorily worked for one of the more powerful attorneys at the firm. She wanted so much to wear her power well but she was clumsy with it—heavy-handed in certain circumstances and a pushover in others. You could tell that she was self-consciously aware of it, which made her a particularly entertaining blend of ostensible power and self-doubt.

I was not, perhaps, her best associate. As much as anyone I have ever encountered, Jane believed that I was undeserving of all that I had accomplished. Whereas she had taken so much effort to dress appropriately (ill-fitting beige suits with shoulder pads), I wore flip-flops and T-shirts at every semi-reasonable opportunity. While she regularly billed as many hours as humanly possible, I exploited our firm's non-existent vacation policy by taking three-day weekends and weeks-long vacations abroad. People were implicitly expected not to take vacations, but I had my own lifelong policy of following only explicit rules, and then only because they're easiest to prove against me. She could sense that I flouted this and other unspoken rules with little consequence by a quick look at my time sheets and my less-than-formal office attire. It wasn't that she hated me; she just didn't know what to do with me. To her, I was walking injustice. It disgusted her, but if I had sold my soul to the devil, she wanted to get his business card and contact information.

I had driven to her office for a meeting, and we met in the lobby by coincidence as she was coming back from lunch. We walked together to the elevator, and when it opened, there were two tall, handsome men already inside. One was French, and both apparently worked at a venture capital firm that shared the building with our firm. You could tell by looking at them that they received multimillion-dollar bonuses and likely arrived via one of the Lotuses or Maseratis regularly parked in the underground garage. Lawyers might be wealthy, but they are almost without exception surrounded by far greater wealth.

The two were in the midst of a discussion about the symphony that they had attended the night before, which I had also happened to attend. I didn't go to the symphony all the time; a friend had happened to have some extra tickets. I casually asked them about it, and their eyes lit up.

"So lucky to have met you! Perhaps you can settle a disagreement between my friend and me," the Frenchman said. "My friend thinks that it was Rachmaninoff's second piano concerto that was performed last night, but I think it was his third. Do you recall?"

I didn't miss a beat. "It was his second. It was incredible, wasn't it?" I actually could not recall, and it turned out to have been his third. Of course, it hardly mattered what the right answer was.

The two men thanked me profusely as they left the elevator, leaving Jane and me to travel up to her office in enough silence for her to contemplate the dimensions of my intellectual and social superiority. It was the kind of elite encounter she hoped she would one day have when she was just a nerdy teenager clasping on to her dog-eared copy of *Mansfield Park*—that she would attend symphonies and be able to speak intelligently about them to handsome strangers. She had envisioned that matriculation at a highly ranked university and employment at a prestigious law firm would make such a moment possible for her, but it wasn't hers. It was mine.

Jane was a little jittery by the time we got back to her office, a combination of caffeine at lunch and worry that she had wasted her life. We were supposed to talk about the project I was working on for her, but instead we talked about her life choices from about the age of eighteen, her worries and insecurities about her job and her body, her attraction to women despite being engaged to a man for several years, and other things that I can't bother to remember. After the elevator, I knew I had her—which is to say that I knew that whenever she saw me, her heart would flutter; she would worry about all of the secret vulnerabilities she had exposed to me and wonder what it would be like to undress me, or to slap me across the face. I know that for a long time I haunted her dreams, and that even now, years later, I could make her hands tremble just by flashing her a smile. Of course power is its own reward, but with this particular dynamic between us established, I was able to leverage a brief cancer scare and outpatient procedure into a three-week paid vacation. Which is also a form of reward.

I think that sociopathy gives me a natural competitive advantage, a unique way of thinking that is hardwired into my brain. I have an almost invincible confidence in my own abilities. I am hyper-observant of the flow of influence and power in a group. And I never panic in the face of crisis. I bet there are a lot of things about which people would want to be a little sociopathic. It frees me from the fear of public speaking or the possibility of becoming an emotional eater. Sometimes it is not clear to me whether I have fear or emotions, but I know they don't affect me the way they do others.

In the book *The Wisdom of Psychopaths: What Saints, Spies, and Serial Killers Can Teach Us About Success,* Kevin Dutton argues that there is a thin line between a Hannibal Lecter–type killer and the brilliant surgeon who lacks empathy. Sociopaths are primed for success because they are fearless, confident, charismatic, ruthless, and focused—qualities that define them as sociopaths but are also "tailor-made for success in the twenty-first century." I used those traits to climb the social ladder from misfit kid to talented musician to high-flying legal student to well-compensated attorney—and who knows where else they will take me in the future?

Sociopaths also think fast on their feet. Recent research suggests that sociopath brains learn in a chaotic way, similar to brains with attention deficit disorder, namely by breaking up the information into small fragments and storing it randomly in both hemispheres of the brain. Perhaps due to this odd storage system, the sociopath's corpus callosum, that bundle of nerve fibers that connects the two hemispheres of the brain, is longer and skinnier than in an average brain. Consequently, the rate at which information is transmitted between hemispheres in a sociopath's brain is abnormally high.

Of course, researchers almost never credit the sociopath brain as having any advantage over an empath brain, despite the demonstrated greater efficiency in transmitting information between brain hemispheres. Instead this efficiency is vaguely insinuated as the cause for the sociopath's "less remorse, fewer emotions and less social connectedness—the classic hallmarks of a psychopath." Normal people, even scientists, won't ever admit that a sociopath's brain might actually be better in any way. Every single article I have seen that even comes close to discussing some of the advantages of the sociopathic brain eventually backs off and makes some pat conclusion about how broken we are. In fact, the title of an article about the sociopath's corpus callosum is "Out of Order." But there are two meanings to that phrase, and I think one of them applies to this sort of bias thinly masked as science.

While I have to admit that I am not exceptional at multitasking (and, really, most people aren't), I have a genius for clear-minded focus. With me, my attention is always on one thing at a time, and I toggle rapidly through thoughts in a way that makes it sometimes seem that I have ADD. Despite this appearance, I am excellent at directing all my attention onto a single focus, particularly when driven to it by adrenaline. This can be very bad, like the time I became entirely fixated on killing that DC metro worker who hassled me for walking on a broken escalator. It can also be great in clutch situations, because I am able to tune out all of the white noise that might distract other people, the daily petty worries or insecurities that might plague other competitors. I can achieve a relaxed calmness in even the most frenetic situations. I believe that my lack of nerves is the reason why I performed so well on standardized tests in school. I don't remember a time when I scored outside the ninety-ninth percentile. During a mock trial competition, the judge remarked, "At one point I wanted to go back there and check to make sure you still had a pulse. You seemed as cool as a cucumber."

During the California bar exam, people were literally crying from the stress. The convention center where the exam was given looked like a disaster relief center, with people sprawled out on any available floor space, in a desperate attempt to recall everything they had memorized over the past eight or more weeks, the contents of their backpacks and briefcases spewed out around them. I had spent those weeks vacationing in Mexico, making a cross-country road trip, and teaching my nieces and nephews how to swim. Despite being woefully underprepared by many standards, I was able to maintain calm and to focus enough to maximize the legal knowledge I did have. I passed while many of my equally intelligent and better-prepared friends failed. Psychologists have described this single-mindedness as "flow" and have opined that champion athletes, master musicians, and other performers function at their best when focused in this way. Through this hyperfocus, I was able, with minimal work, to achieve a level of performance in school and my career that others would have to spend many times the number of hours preparing for, simply because I was able to marshal the exact mental resources I needed in the moment.

But other activities require a broader focus, including things as simple as walking efficiently through an airport, engaging in a conversation with more than one person, playing poker, or navigating office politics during a staff meeting. For these things, I have gradually learned to expand my hyperfocus to include multiple, varied targets via what free divers call "attention deconcentration." I've heard another practitioner refer to something similar as "situational awareness." Unlike meditation, which seeks to eliminate all thought, attention deconcentration focuses the user on everything all at once, feeling everything simultaneously. According to free diver Natalia Molchanova, "What you do to start learning is you focus on the edges, not the center of things, as if you were looking at a screen." She mentions that people who are subject to persistent stress factors where quick decision-making is necessary can find it useful to diffuse their attention and blunt their "emotional reaction in critical situations [where it] can lead to the wrong decisions and panic." When I get closest to achieving deconcentration, I am so hyperaware of all sensory inputs that I reach a total-body experience that one might call ecstasy. It's very pleasurable. And useful, particularly in combating unwanted impulses by forcing myself to see the bigger picture, which makes a single impulse seem so inconsequential in comparison. Hyperfocus achieved a similar effect by keeping me so engaged in one activity that I was blind to other temptations. Attention games became one of the best ways for me to finally liberate myself from the tyranny of my impulses and finally acquire some measure of social and professional stability.

I lived for a long time as an undiagnosed sociopath, trying as best I could to figure out ways to cope with my differences to succeed and to pass as normal in the wider world. But I wasn't doing a great job pulling it off. I was stretching the patience of the partners at my law firm. Ultimately, I was fired for shirking my work assignments. My relationships with friends and lovers were dissolving before my eyes. As I began my period of self-analysis and began investigating what it means to be a sociopath, I realized that though I had brought a lot of suffering on myself and people close to me, there was nothing objectively damning about having these traits. If I could figure out how to direct them in useful and productive directions, I could be true to myself and still live a satisfying life that minimized the harm I did to myself and others. It was time to take control of my life. The obvious starting place was my career.

Despite my laziness and general disinterest, I actually was a great lawyer when I was trying. After I lost my corporate job, I worked for a short while as a prosecutor in the misdemeanor department of the district attorney's office. My sociopathic traits make me a particularly excellent trial attorney, as compared to, for instance, an attorney who must learn and adhere to typeface requirements for court documents or carefully cull through millions of documents redacting minutiae. I'm cool under pressure. I charm and manipulate. I feel no guilt or compunction, which is a handy thing to have in such a dirty business.

In law there are a million and one mistakes you can make, particularly when approaching a trial, particularly as a prosecutor. Prosecutors bear the highest legal burden of proof and ethics and face disbarment or other disciplinary action for errors. Despite this, misdemeanor prosecutors almost always have to walk into trial with cases they've never worked on before. It's like buying a foreclosed home at auction sight unseen—it could be a steal or a nightmare. All you can do is bluff and hope that if there is an issue, you'll be able to scramble through it. No problem. At least for someone like me. The thing with sociopaths is that we are largely unaffected by fear. It's not because I am certain I'll do a terrific job, although historically that has been true. With my intelligence, quick-wittedness, and level head I'm pretty sure that even if I don't impress the judge I'll at least put on a good show.

The stereotypes about the bloodlessness of lawyers are true, at least about the good ones. Sympathy makes for bad lawyering, bad advocacy, and bad rule-making. The prosecution and the defense would both benefit from a little hard-hearted sociopathic lawyering. Whether you're a down-on-your-luck welfare recipient or a billionaire corporate executive, you'd be best served by a sociopathic counselor like me. I won't judge you or your supposed moral failings; I'll just stick to the letter of the law and ruthlessly try to win by working every angle I can—and I like to win as much for me as for you.

Lawyers deal with issues that most people would rather turn away from. Neuroscientist and sociopath researcher James Fallon has lauded sociopaths for performing "dirty work"—work that most people have no interest in doing themselves but that needs to get done, like providing legal representation for people whose behavior is (allegedly) abhorrent or disgusting. Somebody has to defend the Bernard Madoffs and O. J. Simpsons of the world. Not only are the sociopaths willing to do the dirty work, they are often better at doing it than others. Working the slippery spot between right and wrong to my advantage is not only personally satisfying but has the additional benefit of being good lawyering. Lawyers know that a fact can only be made fact if wrestled from a sea of strenuously argued maybes. And like all sociopaths, lawyers recognize the self-interest that hides in every heart, ferreting out the hidden motivations and dirty secrets that underlie criminal acts.

In law we have a word that is rarely used in other contexts: *dispositive*. *Dispositive* means "relating to or bringing about the settlement of an issue," so a dispositive point of law or a particular fact is one that will allow a party to either sink or swim on a disputed issue. For instance, let's say that I walk past someone hurt and bleeding on the sidewalk a mere twenty feet away from a hospital and I do not stop to help. The fact that I have no previous relationship to the victim is dispositive; the law would say that as a stranger I had no duty to help and I am absolved of any legal liability. Case closed. All other facts are worthless: that the victim screamed for help, that I had a phone and could have called 911, that I even had a first aid kit and surgical gloves with me at the time. *Dispositive* is a word that is rarely used outside of law because almost nothing in regular life is so final. Most of life is made up of vague moral and social norms that are annoying in their complexity and their ineffectiveness. Law is straightforward: a flush always beats a straight, and the specifics of each hand are irrelevant. Because of this, law is also powerful. If the law says you did not murder someone, for all intents and purposes you did not, as the O. J. Simpson case famously illustrated. Although the law is fallible, we pretend it isn't. This makes the law a trump card, as long as you can manage to manipulate a situation to where the law is on your side.

Perhaps because it is so high-stakes, the courtroom is the scene of the greatest human drama. But I believe it is to my advantage that I am relatively unfazed by the emotion that seems to sweep up many of the players. In particular, I seem to be immune, if not blind, to the extremes of righteous anger. As a child, my siblings and I would occasionally be shamed and chastised for what, I'm sure, were infuriating infractions. My mother could justify her acts of violence and indignity as discipline and punishment, the prerogative of a parent. It was as if the prickly edges of cruelty could be bundled up in moral righteousness, and in this insulated state, they could be trotted out for their day in the sun when petty child thieves were caught in the act.

It wasn't until law school that I was able to identify this thing and know that I had no real part in it. In every course we took, our casebooks were filled with outrageous stories of fraud, deceit, and oppression, demonstrations of how deeply and creatively human beings can wrong each other. Once in a while some story would prove too much for my classmates, and they would collectively become incensed, getting visibly upset over things that had happened decades or centuries ago to dead strangers. Watching them, I was fascinated but nervous. These people apparently felt something that I did not. From such outrage, I heard the most ridiculous suggestions for my classmates' illogical, knee-jerk calls for vigilantism, in complete disregard for the carefully balanced scales of justice. When my classmates could no longer identify with the child molesters and the rapists in the pages of our casebooks, they allowed righteous anger to determine their decision-making, applying a different set of rules to those people they considered morally reprehensible than they did to people they considered good, like them. Sitting in class, I saw how the rules changed when people reached the limits of empathy.

This impulse plays out not just in the rarefied space of the law school classroom but much more palpably in the public square. Almost every action movie constitutes the enactment of darkly violent wish fulfillment. A son avenges his mother. A father avenges his daughter. A husband avenges his wife. Each act of vengeance is more gruesome than the last. It isn't enough that the bad guy is prevented from doing his bad deeds; he must suffer as much as possible. It is as if the existence of evil—or something that can be designated as such—provides a safe haven for the good to engage in evil. It's a safe space to indulge in inflicting harm, to experience the sublime of suffering.

I do not understand or participate in the rush to judgment and punishment that seems to sweep up empaths, even in their roles as attorneys, judges, and jurors. If you have been falsely accused of a horrific crime, wouldn't you prefer to have a sociopath defend you, or sit in judgment of you? The nature of your presumed crime is of no moral concern to me. I am only interested in winning the legal game we play in sorting out the truth from the jumble of facts, partial facts, and misunderstandings.

Practicing law in front of a jury and judge is much more satisfying than slaving away in an office as one of many anonymous, highly educated drones. Trial is the culmination of everything that came before it, and after it little else matters. It is the quintessence of "dispositive." Trial is do or die—successfully persuade twelve jurors to vote how I want or lose. At trial, I get to perform. I am a lion tamer, the center of attraction in the three-ring circus that is the modern courtroom. It requires me to understand what people want to hear, not one-on-one, but on a grand scale. Trial forces my people-reading skills to go into overdrive, which in turn requires me to use attention deconcentration—focusing on everything at once. To get what I need, I must spin together a convincing narrative. I play off people's hopes and expectations, their preconceptions and biases. I use everything I've learned from a lifetime of lying about what makes a story plausible, even believable, to make my story seem like "the truth" and the opposing attorney's story seem like a pack of lies. And finally, because I don't trust people's rationality (particularly in issues where morality is implicated), I play off the one thing that you can always trust people to respond to—their fear. And I am like a cancer-sniffing dog when it comes to finding exactly which buttons to press to tap in to someone's ready supply of fear.

During jury selection, and depending on the laws of the state, the lawyers are allowed to question jurors about any prejudices before they are empaneled. Jury selection is a juror's first chance to form an impression of me. It is seduction in suits, and like any good seducer I start out casually. I first ask about their occupation, nodding simple approval for those jobs of which the juror is neither proud nor ashamed. For the jobs of which I can sense the juror is ashamed, I make a remark like "That job must be in high demand" to indicate my approval before the rest of the jurors. With this comment, I become his ally and champion. I've done him a favor for which he owes me a certain amount of allegiance. If I can tell that the juror is especially proud of his job, I express surprise and amazement at his accomplishments. The best predictor of whether someone will like you is whether they feel you like them. I like to optimize my chances.

Being a juror is a hard job. Evidence is not presented linearly and is limited in all sorts of ways before trial for unknown evidentiary and procedural reasons. Witnesses show up according to their availability, each telling a story that makes up only a small piece of the puzzle. Often, the purpose of their testimony might not even be apparent.

For this reason, jurors often direct the bulk of their attention to the drama occurring between the attorneys. It's only natural. Lawyers are present the entire time and seem to be running the show. Jurors spend the whole trial watching from the jury box as we move, speak, and act, knowing that there are invisible rules governing our behaviors. They understand that important things often happen in the courtroom while they are sequestered in the deliberation room. And even more maddening are the sidebars in which lawyers and judges conduct whispered conferences out of their earshot. Even in the halls, jurors are not allowed to speak to the lawyers. All of this makes us walking mysteries to them—celebrities starring in the only show in town.

I am always polite to opposing counsel, but never so much so that it would appear I like them. In the halls, I smile lightly and with ever-so-slight coquettishness, signaling that I share with the jurors embarrassment at the awkward situation in which we find ourselves. I am never ingratiating to the judge.

Inside the courtroom, I am likable, too, but armed with power, authority, and knowledge to which the jurors are not privy. People can be afraid of having power. Asked to choose between having power and giving up power to a "trusted" entity, people often prefer to give it up rather than have the responsibility that comes with that power. This is particularly true if they don't feel like they have a specific expertise and are worried about making a mistake, like deciding if a defendant is guilty or innocent. I know that they are unsure of themselves and are looking for someone to trust, to take away the burden of power. I make myself that trusted repository of power by exuding confidence and authority. I make meaningful eye contact with them when I discuss certain disputed issues in the case. I want to convey to them that they aren't hearing all of the story, and that if they knew what I knew they would come to the same conclusions I have about the case. I always make a more compelling character than the other attorney. I imply that, outside of the courtroom, I am a lot like them—the type of person you could turn to when you have a thorny problem you need help solving.

This alliance with the jurors is key when jurors reach the deliberation process. Jurors are instructed that they must reach consensus based on their rational understanding of the evidence presented. If one differs from the rest, he must make his case to the other jurors. The worst thing that can happen to a juror is to appear a fool for believing something that is clearly not credible to everyone else. Good attorneys use this peer pressure in two ways. First, I make myself into the most reliable and powerful ally a juror could have, making him believe he is not the outcast, because his alignment with me, the most popular girl in school, makes such a prospect impossible. I become the invisible juror in the deliberation room, controlling my puppet jurors by ensuring that they respond to any challenge by saying: "But remember when the prosecutor said this?" If I have done my job presenting my story in a way that it seems like "the truth," this should be sufficient to ensure a verdict in my favor.

But because people cannot be counted on to act rationally, I also engage their fear centers by subtly shaming them into believing my version of the story. The message I want to be broadcasting at all times is "You would be an idiot to believe the defendant's version of events." People do not like to feel like they were duped, so a juror's fear of looking stupid overcomes any anxiety about sending a fellow citizen to jail. I'm not a bully about the shaming; rather, I suggest to each and every juror that I believe he or she sees it my way because I can see that he or she is an intelligent, reasonable person. The juror and I are on the same team, and it's the winning one.

I enjoyed being a trial attorney, and I was successful at it. I loved the sensation of risk, for instance the risk of making a misstep that could result in a mistrial or the possibility of being waylaid by a witness changing his story on the stand. There was the seductive aspect of winning over the jurors and judge, not to mention the feeling of power I got from being the center of attention. Instead of seeing trial as a big moral issue, I played it like a game of poker—both sides dealt a specific hand and determined to play their hand better. Law is great that way—there really are winners and losers in clear, defined ways. Doing justice is fine I guess, but beating someone is its own reward. Luckily the justice system was designed exactly for this type of partisanship—an adversarial system in which our closest approximation of truth can only be reached if both parties are putting forth their best efforts at winning.

Indeed, there are a lot of careers for which the skill set of a sociopath is particularly well tailored. Jim Fallon mentions surgeon and investment banker. Sociopath researcher Jennifer Skeem has suggested that the protagonist in the film *The Hurt Locker,* a bomb-disposal specialist in Iraq, is a classic example of a sociopath due to his lack of regard for the rules, his boldness and fearlessness in defusing IEDs, and his trouble relating to the emotions of his team members. By looking at the list of characteristics, I could also add professions like military officer, spy, hedge fund manager, politician, jet pilot, underwater welder, firefighter, or many others. A high risk tolerance allows people like me to take opportunities that others could not, providing us an edge in competitive environments.

And as Al Dunlap, the former CEO and possible sociopath, describes it, those sociopathic traits can be a real boon in the corporate workplace: unemotional, ruthless, charming, confident. Lots of sociopaths are ambitious or are hungry for power or fame—all traits that are lauded in the business world. Joel Bakan, author of *The Corporation: The Pathological Pursuit of Profit and Power,* argues that if corporations have "person-hood" under the law, then it makes sense to question what kind of people they are. He posits that corporations behave with all the classic signs of sociopathy: They are inherently amoral, they elevate their own interests above all others', and they disregard moral and sometimes legal limits on their behavior in pursuit of their own advancement. Organizations of this type would thrive under the leadership of people who have the same traits: sociopaths. And, indeed, a study for a management development program discovered that managers at the highest levels of their companies were seen as "better communicators, better strategic thinkers, and more creative"—and they also scored higher on measures of sociopathic traits. Though they weren't popular with their staffs and were rarely seen as "team players," they were generally believed to have leadership potential. The authors concluded that "the very skills that make the psychopath so unpleasant (and sometimes abusive) in society can facilitate a career in business even in the face of negative performance ratings." Perhaps it can be argued that there is something wrong with corporate capitalism, but that is the system society has settled on, and it's one in which sociopaths can excel.

In my own work life, I've found that my need for constant stimulation means I am excited rather than stressed when deadlines approach. My desire to win whatever game I play makes me ruthlessly efficient, and my unflinching confidence that I will win inspires others to follow me. I am logical and decisive, a natural leader, particularly in crises where others panic or fall apart. I can get angry in a flash, but it is also over in a flash, which allows failing members of my team to realize that while failure will not be tolerated, no one is holding grudges. Now that I have learned to steer my inclinations along useful paths, I am a natural leader and a success in my professional exploits, not in spite of my sociopathic tendencies, but because of them. Commenters on the blog have attested to similar experiences:

> I am the Service and Production Manager for the largest producer of bottled water in the U.S. Before that I started as a laborer for one of the largest concrete companies in the U.S. Within 12 years I had 2 bosses (the owners of the company), and had over 350 people below me. Needless to say the transition from construction has been difficult, but we (Sociopaths) can adjust or rather force adjustments. As a teen, I was told I had a severe adjustment disorder. I don't adjust to my surroundings, I make my surroundings adjust to me. I do, by manipulation or intimidation. We are wolves amongst sheep.

Another commenter suggested that sociopathic managers "want to out-do each other. They don't care about their colleagues or praising someone else at their level. They are self centered. But they get the job done and that's all that really matters and if they are high up the ladder it's unlikely they will be confronted with the way they run their ship."

Sociopathic traits can and do manifest themselves in malignant ways. But particularly in the field of business, one reader suggests, sociopaths might actually create less discord than empaths do:

> I think it's the empaths who are the bigger problem. They engage in bad politics and base most decisions on the whims of their emotions, the main one being the fear (probably not unfounded) that others are out to screw

them over and take away their power. Having worked for incompetent, frightened and greedy individuals (not a pretty mix), and a couple of pathological narcissistic ones, I don't see how a sociopath could do worse. Logic, even cutthroat logic, would be a nice change.

In fact, when corporations or managers mix business with their personal feelings or sense of morality, it can often lead to decidedly negative results, like the backlash against corporations such as Chick-fil-A for their anti-gay-marriage stances and the lawsuits from shareholders against corporate officers for having the corporation support political causes that are unrelated to the company's business. As another reader put it:

The only reason business might be a good fit for people with little conscience is because corporations are themselves purposefully designed to be without a pro-social agenda. Corporations are created to make money. Period. Ergo, . . . corporations self select those who are likely to help fulfill its pro-profit agenda, sociopath and normiopath alike. That's the beauty of it. The company does not care if you have a conscience or not, only that you can put your morality aside to make a profit, if that is called for.

No, at least when it comes to business, cash is king. This doesn't mean that corporations can't do good things. As one reader pointed out, "corporations, like sociopaths, can choose to act in a benevolent manner out of their own best interest—and often do."

I love money. It's so impersonal. In a world where everyone

likes to win, money is frequently how the score is kept. I don't like spending it, necessarily; I don't get much pleasure from buying or owning things. Money doesn't matter to me in itself. But the acquisition of money is a game I like very much. It seems that other people care about money more than almost anything else in the world, and because they care about it so much, they will fight hard for it—against me or anybody else. They're just as committed to winning as I am, which makes the game very fun.

Sometimes all you need is a different perspective to win, particularly in something like the stock market. As Sir Isaac Newton famously confessed after losing a small fortune in the stock market in the early 1700s, "I can calculate the motions of heavenly bodies, but not the madness of people."

I have an incredibly green thumb for money, particularly in the stock market. I fully funded my retirement by the time I was thirty years old. Since I started investing seriously in 2004, I have averaged a 9.5 percent return in the stock market—257 percent better than the 3.7 percent average returns of the S & P 500 over the same period. Beating the market this soundly and consistently is unheard of and many argue it is impossible (or due solely to luck). In 2011, only one out of five mutual fund managers beat the S & P 500, and only a handful of individuals have managed to do so with any regularity. I do it every year. I am not trading on better knowledge. In fact, I am a relatively unsophisticated investor. Instead, I am trading on a special vision. When I look at the world, the flaws or vulnerabilities in people and the social institutions that they've made jump out to me, as if they were highlighted for me and only me to see.

Sharks see in black-and-white. Scientists have suggested that contrast against background may be more helpful than color for predators in detecting potential prey, helping them to focus on crucial spatial relationships rather than extraneous details. I'm color-blind in a way that makes mass hysteria seem particularly striking in contrast to normal, expected behavior. My lack of empathy means I don't get caught up in other people's panic. It gives me a unique perspective. And in the financial world, being able to think opposite the pack is all you need.

Traders laud the "contrarian" mentality. Warren Buffett said: "Be greedy when others are fearful and fearful when others are greedy." Easier said than done for the vast majority of stock traders. And when I'm trading stocks, those are the people I am up against. On every stock trade there is someone who wants to sell and someone who wants to buy, at least at a particular price. Each tends to think the other is an idiot. In simple terms, the person who is selling thinks that she is getting out just in time while the person buying thinks that he is about to make good money.

Because the actual transaction is faceless, I can't practice my usual people-reading skills or manipulation, but I don't need to. The truth is that the market doesn't really reflect some magical perfect valuation of a stock under the efficient market hypothesis. It reflects the mass consensus of how actual individual investors value the stock. It is the sum total of everyone's hopes and fears about what a company is capable of doing. Preying on people's hopes and fears is my métier, even en masse. It's how I played my jurors. There's a desperation to both hope and fear that becomes obvious once you've learned to spot it. With my color-blind eyes, I see these features more starkly than anything else.

And you only need to see this desperation in a few people to know that it has reached a critical mass of people. Joseph Kennedy said that he knew it was time to pull out of the market before the stock market crash of 1929 when even his shoe-shine boy was giving him stock tips. Joseph Kennedy may not have been a sociopath, but he certainly acted like one. In a 1963 *Life* magazine feature on him, Kennedy was described as having the sociopathic traits of being able to mix well "in all kinds of company, against every background," from the very highest of the social elite to the "theatrical unknowns" inhabiting Greenwich Village. "Only the keenest observer" would realize that Kennedy was actually allied with none of these groups—"he belonged to no world but his own." Kennedy was no doubt aided in his stock market exploits by this ability to be both one of the crowd and completely independent. In fact, Kennedy was described by a broker whom he shared an office with as a man who "had the ideal temperament for speculation" because he "possessed a passion for facts, a complete lack of sentiment and a marvelous sense of timing." I may not be as talented as Joseph Kennedy, but I also am blessed with a complete lack of sentiment.

Kennedy and I are not the only cool heads that have been drawn to the stock market. An estimate that 10 percent of Wall Street employees are psychopaths was being casually thrown around the media in 2012, but the research so far doesn't confirm that number. A 2010 study by Dr. Robert Hare of psychopathy among corporate professionals found that about 4 percent met the threshold for clinical psychopathy, versus about 1 percent for the general population, though as Hare has said, "we do not know the prevalence of psychopathy among those who work on Wall Street. It may be even *higher* than 10%, on the assumption that psychopathic entrepreneurs and risk-takers tend to gravitate toward financial watering-holes, particularly those that are enormously lucrative and poorly regulated."

While the fall of Enron and the banking collapse of 2008 are sometimes blamed on sociopathic behavior, it's not clear whether the ringleaders were actually sociopaths or not. On the one hand there are some pretty sociopathic-sounding quotes from Enroners talking about cutting off power to Grandma so they could squeeze more money out of the state of California. On the other hand: (1) most Enroners didn't necessarily break the law but were careful to stay within the letter of the law, and (2) they did what they were supposed to do—make lots of money for the company, even if it involves manipulating markets in unethical ways. Some have suggested that the only reason that most Enroners may not have technically engaged in unlawful behavior was because they used their money to eliminate or change the regulations that they didn't like. The rise and fall of Enron was shocking to people because it exposed the face of corporate hubris and amorality. A sociopath would be well at home at a corporation like Enron. A sociopath might also do something as reckless and risky as being a whistle-blower. In a lot of ways sociopaths and corporations are like the weather: Sometimes rain is a blessing and sometimes it is a curse. The most people can do is hope for the best and prepare for the worst.

I might have been a good lawyer but I gave up practice a few years ago, because it got boring, and I realized I am not very interested in helping people or corporations. I would much rather indoctrinate them, which is why I became a law professor. I was lucky to stumble upon law teaching as an option—one of my friends was a professor and encouraged me to send letters to schools in case they had any emergency teaching needs. And it turns out that I love teaching: the lifestyle, the pay, the power, and most of all the autonomy. Every year a new crop of students arrives to be charmed. I have a small cadre of legal "nemeses" that I play one-sided games with—other academics in my field whom I disagree with or don't like. My scholarship often focuses on ruining theirs. People are often surprised to learn that I teach less than six hours a week, less than eight months out of the year. In many ways it's a dream job for someone inherently lazy and unable to do grunt work like me, but eventually I'm sure I'll get bored of it too. After I do, I don't know what, but I'm sure things will work out. They always do.

As an academic, I work in an institutional setting organized within idiosyncratic parameters. For instance, law professors are the most formal of academics in that they are expected to wear business attire, given the formality of dress that their students will be expected to adopt upon entering their profession; however, they are also less often expected to abide by community norms, since their role is to challenge existing legal regimes. In other words, you should wear a suit, not be one. Some of the biggest legal academic superstars bring their dogs with them to work and some of the biggest losers wear power ties. This is the kind of environment in which I thrive because I am used to both trying to conform and never managing to conform completely.

My students love this charming quirkiness I exude. I am unusually attentive to their needs. My first few years I performed extensive market research, subtly surveying my students on hundreds of topics until my teaching had as much mass appeal as a Big Mac. I always get exceptional teaching evaluations that cite my thoughtfulness and my apparent lack of ego. I am described as witty and never condescending. Even better, I am entertaining—making jokes and livening up dry material with videos or group work. By my second year at my first teaching job, my class enrollment doubled as students raved about my ability to make even the most esoteric subject relatable. It helps that I am, according to one of my teaching evaluations, a "stone cold fox." Not true, but I am well aware of the research that attractive people get treated far better and are perceived as being far more competent than ugly people. Consequently, I dress carefully for class. I shop for clothes that are both conservative and sexy, like a three-piece skirt suit with a vest that fits more like a bustier and a knee-length cigarette skirt cut to fit a pinup model. If I wear a pantsuit, I'll sometimes push the gender lines by wearing suspenders and a tie. To the men, I am an object of desire—a ready-made "hot teacher" fantasy. For the women I am a whip-smart, successful role model, who also has an eye for fashion and is not afraid to say the word *tampon* in class. All of this is a carefully calculated persona meant to appeal to the greatest percentage of the student population possible.

Of course this could all go horribly wrong, and sometimes does. Sometimes I overplay the sex appeal. I had one student accuse me of pandering to the male students. The truth is that many new students are suspicious of my easy charm and what is starting to seem like a cult of personality built around me. This can be a serious danger with sociopaths in the workplace. One blog reader told a similar story:

> I recently had a malignant narcissist as an immediate superior, my little boss as I liked to call him. He hated the fact that those that I was in charge of liked me so much and would do whatever I wanted them to do. They would not listen to him for anything unless it came from me. Even though technically he was their Big boss, it was me their loyalty was to. Because I am such a "nice guy" they loved doing things for me; I gave them

all the credit of course, which only made me look better in the eyes of MY Big boss (who is my little boss's boss; make sense?) and further infuriated the "little boss." My little boss proclaimed me a cult of personality, a cancer to the business, and feverishly tried to defame me with the Big boss. Finally he got personal on a day that my patience was wearing thin and I snapped. I now have to go find employment elsewhere or face assault charges . . . oh, the life.

I don't mind some students' skepticism in the face of my magnetism. They're law students; we train them to be cynics. As with jurors in a trial, it takes a while to build up a rapport with them. I am aware of their distrust so at first I am very straightforward, efficient, and professional. I don't want to seem presumptuous. Nor do I want to seem overly available, as if they are on my same level. I am confident and aloof. If someone is acting out of line, I will put them back into their place with a quick, dispassionate put-down. I will correct some slight misunderstanding of theirs or call on them for a particularly thorny question so the class can see them squirm. The class likes this. They don't like gunners or the teachers who cater to them. Apart from that, there are no power struggles. I have nothing to prove. Their tuition dollars are paying me, and handsomely. They can try to fight me, but in that classroom I am God. I write the test. I give them the grade. If I say something is the law, it is the law. Even so, I show off just enough so that they feel lucky to have me and not someone far less engaging.

My students become interested in me as a person. They develop little crushes on me, which I feed with the selective disclosure of more and more personal information—that I am a musician, that I have an interesting background in the law filled with high-profile clients whose names modesty prevents me from dropping. I am rarely explicit about anything. I make people work for these personal details about my life, drawing their own conclusions, which makes the information seem all the more authentic and valuable to them.

Now, if I had shown up on the first day of class touting my credentials, talking about my personal life, nurturing people's crushes, it would have been disastrous. Every once in a while I forget and make a joke too early, show familiarity too soon, and have to immediately back off again with a renewed period of neutrality, but I've gotten better. Now it's like cooking an old familiar recipe, which makes me worry I'll get bored of it soon.

It seems to me that many people could benefit in their work from this kind of analysis of how to manage people by managing their expectations, how to endear people to you by being respectfully aloof. I don't get wrapped up in the emotional conflagrations that can undermine a serene workplace, and it seems to me that a lot of leaders fail to deal wisely with problems. Once in church I attended an "air your grievances" meeting. Within minutes people were erupting in angry accusations. Although each person's grievance wasn't much on its own, the sheer number of them surprised everyone there. People became incensed that the church leaders remained heedless of all these pressing concerns. Everyone left riled up with grievances that they never knew they had before. I thought this was absolute idiocy. I couldn't imagine a meeting being run more poorly.

When I have little insurrections in class or any other professional environment, I target the biggest complainers individually. I schedule a meeting or write them a quick e-mail saying things like, "I noticed that you seemed really frustrated by X." I let them talk for as long as they need, commiserating with them without necessarily committing to any particular position. I neither justify nor entrench myself in any particular position nor agree with their own position. As part of the commiserating, though, I focus on their feelings: "That must be so exhausting," or, "I understand, the reading assignments are very demanding." I try to use words that sound sympathetic but also make the problem sound either surmountable or like something that should be expected from a lawyer in training, or whatever their position or skill set is. I figure that most people just need to vent, but I am also trying to subtly shame them. I say things like, "Law is hard, that's why you'll get paid the big bucks," implying that the student is being a crybaby and should toughen up.

By isolating the potential instigators and stealing their thunder, I never give them the chance to speak publicly and gain support. Everyone else is left knowing only about their own particular struggles, assuming that any issue with me or the class may have more to do with their own personal failures than a larger institutional failure. I rely on people's need to appear smart in other ways. For instance, it's traditional in law school for lecturers to cold-call on students during class. I don't like to do this because frequently they're ill prepared and it wastes time. If I never cold-call, however, the students will pick up on this and stop preparing as thoroughly for class. What I have started doing is e-mailing a student ahead of time that I will call on them for a particular case. To the rest of the class it appears as if I have cold-called on them. The student performs marvelously. The other students can't help but wonder, Am I the only one who isn't completely getting this material? So they work harder. The student whom I e-mailed has every incentive to keep the e-mail secret because it makes his performance more impressive. This divide-and-conquer approach to classroom and workplace management has been effective for me on many occasions, and I'm surprised more people don't adopt it.

I once worked with a bully. She had no position of real authority but had managed to make herself indispensable in the office where I had just started. At first I was lulled by the bully's seeming good nature and charms; she just seemed nice, asking me about what projects I was involved with, how things were working out. But one of my new coworkers warned me that the only thing she wanted to help me do was fail.

As the bully was saying good night to everyone, I pulled her aside, put my hand on her shoulder, and said, "You know, I have to apologize to you. I made a joke this morning that was in poor taste. You asked how everything was going with my new project and I said, 'So far so good.' I didn't mean to imply that I wasn't giving the project my full attention and skill. On the contrary, I am one hundred percent dedicated to the success of this project. I think I was just trying to be self-deprecating, but I realize now that the joke fell flat." My apology caught her off guard.

She started to spill, "Well, it's true that the last few people in charge of that project got fired, and I was just thinking, maybe . . . but maybe you'll be different . . ." And just like that she showed her hand. She acknowledged that she was aware of what my project was (even though she pretended to have no clue the day before), its history, its importance, and her obvious interest in my failure.

The next day I was all deflection. She asked me a question, and I gave her a nonanswer and asked her questions back, even for the most meaningless of things. "What did you get for lunch?" "Oh you know, same old. What did you get for lunch?"

"What are you working on now?" "Little this, little that. What are you working on?" The terser the answer, the more off-putting it was to her. The bully, now desperate and sensing the shift in power, quickly progressed from "chummy" sideways questions to direct inquiries. "So how did that project turn out yesterday? Did it get approved?" Wouldn't you like to know.

As one blog commenter said regarding bullying:

> [Some] seem to think that sociopaths are the biggest bullies. Any intelligent sociopath should understand that violence and threats are easy, and can backfire horribly if they rely on them. Sociopaths are crowd-pleasers rather than crowd-repressors, bullies make enemies when they gain power, sociopaths make friends.

These tactics may be inspired by a sociopath's selfish desire to avoid emotional drama and upheaval, but they can benefit any organization.

In addition to the pleasure I take in teaching, one of my favorite activities is attending academic conferences. All of the professional action happens there, so everything about the way I present myself is extremely calculated. First, I am careful to wear something that will draw attention, like jeans and cowboy boots while everyone else is wearing business attire. The cowboy boots both emphasize and explain my strut, and I want to indicate that I'm not interested in being judged by the usual standards. This is important because people look at my name tag to see where I teach. Because I don't teach at a top-tier school they don't immediately expect that I will be brilliant, but the truth is that I am. I've also found that, in a predominantly male profession, it's helpful to remember that women are seen as objects. I don't fight their expectations, I just play with them. They like to be played with and I like to force them to see things my way.

I know they underestimate me but I don't fight it. My shtick is that I am just the messenger giving straight facts. "But also do you see how X only looks like Y from this angle? If we looked at it from this other angle, doesn't it look more like X?" I let them see it for themselves. I think it is more convincing. I learned this from my experiences with juries. I'm trying to transplant an idea into their heads. I need to be careful how I present it so they don't reject it as foreign before it even gets settled.

But I also want it to seem a little like magic, the same way an answer to a riddle seems a little like magic. Of course riddles are not by their nature puzzling, they're puzzling due to the way they are presented—leaving out vital pieces of information. Riddles have the appearance of being solvable; that's why people get engaged in guessing and trying to show off. When I present at conferences, I also try to get people engaged in guessing. In fact I specifically ask for shows of hands guessing about the results. When you finally reveal the end of a riddle, it makes you look like a genius, when really it's because you purposefully presented the issue that way.

One riddle I frequently use in law discussions is the riddle of why the Salt Lake City airport has some of the best smoking facilities of any airport in the United States. The majority of the state population is Mormon. Mormons do not smoke; they believe the body is a temple and that smoking desecrates that temple. I ask people to guess why a state full of nonsmokers would build such convenient smoking facilities in an airport. Everyone thinks this is an answerable question and they are intelligent people so everyone hazards a guess, but no one has yet guessed correctly—just me, after I asked myself the riddle one day pacing the halls of the airport during a weather delay. That makes me the magical keeper of the riddle.

The nice thing about this riddle is that it has a very simple answer: the airport has always been nonsmoking since its construction in the 1960s. LAX, LaGuardia, and many of the other major airports in the United States have smoking accommodations that seem like an afterthought. And they were, because those airports originally allowed smoking throughout the terminals. While the main terminals of those airports were a haze of cigarette smoke in the 1960s, the Salt Lake City airport was originally built to be nonsmoking. To appease smokers in a larger society where indoor public smoking was the norm, the airport was built with easily accessible "smoking rooms" spread throughout the terminals. In this way, a good accommodation for smokers actually arose out of a special awareness on the part of nonsmokers. People like this little twist. It seems to be a parable about the difficulty of predicting unintended consequences or a cautionary tale about how quickly the dominant majority can become an oppressed minority (maybe making special allowances for sociopaths is not so ridiculous an idea?). I like the riddle for its moral ambiguity and for the way it reveals the simplistic complexity of the world.

My legal work is not fake, any more than my answer about the Salt Lake airport is fake. What is manipulative is how I present it. I lead them down a particular path that predestines them to reach only one conclusion—my conclusion. They don't know where it's going to end up at the end, and that's part of the thrill. It almost seems like intellectual magic. Really it's just effective rhetoric.

As a law professor, my original ideas represent almost the sum total of my worth to my school. I like to say outrageous things and have people challenge me. I like the controversy. The more controversy, the more people will remember my talk. I have an answer for everything. Their initial underestimation draws them out for my attack. They're used to a world of hiding behind credentials. My point: I am not what you think I am. I want them to hesitate before challenging me again. I want them to be afraid to call my bluff. Law is appearances, and it is rare to have a sure thing, so I make the most of it when I have it.

I know I can't compete with the oxford-shirt types, or even the types who can rattle off the facts of the last dozen decided Supreme Court opinions. Like everywhere else, there is an old boys' club of lawyers and judges who want to hire someone who looks and acts just like them—or at least the younger, more virile version of them. They whip out their knowledge of substantive law in a way that makes it seem like they are comparing penis size. I don't care to engage in legal debates. Most of substantive law is boring, particularly to someone who needs constant stimulation as much as I do. I don't have that type of brain, nor do I care enough to acquire an encyclopedic knowledge of the law. And I don't have any interest in keeping up on any current legal issues. This is why I was not well suited to being a practicing lawyer. I can't make myself do things the way most people can, even very important things that matter a lot to the client. Luckily, as an academic, I have the freedom to learn and teach whatever I want.

Still, I must keep up at least the appearance of competency, which is why, when I am engaged with the old guard of the legal community with my reputation at stake, I am very aware that I must choose my battles. Like the revolutionary army fighting the redcoats, I lure my enemy from their comfort zones and ambush them with my own strengths: reading people, seeing flaws or areas of possible exploitation in a system, and thinking outside of the box. I nod pleasantly at my colleagues until they make a mistake and then engage them on that. It is a little more guerilla warfare than they are used to. Some might say that it is not fighting fair, but I am keenly aware that there will never be a fair fight. Not for people who teach at the school I teach at and can't manage to remember the names of all nine current Supreme Court justices.

Conferences are also minefields of emotional complexities for me. I dread the cocktail parties and sometimes invent a persona for the evening, allowing me to inhabit yet another role. One of my paramours remarked that this paradox was what drew him to me initially—he wanted to know which one of these personas was the real me. He claims that he could tell there was much more going on in my head than met the eye because although I seemed perfectly pleasant when engaged in conversation with acquaintances, I disengaged much too smoothly for it to have not been thoroughly premeditated—as if I spent the entire conversation with a smile on my face and the thought of escape plots in my head. Unless I am actively trying to convey a particular message or to seduce, I would rather not talk to people. There's too much risk of my saying something incriminating and no corresponding benefit, so I will just stay silent.

I actually do prepare anecdotes for the purpose of engaging in small talk at social events that I am frequently required to attend, like my riddles. This has proven to be essential in seducing my colleagues and friends, getting through otherwise painfully awkward evenings, and even scoring career points. I have learned that it is important always to have a catalog of at least five personal stories of varying length in order to avoid the impulse to shoehorn unrelated tidbits into existing conversations. Social-event management feels very much like classroom or jury management to me; it's all about allowing me to present myself to my own best advantage.

As I've learned to satisfy my sociopathic tendencies with more productive professional behavior, I've also reined in some of my youthful impulsiveness. I was reckless as a young attorney, but always with the sense that the downside would be outbalanced by the benefit. I would do stupid stuff like submit easily verifiable fake reimbursements for pittance sums. I got the law firm to pay for my tennis lessons one summer. I tried to seduce one of the lead partners who was in a very happy relationship with her longtime partner. I successfully seduced one of the more obscure partners, but he didn't stay spellbound by my charms after I did subpar work for him. I got away with most of it, and no one ever called me out—until I was fired.

But now I have more to lose if things go wrong—more money, a more stable life, a career, a relatively constant set of close associates. All these figures get crunched in my head and make me aware of a million different risks, which added together are not negligible. And that awareness gives me the symptoms of what is probably best described as "anxiety," even though I used to be completely oblivious to all of it (or didn't care). Every time I have gotten this far in the past I have quit and started over. The older I get, though, the fewer do-overs I have left.

I may still seem reckless, particularly in circumstances in which people are irrationally afraid and I am relatively unfazed. I still like excitement in my life; I tend to seek out new and potentially dangerous experiences, like a recent bungee-jumping trip I went on with friends. But as I have aged, I have admittedly retreated into more of a life of the mind in which my excitement and thrills come more from mind games or intellectual pursuits where the reward-risk ratio is high. I play fewer games with my colleagues' emotions, though I'm not sure I'll ever be able to stop completely, or if it will even be necessary to.

In truth, a lot of lawyering was smoke and mirrors. I play the part that people expect. It's not like there weren't bad parts. There were really bad parts. I'm a little bit of a legal idiot, at least when it comes to certain topics. I have terrible fashion sense. My first impulse in a conversation is frequently a bad one. I've just learned to fake my way through errors, or outsource my fashion (and moral) decisions, or spin misstatements into clever, sarcastic jokes. Like an actress who is aware that she has a good side and a bad side, I was always careful to put on the right sort of show for the right sort of audience, for lovers and employers and friends. And for a while, I pulled off my performance to general acclaim.

Now, many years later, after this period of self-analysis, I have learned to be basically honest with myself, my family, and a few intimates. But for the sake of getting by—holding a job, having a life—I present a mask of normalcy to the world. It can be lonely. I become restless from pretending to be normal for too long and too hard. But going through the motions of being normal and stable does make them true, to some degree. What's the difference between acting the part of a good lawyer and being one? What's the difference between pretending to be a valuable colleague and being one? I've come to realize that the scam I was playing as a new lawyer has acquired the weight of reality—it is my life.

Chapter 7

EMOTIONS AND THE FINE
ART OF RUINING PEOPLE

When we were children, my sister Kathleen and I read *The Wonderful Wizard of Oz*. I didn't identify with Dorothy and her wish to return to her Kansas home. I wasn't the heroine who saved her motley band of companions from the forces of evil. Instead, I saw myself in the Tin Woodman, who began life as Nick Chopper, an Ozian logger.

His troubles began when he fell deeply in love with one of the Munchkin girls. The girl's guardian refused to part with her and made a pact with the Wicked Witch of the East, who bewitched Nick's ax to harm him. When Nick wielded the ax against a tree, it slipped from his fingers and cut off his leg instead. The next day it cut off the other leg, then both arms, then his head, and then finally split his torso in two. Each time his ax betrayed him, Nick would go to the tinsmith to replace his lost flesh with a tin prosthetic. However, when Nick came for the last replacement, his split torso, the tinsmith forgot to include a prosthetic heart.

Tin Woodman was unperturbed. Without a heart, he no longer cared about whether he could marry his former love;

without a heart, he no longer cared about much at all. It was as if the Wicked Witch had given him a gift with her cruel and painful curse. Tin Woodman's new tin skin was more durable than his old soft flesh, and he shone with brilliance in the daylight. He delighted in the beauty and strength of his newly improved, albeit heartless, self. In chopping up his flesh, she rid him of another and possibly more painful curse of wanting what he could not have, of holding on to the Munchkin girl as the answer to his happiness. I often wonder if, like the Tin Woodman, I was also given a kind of gift—a release from the things that seem to torture others. It is difficult to feel dissatisfaction when you rarely look to others for satisfaction. In some ways my deficits have freed me from wanting and not having that which seemed so essential to them—some purpose or identity in the world, some affirmation of the goodness and rightness of my existence.

The only disadvantage that Tin Woodman could see was that he was susceptible to rust, but he was always careful to bring an oil can with him should the weather happen to turn. But one day, the Tin Woodman was careless and got caught in a rainstorm without his oil can. His joints rusted shut and he could no longer move. He remained frozen for a year before Dorothy discovered him. It was only during that motionless year that he began to realize what he was missing: "It was a terrible thing to undergo, but during the year I stood there I had time to think that the greatest loss I had known was the loss of my heart."

It took a long time for me to finally rust over—to reach that period of aimlessness, unemployment, and self-searching that slowed me down and gave me time to think about who I am and what I want. The rusting happened in fits and starts. I had long stretches of bewildering emotional arthritis, through which I trudged onward in my unyielding determination to ignore pain. These were punctuated with periods of success and happiness, of superior performance and pleasurable mastery of the world around me. But as heartless as I am, I have wanted to feel love, to feel connection, to feel like I belong to the world like anyone else. No one, it seems, can escape loneliness. I know enough, however, to understand that getting a heart isn't a quick fix either. Even after Tin Woodman gets his version of one, he has to be very careful not to cry lest his tears cause him to rust. A heart can be paralyzing in its way. It is not at all clear that the Tin Woodman is happier or better after he receives one.

When I think of myself, I feel that I exist first as a will—I am the product of my desires and my efforts to fulfill those desires. I identify more as a sociopath than by my gender or profession or race. In my soul, it feels like I was cast first as this iron-hearted thing, this Nietzschean machine, and then the rest of me came later—perhaps my consciousness next, and then my body, and then the phenomenological awareness that comes with being inside a body and negotiating the world through it. You feel the universe as mediated through the particles of your flesh, viewed from the height of your eyes and touched through the nerves in your fingers. People perceive you in a certain way and treat you accordingly, and so you become a mélange of certain qualities and impulses and desires, all entangled at atomic speeds in the molecular space of your body. But at my heart I feel I am just want, need, action, and my sociopathic traits profoundly impact all of those things.

I have trouble navigating my own emotions. It's not that I don't feel them. I feel a lot of different emotions, but some of them I don't recognize or understand. Often it feels like my emotions are without context. It is like I am reading a book one page at a time, but starting with the last page and moving backward. There are clues to help me understand, but there is no linear logic that allows me to infer simple cause-and-effect relationships between the vague discomfort I feel and the recognition that "I am sad because of X." And if I can't contextualize my own emotions, I have even greater difficulty understanding the emotions of others.

Recent research from King's College London's Institute of Psychiatry revealed that the brains of sociopathic criminals show distinctly less gray matter in the areas of the brain that are important for understanding the emotions of others. Studies indicate that sociopathic brains do not respond emotionally to words such as *death, rape,* and *cancer* the same way that normal brains do. We respond with about as much emotion as we do to a word like *chair.* More research has shown that sociopathic brains have a lower number of connections between the prefrontal cortex (which helps regulate emotions, processes threats, and facilitates decision-making) and the amygdala (which processes emotions), which could explain why sociopaths do not feel sufficient negative emotions when doing something antisocial.

This neurological disconnect between emotion and decision-making can be a decided competitive advantage in most professional settings, where risk taking is often richly rewarded, but it can cause real problems in personal settings, in which sociopaths are expected to make emotional connections. One blog reader said:

I've always worked in sales and my [moral] flexibility has paid off time and again. But I think I've often been promoted to levels where my personal style becomes a liability. When I do well the next logical step always involves managing other people or corporate partnerships . . . stuff that require[s] a great deal of sensitivity to the interests of others over a longer term. This is the level where I seem to make mistakes. Then I have to go somewhere else and start all over again.

I am much like this reader. Because I am largely just mimicking emotional connection or understanding, almost all of my exploits have an expiration date at the moment when pretending to care ceases to be sustainable.

One of my favorite theories regarding a sociopath's emotional world comes from psychopath researcher and University of Wisconsin professor Joseph Newman. Newman has advocated that sociopathy is largely an attentional disorder, where the sociopath is getting all the right input but is just not paying attention to it in the same way that everyone else is, so it is meaningless to him.

In the emotional realm, Newman argues that sociopaths feel the same breadth of emotions that normal people do, but that they do not attend to the emotions as others do and therefore experience them differently. Newman has noticed that if a sociopath's attention is directed at a particular emotion, she can generally feel it the way that normal people can. The difference is that it is not automatic; the sociopath has to make the conscious effort to focus her attention that way. Therefore, sociopathy results in an "attention bottleneck" that allows sociopaths to focus on only one activity or train of thought to the exclusion of other social cues and "perhaps even signals sent over the prefrontal-to-amygdala pathway" that would tell them to stop doing what they're doing.

This theory resonates with me. If I focus on an emotion, I can greatly amplify its force far beyond what it should be. For feelings that I don't care to feel, I just tune them out. It's easy to ignore anything that would be inconvenient or unpleasant to consider.

In this way, my sociopathy feels like an extreme form of compartmentalization. I can shut myself off or open myself up to emotions like fear or anger or anxiety or dread or joy just by flipping an internal switch. It's not like I can't ever experience these emotions in the right circumstances; I just have to know how to tap in to them. It's sort of like looking for a signal by turning a dial, like a radio. All those things are out there, all the time, being broadcast through our airwaves. All I have to do is tune in to the right station. If I want to feel something—despair, anxiety, bliss, horror, disgust—I just have to think about it. It's like seeing a glass half empty and then flipping the switch or turning the dial to look at it as half full. I believe empaths sometimes have a similar sensation and label it an epiphany—a sudden shift in perspective—that changes the way they think about the world. Because the scope of my perspective is so focused, and so limited, I experience this feeling of epiphany many times a day. It can be disorienting, but it keeps things interesting.

Most people have to listen to whatever signal is being broadcast the strongest, both within themselves and in their social environments. By virtue of my sociopathy, I get to choose which signals to listen to. Sometimes it's nice to be able to choose who to mirror or how to feel, but it can also be a burden. If I'm in a social situation, I have to constantly and actively monitor the airwaves. Most people pick up on social and moral cues because they automatically tune in to other people's emotional stations, reading body language unconsciously and displaying appropriate emotional responses in a natural, instinctive way. Empaths are like cell phones in this way—they automatically seek out the strongest signal from the cell towers. Sociopaths, on the other hand, are like traditional radios. I can only hear the strongest signal if I happen to be on that station, or if I'm being extra vigilant about scanning. It's a lot of work; there's a lot of trial and error involved. Often the best I can do is realize I've missed an important cue, then shift and shuffle through my stations to recover.

This happened the other day with one of my students. I had called on her about the meaning of the Latin phrase *duces tecum* because she had previously indicated some knowledge of Latin, but she shrugged the question off. After class she came up to me to say that she would be missing the next class, that her grandmother had died that morning and that she was flying out for the funeral the next day. My stomach sank and I became anxious. I spat out the usual, "Oh, I'm so sorry to hear that," accompanied by a very concerned-looking face (hopefully it was concerned looking—luckily the grieving are not close observers of the authenticity of faces). She lingered. I didn't know what else to say so I kept yammering: "Well, presumably you have asked one of your classmates for a copy of their notes. Also Mr. Smith usually audio-records the lectures; you might want to ask him for a copy of the recording . . ." She wasn't making eye contact, looked down and away. I didn't know what to say and I wanted to get away from her so I finished with, "But I'm very sorry for your loss."

At that she understood that our conversation was over. I didn't understand what the purpose of the conversation had been or whether I had properly met her expectations, but I got more nervous as she walked only five feet away to be comforted by her classmate, now visibly upset, triggered by the slightest provocation of her classmate's small expression of concern. I suddenly had the irresistible impulse to leave the room as quickly as possible, but she was blocking the aisle to the door. Luckily, I remembered that there was an emergency exit at the back of the lecture hall that dumped into a little alleyway and I made my escape, instantly hidden by the night. I threw my stuff in my car and made a hasty exit from the parking lot, determined not to run into the dead-grandmother student again.

So, I can be awkward around strong emotions. But over the years, I've gotten better at masking my errors. I can cycle through possible emotional choices very quickly and come up with acceptable responses like a computer playing chess. But like chess, there is a practically infinite number of pathways and variations in human social and emotional interactions, and I'll never be as fast as an empath in intuiting emotions or applying the appropriate (natural) responses.

Being relatively unemotional can be very useful in professional situations, but it's caused some unfortunate tensions with friends and lovers when things do not upset me that they desperately think I should be upset by, like being worried at the possibility of a breakup. Not long ago when I told my friends that my father had just had a heart attack that day, they were very confused about whether I was being serious and whether it was an appropriate thing to joke about. This confusion occurred only because I did not accompany my statement with the appropriate show of negative emotion. In fact, when I was formally diagnosed, I believe that one attribute—having conversations about very emotionally fraught subjects without appropriate displays of emotion—was one of the most striking indicators of sociopathy that I displayed to my psychologist. It is the one that is often the hardest for me to accurately fake.

A lot of times my lack of emotionality just reads as an increased masculinity. The men I date sometimes lament that they feel like the girl in the relationship. I wonder what my sociopathy would look like if I actually were male—it often seems that male sociopathy exhibits itself as blatantly antisocial in a way that is not always the case in women. Indeed, very little research data exists regarding sociopathy in women, but what has been done reveals that female sociopaths exhibit only two or three main features that are similar to those found in men—usually, a lack of empathy and a pleasure in the manipulation and exploitation of others—but do not often exhibit violently impulsive behavior.

I am rarely tempted to commit violence, but my impulsiveness got me into plenty of trouble in my teens and early twenties, when I would find myself being groped and harassed in seedy concert venues alone and scantily clad, traveling down a heavily trafficked dark hilly road on my back on a skateboard, or caught in a lie (and possession of stolen goods) in a retail store's security office. On occasion I experience bloodlust, in particular when I think someone is trying to force me to experience guilt or shame. One commenter on my blog remarked about impulse: "Once impulse takes control there is no grasp of reality or balance until it's over and you're looking down at what you've done wondering what the next move is to get away with it."

Impulsiveness and fearlessness are defining characteristics of sociopathy. Scientists have explored variations in psychophysiological traits in sociopaths, finding that sociopaths have an abnormally low startle response when confronted with aversive stimuli. It appears that we have a deficit in our ability to feel negative emotion—or fear—in response to threats. I literally do not blink in the face of danger. One time I walked in on two men robbing my apartment. At first I didn't realize what was happening. They of course did and scurried out the back window where they had come in. I ran after them but then realized that most of my things had not been taken, only piled in the center of the room in preparation. There was no point in chasing after these men, and so I stopped. The police came at my neighbor's insistence, but I felt acutely aware that I had no idea how to behave before them. I was not naturally afraid or particularly concerned, though I knew this was what was expected of me. I ended up just being friendly, but it came off as flirtatious. Maybe that's okay. It's these unusual circumstances that are certain to trip me up in my continuing project to appear mostly normal.

My first year of teaching, I said many borderline-offensive things and then I just started intentionally saying them, as if I was being sickeningly sarcastic or deliberately offbeat, like suggesting that I might dress as Condoleezza Rice for Halloween. It's not that the mask slips off and reveals my true thoughts. I don't really have "true thoughts," just good and bad performances as I attempt to say and do things that normal people say and do.

And really, I can't help myself. I am continually shaping my self-presentation so that I can control what people think of me. I have been doing it for so long that I cannot even imagine what I would be if I were not performing all the time, blunting my edges and cultivating tricks of invitation. Even the way I speak is manufactured.

I have an ever-so-slight accent, something of a low drawl colored with unusual inflections, that is nothing like my siblings' or parents' accents. It has no identifiable origins but developed, I think, from my propensity to indulge in the sound of my own voice. If you listened closely to my speech, you would hear the pleasure I take in the textures of consonants and the phrasing of vowels. I have done everything to maintain and cultivate my accent, as I've discovered that it promotes a kind of accessible mystery and captivating vulnerability, an otherness that is attractive and nonthreatening. People often mistake me as foreign, most frequently Eastern European and Mediterranean. One of my paramours actually said that, if anything, I seem like an alien—"decidedly not human."

I meet a lot of people at work and at conferences, and I work hard at putting on the right act to optimize my standing in the profession. Unfortunately, like many, I'm bad at remembering people's faces, typically because I did a quick valuation of someone as a person upon meeting him and figured he was not worth the effort. If he remembers me and I don't remember him, I act like an idiot for the first few sentences. Then I flirt like mad. I touch shoulders. I laugh heartily and repeat his name as often as I can. "Oh, Peter! I like the way you think!" If he compliments me back I accept the compliment with confidence, then quickly turn the conversation to him and keep it on him. I am gracious and generous with compliments and expressions of interest. My accent is more pronounced. I create a rush of attention and flattery, with no apparent origin or goal. I excuse myself abruptly. I always make sure that I leave the conversation. I am careful not to be left.

If I'm stuck where I am, I veer the conversation to an area

of personal expertise. I know what you are thinking. This is what douchebags do. But you would be surprised at how delicate I am about the shifting of conversations. You would not notice it unless I told you. I ask at least a few more questions before I confess my own experience, interest, or knowledge of the subject matter. I am razor sharp. I tell witty stories or interesting factoids.

"You lived in Los Angeles for a year? Isn't it beautiful?"

"After about three months there I got sick of the sun. I felt that every day I had to be out bicycling or hiking or otherwise making the most of such good weather."

"Ah, see, that's the special pleasure of living in that climate, being able to waste a beautiful day by drawing the drapes and watching ten episodes of *The Sopranos*. It's decadent. Like eating gold flakes."

People like to hear words like *pleasure* and *decadent.* They think of Roman orgies or chocolate. I emphasize my point by tilting my chin down ever so slightly while maintaining eye contact. My hand reaches out to touch theirs just for an instant, a half grab or tug that never really materializes. It's unmistakably sensual but too fleeting to be forward. They laugh nervously, wondering for just a moment whether I can read their thoughts. Of course I can.

Sociopaths typically don't make small talk about themselves as much as normal people do. They will direct the conversation back to the new acquaintance as much as they can. When I talk to people, the only thing I really care about is getting what I want. This is true of everybody, but I never am trying to get someone's approval or admiration, unless it is a means to the end. I have no desire to talk. Instead, what I find most useful is collecting a mental dossier about everyone I know. Knowledge is power and if I know even something like where your grandmother is buried, I might be able to use that in the future. Consequently, it typically only makes sense for me to listen. If I'm not listening, I'm probably telling a joke or shamelessly flattering you. I probably would rather not be talking to you at all, but since I am, I might as well be polishing my charm.

A sociopath will reveal "personal" details about himself strategically, i.e., for the purposes of misdirection or a false sense of intimacy or trust. Revelations of actual truths are very rare and may be perceived as a small slip of the mask. I don't like people knowing things about me because it just means more things for me to remember that I can't lie about (or more lies to keep track of if I decide to evade the truth). And if knowledge is power, I want to keep my cards very close to my chest.

Sociopaths are supposed to excel at deceit, and new research might reveal why. The brain is made up of gray matter, which is the groups of brain cells that process information, and white matter, which carries electrical signals from one group of neurons to another, connecting the different parts of the brain. Habitual liars, in a study by Yaling Yang of the University of Southern California, had on average 22 percent to 26 percent more white matter in their prefrontal cortex than both the normal and antisocial controls. The white matter may be a result of liars making connections between things that nonliars would not make, for instance "me" and "fighter pilot." According to Yang, these connections allow you to "jump from one idea to another," fabricating stories from otherwise unrelated stories and ideas. What is not clear from the study is whether these connections facilitate lying in the otherwise truthful, or repeated lying creates these extra connections by "exercising" them.

On the blog, I am careful to disguise my identity. The deepest and most invisible lies are the ones that you never have to say out loud—that others tell about you to themselves. I selectively disclose information about myself for strategic reasons. For instance, I never talk about my gender or even strictly about my ethnicity or other demarcating personal characteristics. I hope that by doing so I will be a blank slate and people will be able to project their own ideas onto me. I want to be a figurehead, a receptacle for people's hopes, dreams, fears. I want people to relate directly to the blog—to think of the sociopaths they love in their lives or the sociopaths they hate. If I got too specific about anything, the illusion would be broken. Instead I stick to generalities and let people fill in the blanks in whatever manner they feel inclined. When people write to me and say that I seem to describe perfectly their own experiences, either as a sociopath or as someone who has known a sociopath, I know I have been successful.

The self-confidence that has helped me become something of a figurehead with the blog also helps in my seduction life. I always do much better than my looks alone would warrant. I don't just walk, I strut. I make solid eye contact. I act as if one of my main purposes for existence is to be admired, and I give people ample opportunity for it. I always assume that people have crushes on me, a belief that has been validated many times by embarrassed confessions years later when the issue has become less sensitive for the sufferer.

Sometimes, though, I'm very wrong, particularly about this. Sometimes I can't see people's disgust for me because I'm so single-mindedly inclined to see adoration. I have natural advantages, but I have my own blind spots, too.

While I can often observe a social situation and gauge each person's place in the power hierarchy or her potential vulnerability to exploitation, I have a very hard time gauging the emotional subtleties of a conversation, in ways that can be harmful to me. Sometimes it is impossible for me to tell when someone is mad at me.

Some researchers, like Simon Baron-Cohen, believe that people with antisocial personality disorders suffer from a degree of mind-blindness, the inability to attribute mental states to themselves or other people, which is intimately tied up with the ability to feel empathy. One reader of my website described being confronted (particularly by strangers) this way:

> When people yell at me, I am confused first and foremost. Bursts of strong emotion take me completely by surprise, and it takes a second or two for me to regain my wits. After that brief moment, my brain immediately kicks into high gear to analyze the situation: Why are they yelling? What are they saying? Have I done something deliberately to harm them recently or ever? Have I done something they could indirectly assume as harming them?

If sociopaths have mind-blindness, how are we able to manipulate so well? Practice. We have to deal with people daily, so we get a lot of opportunities to practice. We're forced to compensate for our mind-blindness in whatever way works for us. Sink or swim.

I can seem amazingly prescient and insightful, to the point that people proclaim that no one else has ever understood them as well as I do. But the truth is far more complex and hinges on the meaning of understanding. In a way, I don't understand them at all. I can only make predictions based on the past behavior that they've exhibited to me, the same way computers determine whether you're a bad credit risk based on millions of data points. I am the ultimate empiricist, and not by choice.

There seems to be some connection between empathy and the ability to understand sarcasm—apparently one's ability to feel for another aids in correctly interpreting hidden meanings behind words. Many sociopaths have a tendency to take things too literally or otherwise not to respond appropriately to nonverbal emotional cues. I am often completely oblivious to sarcasm, to the disbelief of everyone around me.

Although I am often acutely aware of the power dynamics of social situations, I sometimes miss out on social cues that can be glaringly obvious to others. Often they involve customs related to authority, the little tokens of respect that are so bewildering to me as to be invisible.

One time, at an interview for a very prestigious clerkship, I met with the judge briefly. We talked for a while and he suggested that he was going to go off to lunch, but if I wanted to talk some more I should come back after. I never came back after lunch. I figured that we had already said everything we had to say to each other, and so that was that. It wasn't until many years later that I realized that if I was interested in the clerkship, I should have at least come and reaffirmed my interest after lunch. I wish he had just told me that, but I guess the whole point of the test was that I was supposed to know what to do without being told.

Indeed I often am entirely literal, using words in their ordinary dictionary meaning. It's actually odd to me how frequently empaths will say one thing and mean an entirely different thing, expecting their listeners to pick up on the true meaning. Fortunately though, widespread sarcasm and insincerity make it easier for sociopaths to "pass" in society. It allows me to speak my mind quite sincerely and have people laugh it off, apparently because no one wants to believe that someone would admit to thinking such bloodless things. I regularly comment on my desire to exploit my admirers or to kill cute animals, and I don't even need to laugh or smile for people to think I am joking.

Perhaps the best example of this is the first time (and every time since) that I casually admitted to being a sociopath in public. I wrote a humorous article for my law school newspaper in which I not only admitted my own status but conjectured that much of the student body was sociopathic as well. Because I was poking fun at law school in general and mine in particular, no one thought a thing of it. Another blog reader admitted:

> *Try and tell the truth for once and no one wants to hear it. So I've given up, and I tell the truth quite a lot now. In circumstances such as: "What are you thinking?" "How your ear would feel in my mouth if I ripped it off with my teeth." "Haha!" Or the good old: "Do you like me?" "I don't give a shit about you." "Haha!" I tell the truth, and no one believes me.*

Learning to communicate with empaths is like trying to understand and speak a foreign language. When I had taken four years of high school Spanish I figured I could understand the basics of what people were saying and reply back to them, but the truth is that I frequently don't. Sometimes I don't know enough to even realize that I have misunderstood.

When people assume that I am their ethnicity and start speaking to me in their own language (typically Hebrew or Spanish, but not exclusively), I just reply back to them in my

American English, which indicates to them immediately that I am not who they thought I was. Of course I don't dare do that when people speak to me in an emotional foreign language. I don't dare tip them off that I don't speak the language natively, that I am not who they think I am. So I say my one or two rote phrases that I've learned for the most common situations and try to quickly leave or change the subject. It's not ideal, of course, but nothing about my life is.

But despite these handicaps, sociopaths have a unique talent for getting under other people's skin. I am often asked how sociopaths seem to be able to "see" someone's soul and view them as they truly are. It's a good question and a common complaint (compliment?) regarding sociopaths. I don't think that sociopaths are any more perceptive than other people, they're just looking for different things—weaknesses, flaws, and other areas to exploit—and concentrating a good deal of effort on it. Sociopaths are dangerous because they are such keen students of human interactions, closely studying others with the goal of picking up on the right social cues to blend in, imitate normal behavior, and exploit where they can. The more you pay attention to something, the more aware you will be. I am a musician, and I can listen to a recording and tell exactly what is going on, who is playing what, even the way the music was mixed in the studio. You could learn that too, if you practiced as much as a musician does.

R*uining people.* I love the way the phrase rolls around on my tongue and inside my mouth. Ruining people is delicious. We're all hungry, empaths and sociopaths. We want to consume. Sociopaths are uniformly hungry for power. Power is all I have ever really cared about in my life: physical power, the power of being desired or admired, destructive power, knowledge, invisible influence. I like people. I like people so much that I want to touch them, mold them, or ruin them however I'd like. Not because I want to witness the results, necessarily, but simply because I want to exercise my power. The acquisition, retention, and exploitation of power are what most motivate sociopaths. This much I know.

What do I mean by ruining someone? Everyone has their different tastes in regards to power, just like everyone has their different tastes for food or sex. My bread and butter is feeling like my mind and my ideas are shaping the world around me, which is of course why I bother writing the blog. It's my daily porridge; it keeps me from starvation. But when I indulge— when I am hungry for the richest, most decadent piece of foie gras—I indulge in inserting myself into a person's psyche and quietly wreaking as much havoc as I can. To indulge in malignity. To terrorize a person's soul without having any real design on the person. It's a pleasure to build something, to see the physical embodiment of your work. It can be equally pleasurable to destroy, to see the devastation that your hands have wrought, like swinging a pickax at a discarded wooden door with careless abandon. Both make you feel powerful and capable. But there is a special pleasure in destruction because of its rarity—like dissolving a pearl in champagne. Every day we are expected to be productive, pro-social. But if you've ever had an impulse to tell your best friend that yes, those pants do make her look fat, you understand how liberating it is to unrestrainedly lash out at another's softest parts.

How many times have I done this? It is hard to say. Often when I was young, I did it without being aware of what I was doing. I remember I always liked being in friendship groups of three because they were so unstable. I used to invent drama so

I could pair up with one or the other against the third. There's nothing too sociopathic about that. Every little girl likes to indulge in that sort of drama and many never grow out of it. People sometimes express shock to learn that there is someone out there who is not only actively working against them, but is doing so for no other reason than the enjoyment of flexing their power. In fact, I think that toying with people is something that comes naturally to all of us. I am sure you have done it or had it done to you—the way many people we admire can callously disregard our feelings, thriving on the self-importance they feel from the interactions without being self-aware enough to realize what they are doing to people around them and why. We can all tell when people have crushes on us, sexual or platonic, and we enjoy wielding that small amount of power over them. If anything, sociopaths are just a little better at it and enjoy it in a particular way.

When I have such thoughts of ruining people, I typically have a small tell—my tongue caresses one of the sharp points of my teeth. I grind my teeth like a champion and I've ground one of my upper canines down flat except for one jagged, needle-like point. (One time when I was a teenager, my dad accused me of being in a gang and filing my teeth down on purpose as some sort of sign of affiliation.) I love tonguing that tooth; it gives me shivers of pleasure. The physical sensations of sharpness on the soft flesh of my tongue would be enough, but what I really like to think about is how secret it is from the outside world, safely hidden inside my mouth. My teeth present as a whole, their dominant characteristic being an eerie but natural perfection. The sharp little point gets lost in my sea of gleaming white teeth. It reminds me of Bertolt Brecht's lyrics about the charming serial killer Mack the Knife:

And the shark, it has teeth
And it wears them in its face.
And Macheath, he has a knife,
But the knife you do not see

I wish I could tell stories of ruining people, but they're the stories most likely to get me sued—situations that involved the police and restraining orders and professional lives derailed. Or they are failed attempts in which the person only suspects me of not having their best interest at heart and stops associating with me, and so are too boring to relate. Still, I think even my attempts to ruin people perhaps best reflect my sociopathy, and are the most consistent deviation from my current, relatively pro-social lifestyle.

I do have a moral code that I try to adhere to, but ruining people is my practical reality, the same way that picking up men in airport bathrooms might be the practical reality for a closeted gay, married Christian evangelical. I think that my adherence to my prosthetic moral compass is similar to the way most people adhere to their religions. I was recently at a conference with a woman who is Jewish. We went to a burger joint and she ended up ordering a grilled cheese sandwich. Why? She says that she keeps kosher, but when she travels she just tries to approximate. To her, kosher eating is an important moral goal, perhaps a good rule of thumb, but she accepts that no one can be perfect in everything. She understands that she is just human, that we are all just human, and that people will fail no matter what sort of code they set for themselves. If you didn't fight constantly to maintain the code despite slipping up here and there (sometimes just to give yourself a break), you wouldn't need a code in the first place. If you just naturally behaved in a certain way, you wouldn't need to consciously try to fight your natural inclinations with some rigid framework. You'd just live however you were inclined to live.

For me, I don't feel a compulsion to break with my code in typical ways: I am not a compulsive gambler, I am not an alcoholic, I am not a sexaholic, I am not a drug addict. Most of my cravings are usually sporadic or harmless. To the extent that I crave something consistently, it is to cease my tireless efforts at impulse control. In other words, what I really crave is to be able to act in whatever way I want without having to worry about the consequences. I typically fight that craving. The worry is that if I let myself go just a little bit, I will revert completely back to the way I was before, which I know isn't a sustainable way to live. But even so, I have to have a way to blow off steam. So I ruin people. It's not illegal, it's difficult to prove, and I get to flex my power. It feels good to know that I can and that I am good at it. The fact that it is wrong or can hurt people is not necessarily the point. No one has ever died from my ruining. I think some people have barely even noticed, or if they have noticed it is because I have had all the effect of a fly buzzing in their ear. This was probably true of one of my favorite experiences, a love triangle I constructed between me, Cass, and Lucy.

I dated Cass for a while, and though we considered the possibility of a long-term arrangement, I ultimately lost interest. Cass did not. He was sure to keep in touch and in passive-aggressive ways always seemed to be part of my life. Cass wasn't going to tire easily, I could tell, so I tried to find other uses for him. One such use appeared on a night when Cass and I attended a party together where people were playing kissing games. As soon as we entered and got separated in the crowd,

Cass was accosted by someone as part of one of these games, a person who was later introduced to me as Lucy.

She was striking, particularly in her similarity to me, which made me want to ruin her. In my mind I quickly did the calculations—Lucy was smitten with Cass, Cass was smitten with me, which meant I had an unexpected power over Lucy. At my direction, Cass began pursuing Lucy. In the meantime, I found out everything I could about her from her well-meaning friends. These little forays with the friends were not only a means to an end but their own independent sources of pleasure. It turned out Lucy and I were born hours apart on the exact same day. This information fed my obsession in the most delicious way. I began thinking of her as not just a doppelgänger, but as an actual extension of me, like a walking mirror image. We had the same predilections, the same pet peeves, the same style of distracted, quasiformal, slightly awkward communication. In my mind she was my alter ego, which, of course, made her exceedingly interesting to me.

For as long as Lucy dated Cass, I kept him as my side piece. I would induce him to make and then break dates with her in favor of being with me. He was complicit through most of it—he knew that I was using him to mess with her. When he started feeling pangs of conscience, I broke it off with him. I waited until he focused all his attention on Lucy again, waited until she got her hopes up that he had turned over a new leaf, then called him up again. I told him we were meant for each other and I was just testing his resolve. I had no respect for him.

Lucy was just as bad in her own way. She had no sense of keeping personal things private, particularly with people like me who would use that information against her. I felt like she must have been emotionally damaged. It was almost farce, like a campy vampire movie where the love interest/victim is always traipsing along giving herself paper cuts, or tripping and scraping a knee, or cutting her finger while chopping onions, that sort of a thing. And if it wasn't Lucy telling me things herself, it was her well-intentioned friends. It was such a head trip. Sometimes I wondered if I was being punked, because things could not have gone more perfectly for me.

The thing that kept it all interesting was that I was genuinely fond of Lucy, smitten even. Her Pollyanna attitude was captivating. I almost wanted to be sincere back to her, almost wanted to be a true friend. There were so many interesting psychological angles going on, at least in my own mind, such that even the most mundane of conversations was absolutely thrilling to me. Just thinking about it makes me salivate. In fact, after a while, I began to avoid Lucy. She became a dessert too rich, too painfully pleasurable. Lucy gave me a stomachache, so I made Cass break it off with her for good.

And this is what I mean about ruining people being relatively harmless. What did I actually do to Lucy? Nothing. From Lucy's perspective, here is what happened: She grabbed a boy and kissed him at a party. She liked this boy and they saw each other a couple times a week after that, sometimes with his creepy friend (me). After a while, it didn't work out. The end. I didn't ruin anything about her, really. She's married now, has a good job. The worst thing I did was propagate a romance that she believed was sincere but was actually staged (as best as I could manage) to break her heart. And that's the thing. I don't just manipulate others; I manipulate myself. I mess with my own emotions as much as I try to mess with other people's. In fact, in enacting the ruination of others, I concoct elaborate psychological fantasies that may or may not be happening. And the thought of the possibilities is often enough to satisfy me.

Someone once suggested that I expand my emotional horizons by taking MDMA, the pure ingredient in the drug ecstasy. I told him that it was an interesting idea, but that I sort of already manipulate myself into feeling other emotions via film, music, and art, and I wasn't sure if it would be all that different.

I love music. There's no doubt that music is manipulative, as is film (possibly because of the music in it). The whole purpose of music seems to be to evoke some feeling or sensation in the audience, if you let yourself get caught up in the experience. I have found that it can be a good way to learn about other people, allowing me to experience emotions the way other people experience them or the way the composer or lyricist experienced them. Music is like a drug in some ways because it forces me to feel something different from what I usually feel; it's an artificial entrée into an alternative sensuality.

When I studied music in school, I even liked being critiqued, to get detailed judges' sheets back after a competition. I liked that these people were compelled to pay meticulous and thoughtful attention to me and my performance; it hardly mattered whether they liked it or not.

As I have grown older, music has played a different role in my life, offering an avenue of human interaction with other musicians that is devoid of guile or artifice. The connection between performing musicians is mediated by sounds and instruments—musical acts in time—rather than words or facial cues. Playing music provides me with a level of pleasure and enrichment that I rarely feel when interacting with people in any other way. It also offers a means of avoiding casual social interaction with nonmusicians, since I can set up shop at a piano at almost any social function that has one. It is such a relief to see them in the corners of hotel lobbies or old-timey bars.

The truth is that I hate small talk. I care even less than most people about your eight-month-old baby making all of his developmental milestones or your trip last month to Colorado. And it is even worse for me because when I am forced to engage in small talk, I feel compelled to excel at it—smiling, nodding, and coming up with clever and complimentary anecdotes. But with music, I know that the impression I make on others while playing the piano is much more effective than what I could manage on my most impressive day of banter. Receding to the edges of parties becomes introspective rather than antisocial, artistic rather than awkward. It is sometimes easier to beguile without speaking. There is something about music that is so mystifying and alluring, and performing it is one of the very few acts of self-involvement that is universally perceived as generosity.

I often wish I could just passively watch people without being expected to participate myself, like television. I actually do spend a lot of time in front of the television for this reason, and I am pretty undiscriminating in what I will watch. I like the closed universes and conventional plot devices of television series, knowing that there is nothing for me to do but to passively watch what happens, having no stake in the outcome. I find it easier to identify with characters in movies and books than with people in real life. In movies, you can watch and analyze people freely and without detection. In books, you can listen in on their inner thoughts, take the time to contemplate them, and listen in again if you are so compelled. I have learned more about people from books, television, and movies than I ever have in real life. I have enjoyed people more that way, too.

People mistakenly assume that because sociopaths don't empathize, they don't have emotions. I've never heard of a sociopath not having emotions. I do think that sociopath emotions are frequently shallow and stunted, childlike even, but how many people do you know who are emotionally stunted and are not sociopaths? If I didn't have emotions, how would I be so good at playing the emotions of others?

And what are emotions anyway? They're at least partially contextual. They at least partially originate from the stories we tell ourselves. If you have "butterflies in your stomach," you could be nervous or excited depending on your interpretation of your situation. And there are certain emotions that exist in some cultures that don't necessarily exist in others, for instance the nostalgic *saudades* in Brazil or the intense aspects of shame in Japan. Are emotions just an interpretation of the body's evolutionary fight-or-flight reactions? Are emotions only releases of adrenaline that we interpret as anxiety? Or endorphins that we interpret as satisfaction or pleasure?

One theory of why we dream suggests that dreams are the result of the brain trying to interpret external stimuli during sleep. For instance, if we are cold, we imagine that we are walking through snow. Our subconscious concocts a story to explain things we are sensing during our sleep—trying desperately to make random and incomplete sensory inputs fit into whatever fictional scenario we have literally dreamed up. Are our emotions the same? Are we just interpreting sensory inputs, making up explanations that support the stories we tell ourselves?

But as much as I want to believe that everyone else lives in a collective delusion, I know that love exists.

In his tragic narrative poem "Lara," Lord Byron wrote a semiautobiographical narrative of a wayward count, describing him thus:

> *Tis true, with other men their path he walk'd,*
> *And like the rest in seeming did and talk'd,*
> *Nor outraged Reason's rules by flaw nor start,*
> *His madness was not of the head, but heart.*

I've always known that my heart is a little blacker and colder than most people's. Maybe that's why it's so tempting to try to break other people's.

Chapter 8

LOVE ME NOT

When I was eighteen years old, I was an exchange student in Brazil. There I was enthralled by a new way of thinking of love. Naturally, I saw love as something to be achieved, because achievement was the lens through which I viewed everything. This meant that my study of love would be a study in seduction.

Watching the endless string of B-movies on Brazilian TV gave me a rough blueprint of what love was, and of course, I was a quick study. You really can learn almost all you need to know on television. Love is not a hard kind of con; it doesn't require all that much subtlety. People are so starved for love that the usual manipulations really do work—the fleeting touches, the vague statements of feeling and devotion, the powerful embraces as passionate in parting as in their initial entanglement. Any soap opera could show you that love is most tantalizing in its evanescence. Its nature is to shift constantly through states of being—condensing into dense beads of sweat on hot skin only to disappear into the air, thick with promises of something more, of something better simply because it has yet to come.

Brazil was the perfect place to learn about love and touching. By the time I arrived there, I had forgotten—or never really knew—what it felt like to be touched tenderly. The sense memories of the kisses my mother must have given me in my childhood were eclipsed by the sensations of playground fisticuffs I regularly experienced as I grew older. But those knocks were replaced in my adolescence by the constancy of hardly ever being touched at all. And I didn't like any extreme shows of emotion—not the stumbling, ogre arms of my grandparents reaching out to wrap me up in their old-person auras, nor the ugly contortions of anger or sadness or incipient tears that would regularly crumple the faces of my family members through our various sagas of dysfunction. It felt like people were manipulating or even bullying me to react in some way of which I was uncertain, as if they were pushing me to the edge of an emotional precipice. I rarely jumped.

That was the life I had left behind. But thousands of miles away from home, touching and physical displays of emotion were a part of the intrigue of love. And love was such a thrill—a page turner—that I knew I wanted to play. Brazilians kissed and embraced upon every meeting and departure. They played with each other's feelings like it was nothing or everything at once, at turns feigning sympathetic outrage or passionate emotional bruising. Their hips were sexually possessed: At the time, a popular dance was hitting the clubs of Rio called the bottle dance, in which a woman or man would gyrate over an open beer bottle placed on the floor. Sensuality was everywhere. I was not prepared for the three-year-olds I would see dancing the samba in the middle of the street on workday afternoons.

Brazilians were beautiful or very ugly in interesting ways. The young people were shiny, slender, and flexible, like willow switches in shades of pale amber and dark coffee. The old and the infirm were wretchedly dehydrated, hardened in the heels of their feet and in their lower backs like petrified wood. There was a smile, or a hint of a smile, or a memory of a smile on every face I encountered. Set against such apparent despair and abject squalor, you could not help but notice a strong corporeality in the way people lived that you simply do not see in the States. Bodies—and the stuff of bodies—so saturated every molecule around you that oftentimes you felt like you were living in a baroque fantasy, except that instead of Italian marble you got tons of haphazardly poured cement, and instead of St. Theresa in ecstasy you had seminaked strangers copulating in the street. It was a wonder that people did not cry or laugh or scream or sing all day and all at once.

Part of the freedom of Brazil, besides knowing or being accountable to hardly anyone, was being immersed in a culture of ambiguities. There were not white or black people, but people of varying shades from so many generations of mixed race and ethnicity that you could not define them if you tried. I came across many transgendered people, who defied the gender norms and conventions by which I had so long felt entrapped. Some people had penises and breasts; some had neither. Having either/or was not a condition of being human. As a person who felt ambivalent about her gender, I felt kinship with these people. They offered me possibilities that I had hitherto not considered.

I had never seen such an array of human life, and it made me interested in people in a new way. Brazilians were much more than just mirrors for me to try on different personas in front of, as everyone else had been back at home. They were so different from me, viewed the world through such a foreign lens and daily engaged in such strange behaviors, that I was forced to put away the lazy, naïve thought that I had already learned all there was to know about people.

They were their own species and I was a scientist embarking on a mission to discover their secrets. The most beautiful people were always the ones who seemed happiest and most satisfied with their lives. And the most attractive ones were the ones who carried around with them a cushion of humor and goodwill, so that the particles in the air around them floated a little lighter and danced with a little more joy than anywhere else. I wanted to be like this.

I understood so much, and I practiced a lot. I was in a place filled with people I would never have to see again, so I could do whatever I wanted without any real consequences. It's why American students abroad are often so well liked (girls) and so despised (boys). I could hardly be blamed. In the *cultura de ficar,* I was young and unattached and therefore expected to share my body with other young people as part of a communion of bodies, a celebration of sexuality and sensuality and intimacy. At the end of the night, individuals would become couples locked in deep, exploring kisses, and I was one of them. I learned all kinds of things in these experiments—how to suck on a person's tongue, how to let your own tongue be licked and sucked, how to tickle the roof of a person's mouth so that it is almost irresistible for them not to lap up more of you. I came to understand kissing as a conversation. Sometimes, it can be small talk or playful banter between goodwilled strangers. Other times, it feels like you are forging an intimate connection with another human being, reaching as far as you can inside them.

I treated love like it was something to be mastered, like

becoming fluent in Portuguese. Just as I developed my language skills, I devised milestones and challenges for seduction. I would go to clubs with goals in mind, testing how close I could get to a person without saying a single word, or how frustrated I could make them without touching. I practiced on sweet high school boys and jaded exchange students, old men and transvestites.

The first person I kissed was a man in drag. He was magnificent, his body bronze from glitter and paint. He wore a golden, ornate breastplate and thong, and there were vibrantly colored feathers and gemstones in his long, black hair. It was natural for me to want to touch his red-stained lips with mine, to be attracted by his peacock confidence because it made me want to take possession of him. It was like winning a prize or a trophy, and an uncommon one, like me.

In my short life I had not met a man so magnificently adorned. I imagined him in a tiny, run-down apartment, carefully orchestrating his appearance by placing each rhinestone just so, applying each shade of eye shadow to complement the others. My attraction had nothing to do with his masculinity or femininity—it was his attention to beauty that screamed for appreciation. There was a kind of seamless courage in him that I admired and a trembling vulnerability that I wanted to exploit.

Perhaps in some way, I envied his ability to embrace his strangeness and to display it to the world, or even to know what and who he was in order to do so. I did not have this ownership of myself, not yet. Outwardly I was all confidence and openness; inwardly I was spiteful and lonely and unaware of how to relate to the world. I wanted so much to be good but only knew how to appear that way by being bad. I knew no other way to live but to dissemble and to violate. So in kissing him,

I momentarily captured his earnest effort, his honest beauty, the phantasmagoria made human by his mere existence in the world. All that good intention and energy cast out into the world—I wanted to taste it in my mouth and swallow as much as I could.

It wasn't the kind of possession that needed to be enduring. I only wanted a moment with him, to gain the feeling that I could understand or comprehend him in a certain physical way. It would not have mattered to me in the slightest if he had dropped dead the moment we stopped kissing. If a gang of teenagers had appeared that night to kick in his organs and slash his throat, I would have stood by to watch in order to enjoy the enthralling violence of it. If I had not been a young girl with a future to lose, I might have joined them so that I too could feel the satisfaction of his bones cracking and muscles bruising from my blows, these human parts I had caressed only moments ago.

After that first drag queen, I moved on to others, practicing physical affection with strangers so that I could use what I learned to cultivate emotional love with my few acquaintances. I could not even experience a kiss without making it contribute to some kind of agenda I formulated having to do with gaining power over other people. I was a calculating, ruthless animal, after all.

I now realized that love and sex had everything to do with the kinetic energy that I had admired and tried to understand in my drag queen. All I had ever read or heard or saw (not least of which were the soap operas and movies I watched day in and day out) told me that love could not be bad, that it made everything worthwhile, that it was the greatest thing in the world. And sex, though it had so long been stained in my mind with the bad, I now understood was a vital part of love. It wasn't just the stuff of perverts and male oppression, but a means of singular connection. And all of this, wonderfully, was a means to awesome, delicious, euphoric power—for which I had a knack. Formulated in this way, the pleasure I had in the manipulation and exploitation of others—the principal stuff that made my life worthwhile— could be described in a narrative of love. What could be more redemptive and human than this?

It was such an amazing discovery. I found that I had spent almost two decades overlooking a vital entry point into the inner worlds of other people—the universal Achilles' heel. I finally understood what it meant to kill people with kindness. People are so hungry for love; they die a little every day for want of it—for want of touch and acceptance. And to become someone's narcotic I found immensely satisfying.

Love was an addiction for me too. I loved being adored; I loved to admire. I did not understand why people didn't rip their hearts out and shout declarations of love in the streets, why they did not write pages and pages of love letters every day. It was so easy. It cost me nothing and gave me such thrilling satisfaction. The deeper I went with my love interests, the more they relied on me for their daily happiness, and the drunker I became with power. I generated their smiles and sighs, as if fashioning their moods from clay—I did this to them! The ecstasy of that thought was incredible.

I discovered that you could love almost anyone, really, and make them your reason for living at least for a time—whether it is an evening or a week or a few weeks. It wasn't just that you could have more power over someone through love than through any other means, but you could have access to more parts of them. There were more levers to pull and buttons to push, endless modalities. I could bring relief to pain of which

I was the direct and sole cause. I thought nothing of deceiving or manipulating them.

My love interests disappeared from my thoughts immediately upon my return to the United States. Back home, I had to do a few things. I didn't want to have what I learned in Brazil corrupted by contrary American sensibilities. I wanted to expand and deepen my Brazilian operations, including trying to form relationships with real people in my life.

I realized I had thus far been blind. I had unknowingly denied myself the pleasures of really leaping into and consuming the emotional inner worlds of others. Why did I ever think that it was sufficient simply to make people do things for me when I could make them *want* to do things for me? Now that my eyes and mind were opened, I wanted to keep them open forever. Love was the newest thing to add to the long list of things I wanted to be so good at that people would cry.

I did become pretty good at it. But when you are back in your home country, you can't start shoving your tongue into the mouth of every person you come across, especially when you attend a religious university with strict rules about that kind of stuff. On the flip side, however, because everyone around me was starved for sex, people were almost too easy to snare, especially the boys.

I remember a date with one especially innocent boy. He had all-American quarterback good looks—a dimpled wide smile showing straight rows of white teeth and fluffy blond hair bleached by the sun. After a movie, we sat in my car for a long time, because he wanted an invitation into my apartment and for access to my body (in particular, my breasts). It was long past the university-imposed curfew and against several moral code rules, and I had no real interest in him. About fifteen minutes into the date, I'd known that I had him, so I was really only going along for the ride, taking the opportunity to observe him and therefore collect information for later use. I was in it more for the chase, and he was too sick a gazelle to provide any real challenge.

As he sat there across from me, I wondered what he fantasized about in the shower and what kinds of girls he'd kissed. He was almost too generic, like he was acting out youthful boyish nervousness for a television show. With people like that, you've got to wonder if they have inner lives at all, or if the extent of their consciousness ends when the television writers shut off the office lights and go home.

I unsettled him. He couldn't understand why I was so confident or why he was so attracted to me. On the surface of things, I was nothing special. I wasn't particularly striking, nor did I have any real popularity to speak of; I in fact was odd enough that I could see flits of doubt flutter across the surface of his skin as he tried to decide if he even regarded me as a worthwhile person. With his traditional good looks, he could have attracted the attention and affections of many a blond coed, his female counterparts, so the fact that he felt so disarmed by me bred a lot of insecurity in him.

Just like the junior associate version of me had Jane, the nineteen-year-old me could have had the all-American quarterback if I'd wanted him. I could have made him do my homework, buy me things, and marry me. But I didn't want him. That night outside my apartment, after a long while of patiently humoring him, I began to wish he would get out of my car so that I could go home to sleep. He tried to contact me many times after that date, but it was too late for him. He had already vanished from my thoughts halfway through the night.

That's the trouble with seduction as a game played for the thrill of it. You can innocently go about seducing people, even enjoy the attention and affection for a time, and then suddenly, when you're ready to move on, you're left with this dependent besotted person who can hardly stand to live without you.

Typically when I set out to seduce someone, I cut the target loose as soon as I know I have won. My rationale is to treat it like sport fishing: the fun is in catching the fish, not in gutting, cleaning, and cooking the fish afterward, so why not throw the fish back to be caught another day?

I try to cultivate a persona that makes seduction easy. People are attracted to my confidence, but the thing that really hooks people is how I don't seem like anyone else they've ever met, and in deliciously exotic ways. My accent is unplaceable. I am darker than most white people, but not in a way that would clearly indicate "other." My natural style is androgynous, but I don't care to have my clothing reflect my personality too closely so I rarely choose it myself. Consequently I frequently wear the soft, flowing dresses and structured heels that are more my friend's taste, a fashion-forward woman who is happy to select most of my clothing. Underneath the lush material, it's clear that I am firm, even muscular. I have remarkably beautiful breasts. But I have always been acutely sensitive to the beauty of things—in bodies and faces, and in numbers and landscapes and logic, too. Pleasure to me is paramount and I am always looking for new sources of it. The pleasure of a seduction conquest lies in both the physical satisfaction and the mental challenge of completely occupying a space in a person's mind until it's yours, like a squatter. The one caveat is, you may find that the space you're occupying is more trouble than it's worth.

When I met Morgan, I didn't know she would be so much trouble. She had the same name as me, which constituted 90 percent of my interest in her at the beginning. It amused me to think that I could be making love with myself. She was a senior trial attorney in an office in which I was very junior, and her apparent abilities, as viewed from a casual distance, were pretty sexy.

The first time we actually had a conversation was when we ran into each other leaving the office early on a Friday afternoon, like being caught red-handed by someone you know could never tell on you without revealing her own misdeed. I knew we would take the elevator together, then walk through our building's maze of halls for at least five minutes more, and then walk in the same direction toward the parking garage. Because I had already begun to admire her, I was a little nervous making so much small talk. I had nothing to worry about, because she instantly shared her life story with me in the time it took to get to our cars. I just listened. It's amazing how much more effective listening is in seduction than anything else. It helped that her life had been tantalizing in a way that fed into my desire to know people's vulnerabilities—abusive relationships, crimes, gender identity disorder, and so on.

The infatuation between us quickly became mutual. Mine was firmly rooted in my own narcissism and a desire to exploit the weaknesses in someone I had initially admired, hers in an apparent attraction to people who enjoyed hurting her. I've never had someone react so strongly to me as Morgan. Her growing attachment to me even warped her appearance. Her once-firm jaw began to appear weakly skeletal, and her steady brown eyes now flitted about in avoidance of mine, hesitant to rest on any one thing. I think her hair even began to fall out.

It was puzzling because she had seemed such a strong and confident person in doing her job, facing judges, juries, and some pretty tough lawyers with self-possession. Morgan had a social power at work of which I wanted to have a piece, and in particular, an outsider's hard-won respect that I in many ways wanted to emulate. At first, I really relished the power I had over her. I got sick from enjoyment every time I noticed a crack in her voice or a nonsensical sentence escape from her lips. In those moments my breath would catch, my eyes half-lidded. My pleasure in her discomfort was very visceral, my tongue instinctively running over the jagged edges of my teeth the same way one might salivate and even become overwhelmed a little at the smell of a succulent slab of meat. I think I ran away with it a little.

Morgan couldn't recover. I was winning by too great a margin for her to remain interested in playing the game. I tried to alleviate her nervousness in the same way you'd try to calm an overexcited animal or child—making slow movements, explaining what you are doing, assuring her that there's nothing to worry about and no harm will come. There was a certain amount of condescension in it, an active effort to shame her into seeing how ridiculous it was to be scared of little ole me. The whole thing was a lot of work. I made things worse by getting increasingly disgusted by how weak and afraid she was. One afternoon, she canceled her dinner plans with me, and I could see that it was for no other reason than that I made her nervous. I sat in her office, staring at her with motionless judgment, unable to let myself let her off the hook. It was too satisfying for me to feed her masochism. I pushed the shame tactic too hard, and she stopped speaking to me. I can't remember what in particular I did that ended it. Maybe I implied that she was worthless and teased her about the poor quality of her skin. I was genuinely surprised that she wanted to end things, but I shouldn't have been—I had inadvertently made it more appealing to forfeit than to surrender.

I knew I had only one chance to get her back, so I let things cool off for a couple of months before I sent her a seemingly heartfelt but factually insincere e-mail confessing my love and apologies. The apologies were profuse but vague, so that she could apply them to whatever thing she perceived I had done to wrong her. The love was dripping with honey-hued affirmation. I named all the things that I admired about her, or rather, the things that she hoped to have admired. I was sure to include confessions of my own "vulnerabilities," that I thought about her every day—though I thought about her almost every day as a lost object I needed to reclaim. In the e-mail, I said that I loved her several times and made sure to use the past tense, because I wanted her to feel regret for something she didn't even know she had. There isn't anything more crushing than lost love, and there are few more compelling motives than to recapture it. Because she never knew I loved her, and because I didn't, she never even got to savor it. At the end, I threw in a few mild recriminations disguised as insecurities (she made me feel abandoned and bereft) and suggestions that things would be different were we to reunite (though I claimed I had no reason to believe or hope that we would). It was an effective e-mail.

A few weeks later, I heard back from her. She had received my e-mail while on an island vacation with a new girlfriend, the arrival and discussion of which precipitated a minor spat and then a breakup. It gave me satisfaction to know that thoughts of me plagued her while she lay on the beach with her lover. When she came back, we took up again. Her self-devouring weakness hadn't gone away but seemed to have grown exponentially. She wanted more and more hurt from me, and because I was sufficiently disgusted with her and wanted to oblige her wishes, I was happy to deliver.

After a few months we drifted apart. Morgan quit or was fired from her job and fell into an abyss of eating disorders and substance abuse. I was shocked by how quickly she fell from excelling in her career as a successful trial attorney to jobless dysfunction—it was really only a matter of months. It's a wonder that she's still alive. I cannot take all of the credit for this extreme decline. It was inevitable in her life, due to her desire to be abused. She has almost managed to kill herself so many times you would think she would have succeeded by now if she really set her mind to it. But I guess if she died she would lose any further opportunities to suffer, and the prospect of experiencing more vast and varying shades of pain is what keeps her alive. I guess that made our relationship mutually positive: She wanted to be hurt and I liked to hurt and watch her sink further into depravity. I was only sated when she hit absolute bottom.

I still see her sometimes, but the thrill of the chase disappeared a long time ago. I never loved her of course, but she loves me in her twisted way. I made her believe that I understood needs and desires that she had kept hidden from most everyone else out of fear and shame, that I looked at everything about her and wasn't scared of what I found. It's true that I did. People always say to be careful not to confuse sex and love, but I think they should be more wary of confusing love and understanding. I can read every word of your soul, become deeply engrossed in the study of it until I've comprehended every nuance and detail. But then when I'm done, I'll discard it as easily as if it were a newspaper, shaking my head at how the ink has stained my fingers gray. My desire to know every layer of you isn't feigned, but interest isn't love, and I make no promises of forever. Perhaps I do every so often, but you have no business believing me.

One of the manifestations of sociopathy in me is an ambivalence in regards to sex and sexual orientation. Sociopaths are unusually impressionable, very flexible with their own sense of self. Because we don't have a rigid self-image or worldview, we don't observe social norms, we don't have a moral compass, and we have a fluid definition of right and wrong. We can also be shape-shifters, smooth-talking and charming. We do not have an established default position on anything. We do not have anything that we would call conviction. This extends, at least in some degree, to our sexuality.

Indeed, the characteristic of asexuality or sexual ambiguity is noted as one of the symptoms of sociopathy under many of the diagnostic criteria. For example, Cleckley's criteria for psychopathy include sex lives that are "impersonal, trivial, and poorly integrated." I would say that this accurately describes mine. But I feel pretty okay about it.

A friend tells me that what she dislikes the most about my religious values is the ban on premarital sex. Of course I still manage to do a lot of things, but she worries that because sex is so much fun, it's a shame for me to be missing out on any of it. She's a deeply emotional person, though, and I am not at all. I can't help but think the emotional component of sex for her is what makes it so great, whereas the emotional connection I have from physical intimacy is roughly the same as I have while eating junk food (cheeseburgers are great, too!). This is true even when I am in a serious relationship. And because it's that way with me, being physical with someone is pretty fun, but it doesn't mean anything to me in the way it *means* things to other people, and it never leads to tears (for me). This is also why seduction for me is more about the chase and less about the final act.

My lovers, if you can call them that, can sometimes be put off by this nonchalant attitude. I am shockingly comfortable with my body, which I think is a turn-on for a lot of people. I try not to be too reckless, but my indiscretion with things like nude photos must seem unusual since I'm neither a stupid teenager nor a drug-addled stripper. But then again, I have always related better to people who feel they have nothing to lose. Once it becomes clear that I just have no sense of shame or emotional attachment to physical intimacy, though, I suspect I just seem damaged, in the way of teenagers and strippers, or women with sexual hang-ups or abuse in their background. If anything, you would think that my religious beliefs would have encouraged me to think of sex as a special communion of souls, rather than the emotional equivalent of a massage.

My cavalier attitude toward sex extends to my choice of gender in partners. I was not always sexually attracted to women. I was always open to it, always was attracted to certain people for their strength or for their unique worldview, but I didn't feel much of a sexual pull to members of my own sex— not at first. As an adult I realized that there was such pleasure to be had in expanding my horizons, so to speak, and certainly no point in making fine distinctions based on the equipment people were born with. So I trained myself. I started incorporating members of the same sex into my fantasies, substituting women for men gradually more and more until I could have a completely same-sex fantasy. Now same-sex attraction is second nature to me, and I am very satisfied with the expansion of my opportunities.

As a sociopath, I feel I have no particular sexual identity. Even the term *bisexual* is misleading as it implies some sort of preference. I think *equal opportunity* is a more apt label in that I see no reason to discriminate. In fact, I like to think of the sociopath as the bonobo of the human world—engaging in frequent, casual, utilitarian sex. I believe that ambiguous sexuality is one of the best identifying traits of a sociopath.

In fact, early in its history as a psychological disorder, sociopathy was thought to be connected to homosexuality or other "abnormal" sexual behaviors. The original *Diagnostic and Statistical Manual of Mental Disorders (DSM),* released by the American Psychiatric Association in 1952, listed homosexuality as a sociopathic personality disturbance. By the second *DSM,* the link between sociopathy and homosexuality was abandoned, and homosexuality was removed completely as a mental disorder from the third *DSM.*

In later editions of his book, Cleckley criticized this early association of psychopathy with homosexuality, arguing that homosexual tendencies, "though of course occurring in psychopaths, are not sufficiently common to be regarded as characteristic." However, he also acknowledged that "[t]he real homosexual seeking an outlet for his own impulses often finds it possible to engage the psychopath in deviated activities, sometimes for petty rewards, sometimes for what might best be called just the hell of it." Cleckley related several stories of sociopaths engaged in homosexual acts, like Anna, and the story of this wealthy young scion, for whom "any idea that he might be a homosexual seemed absurd":

In the absence of any persistent or powerful urge in this specific direction, the patient, apparently without much previous thought, hit upon the notion of picking up four Negro men who worked in the fields not far from his residence. In a locality where the Ku Klux Klan (and its well-known attitudes) at the time enjoyed a good deal of popularity, this intelligent and in some respects distinguished young man showed no compunction about taking from the field these unwashed laborers, whom he concealed in the back of a pickup truck, with him into a well-known place of amorous rendezvous. At the place he chose, "tourists' cabins" were discreetly set up in such a way that women brought by men to them for familiar purposes could enter without the possible embarrassment of being identified by the management. Despite these facilities suspicion arose, and the patient was surprised by the man in charge of the resort while in the process of carrying out fellatio on his four companions. He had chosen to take the oral role.

Upon being confronted with his crime, the young man laughed it off, remarking, "boys will be boys."

Even though ambiguous sexuality doesn't appear in any of the diagnostic criteria, I find it is much more useful as a litmus test for sociopathy than some of the more publicized traits. I have met many sociopaths, in person and from my blog, who all seem to swing both (or any number of) ways: anarchist ex-cons acquitted on a technicality; big macho, married black guys; ruthless Asian American entrepreneurs; fellow academics; impoverished soldiers. In fact, I can't think of a single sociopath I have met in person or online who has denied having same-sex experiences. This leads me to believe that this is one of sociopathy's most consistently present traits. In fact, I rely on it more than any other one trait in making my own opinion about who is and is not a sociopath.

Surprisingly, there are a good number of sociopath wannabes who frequent my blog. I guess it is because sociopaths are often portrayed as ruthless, efficient, and powerful—all desirable attributes to a great number of people both ordinary and deviant. Visitors to my blog sometimes write to me asking whether I think they are sociopathic. I often probe the sexuality issue. I make fun of them a bit. Maybe I ask them how many same-sex partners they have had, as if I was just waiting to insult them. If they turn squeamish or defensive, I usually discount all of the other evidence indicating that they are sociopathic. Usually a sociopath wouldn't be offended about a challenge to his masculinity or her femininity, since he or she isn't particularly invested in the cultural norms that draw bright lines around gender roles.

Sexual ambidexterity, although not indicated often in clinical literature, is frequently a feature of fictional sociopaths. The very talented Tom Ripley is bisexual, as is the Joker from *Batman* (depending on who writes him). Real-life examples of murderous bisexuals are Leopold and Loeb, lovers famous for attempting to adopt the Nietzschean concept of Übermensch morality in committing the senseless murder of a young boy, immortalized in the Hitchcock thriller *Rope.* Fictional depictions of vampires, those allegorical sociopaths, often contain prominent allusions to a flexible sexuality, with lesbian vampires being so common that it is almost canonical for mythic vampirism.

An interesting example of a celebrity whose sex life seems to fit the sociopathic mold is Sir Laurence Olivier, who, although married three times, also had many male interests.

One of his male lovers explained: "He's like a blank page and he'll be whatever you want him to be. He'll wait for you to give him a cue, and then he'll try to be that sort of person." Olivier may not have been a sociopath, but he illustrates well how a person with a weak sense of self, fully occupied with the stunningly accurate enactment of many other selves, could himself have an amorphous sexual identity.

So it was easy to want to seduce Morgan, who resembled me enough that she could have been a role I had played in another life. But although I love myself, I would never have considered the possibility of loving Morgan. She was always a target for me. Seduction is about reminding myself of my own desirability, not about increasing my acquisitions. It is the fuel I feed my own self-love.

I see relationships with people in terms of possessions or exploits. Like the Greeks and their many words for love, I have my own brand of feelings and behaviors for both groups. The former is typically reserved for my family or people whom I call friends. For these people—possessions—I have a sensation of ownership. Also gratitude.

The latter—exploits—is for my seduction or other romantic interests. Seduction has traditionally been an all-or-nothing endeavor; at least I can't really control it. Seductions are like wildfires: I only get to choose the beginnings and then they take on a life of their own or flame out. So I don't typically do them with people I hope to keep around for longer than a few months. For the exploits, the pleasure is in gaining and exercising influence over them. I am never infatuated with my possessions, but I am with my exploits. And I can feel possessive of my exploits. I pursue them because they give me a thrill. Will I win them over? What might that look like? Success is valuable only to the extent that it is evidence of my power. As one blog reader said, "There really is nothing more amusing or exciting or fun than turning a smart, beautiful, resourceful person into a personal plaything." It is a game, but I am not necessarily interested in the spoils so much as the maneuvering.

The distinction is well illustrated by the literary character Estella, from Charles Dickens's *Great Expectations*. Miss Havisham raises Estella to break men's hearts in a form of vengeance for being jilted at the altar, and Estella willingly does so with everyone but the protagonist, Pip, who is in love with Estella. Pip notices that Estella does not actively attempt to seduce him like she does with other men. He complains, and she reprimands him:

> "*Do you want me then,*" *said Estella, turning suddenly with a fixed and serious, if not angry, look,* "*to deceive and entrap you?*"
>
> "*Do you deceive and entrap him, Estella?*"
>
> "*Yes, and many others—all of them but you.*"

Like Estella, I do not seduce my possessions because I don't want to lose respect for them and because that would be unsustainable long-term. As one blog reader wrote:

> *You find it hard to not objectify people, however it's important so you just try with a few people that understand who you are. All the rest of the people who don't understand you are fools to you.*

I have had a few relationships that have begun as seductions and morphed into something more serious. My last boyfriend was like that, but due to the way the relationship started, he never could be satisfied that he knew the "real" me.

Both possessions and exploits get to see a special side of me that I do not bother to show others. Sociopaths often have a genius for adoring. Not all sociopaths care to use their talents so generously, and even when they do they can be possessive and fickle—devoting themselves to a relationship as long as they feel in control or benefited, but once they get bored or annoyed they're gone. Still, when we're trying, our understanding of your wants and needs matched with our charm and flexible personality means that we can and will literally become the man or woman of your dreams. In fact, when I love, my first step is to gather as much information as possible about every aspect of the person's life in order to more closely resemble their ideal mate. As one blog reader noted, it can become an addiction:

> *You know all their insecurities and you fulfill them. They become dependent upon you, because of it. They start feeling empty without you. They get captured in the moment.*

The closest analogue to a sociopath's love is probably the love of a child: intense, accepting, selfish. And finally, like a child, the sociopath will be extremely loyal. A sociopath will never put you above himself, but if you're worth it to him he will readily put you above all others. I confirmed this with my friend, that with regard to being friends with a sociopath, "the pros outweigh the cons."

This is not to say that my loved ones do not know who I am; most of them know me intimately and are well aware of the particular attributes that set me apart from them and most of humanity. In fact, many of the people dearest to me are extreme empaths, individuals who—with full knowledge of the tiny blackness of my heart—cannot help but place their soft, fragile hearts in my care. I reciprocate with my own brand of acceptance and devotion. I've learned how to do the things that constitute being generous and kind. It's the ones I love most who are able to see how hard I try.

There's nothing wrong with the way I approach romantic relationships, but there's something not quite right about it either. But I guess it also depends on whom you ask. One night, I strangled my "date" in my car. We were returning from dinner, parked on the street outside of my apartment. It was late, and I remember the quiet darkness, punctuated by the brilliant headlights of passing cars. We had talked before about sexual domination, and so by then I felt I had implicit permission to bruise and strike, which is to say that I was reasonably certain that there would be no retaliation for my violence. But I had waited to act. Waited until the time was right, until that moment when I turned off the engine and hesitated. She had reached immediately for her door handle but stopped at my hesitation. I turned toward her and could see the question in her eyes; were we about to kiss?

I slapped first—hard across her face so that I could feel the memory of high, sharp cheekbone on the palm of my hand for several seconds afterward. I could see the shock flash across her face, then turn into fear, finally settling into a soft understanding, and then an open and hungry desire. She later told me that she did not feel out of control until I wrapped my hands around her neck and began to squeeze, because she knew that I was strong enough to really hurt or kill her. She said though that she trusted I wouldn't hurt her and therefore felt adored. I wonder if this is the kind of thing that all masochistic empaths feel. If it is, a great number of people would live in silent dissatisfaction if there were no sociopaths to smack them around once in a while. She seemed to enjoy the experience even more than I did.

Her neck is beautifully long, narrow, and muscular, and especially with her short hair, I could get my hands around it with amazing ease. I might have killed her if I thought there would have been no consequences, but there were a myriad of reasons for not hurting her that had nothing to do with my feelings of adoration, not least of which was her prohibiting me from doing it again. I wanted to do it again, and I would several times after that night. I have strong arms, but more important, strong fingers from years of musical training. They are adept at applying equal amounts of steadily increasing pressure, so that the sensation one has under their grasp is of an unstoppable mechanism without regard for the thing inside it.

Erotic asphyxiation is such a sitcom punch line, but people shouldn't knock it until they've tried it. A man I once saw choked me from time to time. It caused a sensation of even, measured pressure—a kind of touch that was full, solid, and constant. A gradual lightheadedness descended, fluttering sensations emerged from my depths to float up to my surfaces, and there was something like euphoria.

Dating my current boyfriend helps me to appear normal and socially well adjusted. He is of average height and has a respectable middle-class profession. He is handsome and well built, because I would never stand to have someone with whom I am so intimately associated be otherwise. Also, I enjoy his beauty immensely. His smile appears almost as sincere as mine, and he carries himself with a physical strength and self-competence similar to that which I have always admired in myself. We see each other several days a week, and whenever we go out, he opens doors and pays for meals and does all of the things that a gentleman would do for his lady.

In a lot of ways he looks and speaks and behaves like many of the men I have dated in the past, because I chose them to serve the same function in my life. I do not love him the way that he loves me, but that is not to say that I do not or cannot love him in my way, or that I did not love some of the men who came before him. For the most part, I treat him with kindness and generosity.

I occasionally have liaisons with men or women outside of my principal relationship. Not all of the time or as a matter of course but just when a person happens into my life whom I feel a desire to possess. I do not view these relationships as cheating, but I keep them a secret anyway to avoid drama. In my mind, any extracurricular activities would be classified as exploits, not possessions, so there's no concern that I'll become emotionally attached. Because they're by their nature temporary, I don't feel like my paramours need concern themselves with them. I understand that not everyone feels this way about relationships, so I just keep quiet. And in return for their devotion, I provide my romantic partners something they can't seem to get from anyone else; to see a person's hidden need and to answer it must be some form of public service. In return, they give me whatever I want—attention, adoration, money, good advice, the pleasure of their body, access to more potential targets (their friends and family), or even just someone to carry bulk food items from my car into my apartment. It's not quite an even quid pro quo, but remarkably, no one has seemed to mind too much.

My first memory of using someone who was romantically interested in me is from kindergarten. I gained the acquaintance of a Mexican-national kid who spoke almost no English. He had a very serious crush on me and expressed his devotion through daily gifts. My favorite gifts were shiny, decorative pencils that could be purchased out of a machine for twenty-five cents.

After he presumably ran out of quarters, he would give me little Matchbox race cars that must have come from his own toy stash. I would give them to my brothers in exchange for favors or the more desirable items out of their lunch bags. It had been weeks of this when my brother Jim told me that I should tell the Mexican kid I didn't like him, but I didn't see why. What kindness would that have been? I would likely lose the steady supply of toy cars and pencils and whatever else he had in store for me. And he would lose whatever mysterious thing it was that he got from me, the hope of reciprocal love or the opportunity to admire me—it was not at all clear to me. Either way, I liked his love. I liked being loved, just like anyone else.

I get something different out of everyone I am involved with, and I have a remarkable tolerance for people's idiosyncrasies. Many years later, in the twilight of my high-powered job, I met a man whose devotion reminded me of the Mexican-national kid. He was beautiful—chiseled body and features with penetrating blue eyes and short blond curls swept forward like there should have been a laurel wreath framing them. He lived with his brother in a one-bedroom apartment with two twin beds, Ernie-and-Bert style, and had been unemployed for approximately six years. At every meal every day he ate two plain cheeseburgers from the McDonald's half a block away from his brother's apartment. As a result, or so he guessed, his hair was falling out, so that when we made out it would regularly end up in my mouth. He spent his days playing first-person shooter games and listening to action movie soundtracks. He liked that I wasn't put off by his quirks, although I did once tell him that there were only so many times I could listen to a complete summary of the plot of *K-PAX*.

I sent him a book on confronting life with Asperger's. He had never been diagnosed, but to me it was obvious. In some ways he was my damaged twin, and that's why I had hoped that it would work out.

Like the Mexican boy, he wore his heart on his sleeve. Unlike with the Mexican boy, I was willing to consider the possibility of a long-term relationship with him. He satisfied all of my criteria: beautiful, easygoing, nonjudgmental, malleable. But he was needy, demanding. I needed him to accept me and my needs the way I accepted him and his. Even after I was officially unemployed and didn't have much going on, I still thought he wanted too much of my time. It was such a small point of contention, but it made all the difference in terms of keeping me happy. And I really wanted to be happy with him. He was the first person I dated seriously after fully embracing the sociopathic label. I'd had so many relationships recently fail and I wanted to believe that I could make a relationship work if I really wanted it. But I had no clue how to go about a sincere romantic relationship.

I finally decided that maybe the best way for us to understand each other was to speak our common language of rationality. I explained to him that our incentives for spending time together were misaligned. He had nothing going on in his life so he always wanted to spend time together. I didn't feel the same way. In order for him to see my perspective on the value of my time, I told him that he should spend one hour doing something he wouldn't otherwise do for every hour he spent with me. I even took the time to devise an eighty-item list of optional activities, which included reading specific books I had selected for him, taking up photography, or listening to NPR. I didn't really want him to do those things, I just wanted him to see my point of view, which was that my time was roughly twice as valuable as his.

I was surprised that he didn't take my offer. In retrospect, I gather that his feelings were hurt by my spreadsheet. I guess I had hoped that, as a high-functioning autistic, he would regard it as an effort at saving the relationship rather than an insult to his personhood. I had hoped that the trade-off to dating an Aspie was that his feelings would not be the veritable minefield that empaths' emotions are. I had hoped that I would be able to have the stable relationship with him that I had been unable to find with empaths. I still wonder whether it is possible to have a normal, long-term relationship with someone. Will I ever be married? For longer than a few years? It seems like all I ever end up with is a string of bad breakups.

I am terrible about breaking up with people. Once I lose interest in someone, I usually prefer to string them along until they leave me alone of their own accord. I would rather have the inconvenience of this than the possibility of an emotional scene. I don't really understand when people get emotional about things, and I can't stand it when people cry in response to something I have said or done. I feel like it is such a cheap shot, particularly since if they know me at all, they should understand that I am not going to be able to deal with those emotions. It's like expecting someone confined to a wheelchair to walk up the stairs, or maybe being mad at your child for not being the gender you wanted him or her to be. As one of my blog readers put it, "All emotionally stunted people get frustrated with overly emotional people. It's like being yelled at in a language you don't understand." In fact, one of the only surefire ways to make me upset/angry is to cry when in a confrontation with me. So, because I want to avoid the loss of control and damage that can be done when I am upset or angry, along with wanting generally to avoid unnecessary unpleasantness, I try to avoid an emotionally charged dissolution to a relationship.

Most psychologists think that sociopaths cannot love, but that theory seems silly to me. Just because it is a different kind of love, more calculating and self-aware, doesn't negate its existence. This misconception springs from some illusion that the capacity to love is a form of goodness—that one's love constitutes an unadulterated gift that arises out of selflessness rather than selfishness. But I do not believe this is true.

For example, most people do not have children for the benefit of those children. You cannot give to that which does not exist—that which would never risk torture, illness, or heartache had you not brought it into being. But when I see my sister unable to resist smiling in the company of her shiny-blond, rosy-cheeked toddler, I can imagine no greater love. I, too, am overrun with feelings of love for this tiny, just-formed being, knowing that there are genetic landscapes written into my heart that make it so. She's endlessly charming to me. Her mere existence in the world pulls chemical levers and pushes enzymatic buttons that produce in me immense joy. Generosity and affection are simply its symptoms and side effects. Evolutionary biologists have long puzzled over the adaptation for love and its attendant expressions of generosity and kindness, theorizing that altruism ensures the survival of genes through one's kin. So-called inclusive fitness theory basically holds that you are willing to be altruistic to another person in proportion to the advantage it will give your own genes in survival. In other words, you share half of your genes with your siblings, so you should be more willing to help them than, say, your cousin or even your nephew. This theory, however, has lately been the subject of much controversy, as some scientists have begun to challenge the theory on the basis that the math doesn't add up. Still, for whatever reason it pleases me to promote my niece's existence. It behooves me to give to her whatever I can to induce pleasure in her, which infects me with a glittering, light-filled happiness. Mirth, ecstasy, whatever you want to call it. We all want this for ourselves. Sociopaths, too.

When I was in my early twenties, I learned to love a girl named Ann who had beautiful eyes and soft overgrown hair that covered her face. She was a musician. She played one of those unpopular nerdy instruments that never garner any glory or fame, but she played it beautifully. For a time in my life, my skin crawled and my body ached when I was away from her for any stretch of time: a few hours of not being able to lazily brush my fingers against her skin, a weekend of not feeling her even breath in my presence—unbearable. I felt like she was the first person who really saw me, and that allowed me to trust her in a way that I had never managed to trust a person before.

We met on a music tour together, but she didn't pay much attention to me until she noticed me messing with a damaged person in the group—another musician, with red hair, moderate skill, and clear psychological problems. Ann wasn't mad, only curious. To me that was a sign that she was susceptible to me—reacting with curiosity where most would react with judgment. I asked her why we weren't friends, knowing she would appreciate directness as a sign of honesty and courage. She was charmed. "There's no reason why we aren't friends."

We spent the next three and a half weeks together. This was in the midst of my ostracization, when the other students in my program had decided to have nothing to do with me after I had read that girl's diary. I hadn't realized how lonely I had been, how much I missed connecting with other people. I tried to be around her as much as I could, so much so that her friends got concerned, asking her if I was bothering her, wondering why such a good person as herself would allow such a bad person as me to keep her acquaintance. When we rode on buses together for long trips, I would sleep with my head in her lap. It was such peace. It was as if I had found a port in a storm that had been raging for so long I did not know what it felt like to sail in fair weather or to touch my feet on solid, un-shaking ground. From the comfort of land, I could see how wet and cold I had been, how bereft of human contact, how sick— and I never wanted to be those things again. I cannot describe those first days and weeks with Ann without feeling an acute pain. Loneliness is never as awful as its immediate aftermath, because at the time, you are so occupied with enduring it that you can't bear to comprehend its awfulness.

Ann saw me as a broken thing, a thing to be fixed. And in a lot of ways, she did fix me. She taught me that there were more sustainable ways of meeting my needs and that self-control was a prerequisite to them. Before her, I had been so impul-sive. I used to just leave and hope things worked out. I walked in front of cars to make them stop. I traveled with no money. I hit people. Things often didn't work out. Watching Ann live her life, I realized that it was okay to consider the future—that living without thought of it ensured nothing but discomfort. And I wondered why I had lived in discomfort for so long.

Part of it was that Ann sold me on forever. She said we would always love each other and that she would make sure of it. I had never heard anyone speak so certainly about some-thing so inherently uncertain. I didn't believe her, but she saw my thoughts and replied, "No, I mean it. Even if you killed my mother. I'm not saying that you should kill my mother, of course, because you really shouldn't. But if you did kill my mother, I would be very angry and very sad, but I would still love you and I wouldn't leave you."

It was so absurd that it seemed true. I trusted her, and I had never trusted anyone. Unlike anyone I had ever known, she told me she didn't want to be shielded from my thoughts, listening for hours to my megalomaniacal rants about "ruining people" and other hobbies. It was so refreshing to not have to wear a mask, but I kept waiting for the other shoe to drop. Part of me wanted to test her tolerance, maybe even prove her wrong about always loving me. I kept confessing sin after sin, but she never recoiled. I was so used to the opposite reaction from people. I had, in fact, just been severely socially sanctioned for something as small as stealing a diary. Ann didn't think I was a monster for these things, or perhaps she did but professed her love to me anyway.

She taught me how easy it is to give. I gave her as much as I could think to. I bought her boots and made her things to eat and drove her to the airport. I helped her move, rubbed her shoulders, and ran her errands. I finally understood the Mexican kid's compulsion to give me shiny pencils or why people bother keeping pets.

It was a kind of puppy love. I was a kid and she was a kid, and we believed kid things. We reveled in finding each other, because our respective abilities to detect the specialness in each other made each of us feel all the more special. Ann loved seeing the good in someone so very bad. She loved loving someone whom the whole world wrongly thought was undeserving. Her earnest willingness to listen and to try to understand my honest ill will made me think that I wasn't able to hurt her, but of course I was.

Once we were in the car when we fought about something I forget now, and she began to cry. I got so angry at her. She knew that I do not respond to such emotional cues like crying. I felt betrayed, and something in me turned off. I pulled over and told her to get out. I remember reaching over her to unlock and open her door, feeling the precariousness of the city in the draft of outside air.

She screamed at me, "What is wrong with you?!"

This wounded me. I thought she knew.

"You're going to leave your friend in the middle of a strange city?" she asked accusingly.

I didn't understand what had happened. I didn't understand what she was saying to me, but I understood that there was judgment in her voice. She was deciding whether I was a good or a bad person, and leaning toward bad. This was something I thought she would never do to me. I realized, after all, that she was not so different from everyone else. I could have left her there and hoped that she, too, would leave me forever so that I could throw away all of the feelings she had made me feel. As I looked blankly into her tear-stained face and she gasped for breath through her sobs, her clothes disheveled, as if her wretchedness had seeped into their fibers, it would have been easy to let her go.

"No, of course not. Can you close that door?" And she did.

I saw that I could hurt her, that she had to be taken care of if she were to continue loving me. But I saw something else. That she was just like everyone else made her crossing the divide to my corner of the world all the more valuable to me. It was not until then that I began to regard Ann as a person, a human being, rather than just a thing that healed me. And if she was just a person, then maybe there were many other people whom I could learn to relate to as well as I did with Ann.

After I finished college, I went to live with Ann in the Midwest, a place that seemed so characterless it was as if it had been fashioned out of cardboard. My parents had kicked me out of the house. I don't know why really, but I suspect that they thought I was a bad influence on my younger siblings— I had not yet achieved my current level of self-control and at that point in my life most of my interactions were dripping with raw antagonism. I had given up pursuing music seriously, so I spent my days doing odd jobs.

During this time I met a very sweet boy. His speaking voice was at least an octave lower than any other voice I had heard in my life, quietly rumbling below the din. Ann and I had an old dingy couch in our apartment, a dull rose color made duller by dust and wear. When I sat with him on it, his voice would vibrate through the cushions onto the skin on my back, touching me in an oddly corporeal way. I would have loved him less, maybe, if not for his voice. It was a sound that made me tremble.

In many ways I responded to him the way that I responded to music, asking him only to fulfill me with the nuances and complexities specific to his medium. He was a working-class boy. His sturdy military build combined with a fair-haired, blue-eyed innocence fed into common American delusions about the honor and purity of soldiers fighting for God and country. He had never gone to college or learned very much in school. He wasn't smart and couldn't understand math or law or any of the things that I had spent so much of my life learning. But one night the power went out in our neighborhood, leaving us in the pitch-black. I don't remember if he kissed me or if I kissed him, but we kissed each other in the dark.

I was very happy then. I loved Ann because she understood me. And I loved him because I understood him. I could not have loved him if I had not found her first, if she had not illuminated for me what it meant to love another person, to have a stake in their existence in the world. I went from him to Ann and back again, with my only goal in life to be happy and to make them happy. I was spoiled, to be exposed to love in this way, having all of my needs met by two people who didn't believe in labels or boundaries for relationships. Neither of them expected anything that I was incapable of giving.

Ann is married now and has several children. We grew up together, and the friendship that began so desperately evolved into one of trusted consistency. The boy left me. I no longer yearn for either of them, having long been accustomed to their absence to the point where it is difficult for me now to remember how it was to feel that way about anybody. But both relationships were immensely rewarding—rewarding enough for me to finally see that long-term relationships could be worth the special effort I had to pay to cultivate and sustain them.

Still, I am not used to long-term relationships. I still have not managed to keep a romantic relationship going for longer than eight months, which is a problem because I am supposed to get married. It's not just about familial pressure. It's a religious commandment, as important as getting baptized. I have known this and have kept it on my list of things to do. My parents don't mention it really anymore. They got married at twenty and twenty-three respectively. They find it hard to imagine someone well into her early thirties not having a family. My mother was twenty-six when she had me. I thought she was so old when she had my last sibling, a little caboose that came along when she was thirty-seven.

There have been instances in which I would have said yes to marriage. The intelligent Mormon sociopath lawyer, the ruthless Mormon investment banker, the intelligent but gentle non-Mormon lawyer who is generously still footing the bill for his ex-girlfriend's daughter's private school. The beautiful Aspie. There was the midwestern boy whom I loved, I thought. It's hard to remember now what that love felt like.

I might marry the current man. He has that sort of ambiguous attractiveness that seen from certain angles is Hollywood dreamy and from others reflects the usual sag of aging. His best look is four days of scruff, his hair a little longer than the high-and-tight he sports for his one weekend of National Guard service a month. (Military men are disproportionately attracted to me. Is it the perceived challenge? Or the promise of punishment if they aren't diligent?)

We met at church, of course. I wouldn't preface him with *intelligent,* as I did my other hopefuls. He does not represent a source of genetic wealth to me, but I have also become less interested in raising a brood of supergeniuses. Even if I started now, I would probably only be able to eke out two or three children anyway, and so it's not as important. He is clever, though, and handy. He is blue-collar in a middle-class way that seems to have gone extinct sometime in the late 1980s, the start of the diaspora of American manufacturing jobs. His hands are refreshingly rough in mine, in a way that most readers of this book will likely not have ever experienced. I like that we are from different classes, but it might bother him sometimes.

Recently I have been thinking about the proper role of manipulation in a relationship. I have always said that everyone wants to be seduced. With this current relationship, I performed the seduction perfectly. To use a baseball analogy, it's been my no-hitter. It was not easy and it was not always clear that it would turn out so well. (I almost think that, because I felt no expectations about the relationship, I felt no performance pressure, so I performed nearly perfectly.) I'd tell you

about it, but like a baseball no-hitter, the story of a perfect seduction is actually sort of boring.

But now that I have a relationship that seems like it could
last, and I am interested in exploring that option, do I keep seducing him? I have already gotten more real, more true to myself, as the relationship has progressed. I wonder if I should
step back in and "fix," seduce, or manipulate when the situation warrants it. But sometimes it backfires: Some people
would feel betrayed if they ever did find out that they were
being "managed," and I tend to respect people less in proportion to the amount that I manipulate them. Mutual understanding, however, usually means the other person is getting
better at pleasing me. It is not clear to me how this relationship management is different from what people mean when
they say love takes work. Why are my seductions and manipulations in the service of maintaining our good relationship
seen as betrayal, but all the marriage therapists and self-help
books teach people how to better communicate or get what
they want out of a relationship? And yet there is something different to my paramours. Somehow they can just sense it and
it bothers them in ways they can't quite name. And eventually
they all decide that there is something a little off about me,
and they leave.

Love always finds ways to disappoint. Or I find ways to
disappoint love. You can kiss and touch and promise. You can
give away all of your Matchbox cars and your metallic pencils,
and it's still not enough. At a point, there is nothing you can
do to make someone love you, nothing you can do to make
your love better or lasting, but you want it, search for it, and
make every effort to sustain it regardless. There was nothing
Morgan could do once I was done with her. And there was nothing I could do with the boy whom I loved in the Midwest, who

played with guns, built houses, and barely knew how to use a checkbook. I wanted to marry him and make babies with him. I wanted to sit next to him for as long as I could for the rest of my life. I had little desire to manipulate him, because he gave me everything I wanted without my trying to wrestle it from him. I did not seek power over him, because I had all the power I wanted. I think he loved me. And I had no desire to break his heart. But I think I still might have.

Chapter 9

RAISING CAIN

Though my dream of birthing a large brood of supergeniuses is no longer feasible, I still take seriously the Mormon doctrine to multiply and replenish the earth. I like children. They're still figuring out the world, so they don't have many expectations of me, and I'm able to behave more authentically around them; I don't have to work on keeping my mask up the way I do with adults. As much as anyone else, I like the idea of raising little people whom I could influence and shape, though I rarely think of it in terms of producing "good" men and women. There will always be another generation of sociopaths. Children are being born every day with a genetic predisposition to feel no guilt, no remorse, no empathy. And is that really so bad?

There is nothing keeping a young sociopath from being a great, high-achieving, functional member of society. I excel at many things, I have meaningful relationships with people, and I have a very full life. I also suffered a lot to get where I am, and most sociopaths have similar stories; as I was learning to manage my impulses and redirect my desires, I fought with family, alienated friends, and lost out on opportunities I should have pursued. Luckily for me, my parents managed to do a lot of things right in raising me, and I love them for that. It could have gone very badly, I think, and I appreciate the fact that it didn't.

To early sociopath researcher James Prichard, originator of the term "moral insanity," no one was born evil; bad people were born good but cultivated in error in an unending cycle of well-intentioned human folly. And for decades, researchers thought that children were blank slates to be written on, for good or ill. But we're now aware that these traits are likely encoded into people like me from birth. Knowing that I carry my sociopathy in my genes, I often think about the kind of child that I would have. Like pregnant women who have nightmares of birthing half-goat babies, I dream of nucleotide chains replicating into the future with indifference. My genetic code will ensure that it lives on, sociopathy and all.

I once visited Tulane medical school and their collection of fetuses and embryos, fifty specimens in jars preserved in a milky yellow liquid, both the bodies and the means of their preservation relics from the nineteenth century. Approximately half of the specimens demonstrated normal gestational progression, but the other half represented abnormalities, the diagnoses for which were scrawled on yellowed, crinkly note cards—for example, encephalitis for one large-headed baby or ectrodactyly for one with lobster-claw hands. Babies with no specific diagnosis were labeled, simply, "monster." Some were double-headed monsters or four-legged monsters, but miscellaneous monsters they were.

John Steinbeck wrote of monsters in his novel *East of Eden*:

I believe there are monsters born in the world to human parents. Some you can see, misshapen and horrible, with huge heads or tiny bodies . . .

And just as there are physical monsters, can there not be mental or psychic monsters born? The face and body may be perfect, but if a twisted gene or a malformed egg can produce physical monsters, may not the same process produce a malformed soul?

Steinbeck identifies the sociopath Cathy as such a monster. Of her, he writes:

Some balance wheel was misweighed, some gear out of ratio. She was not like other people, never was from birth. . . . She made people uneasy but not so that they wanted to go away from her. Men and women wanted to inspect her, to be close to her, to try and find what caused the disturbance she distributed so subtly. And since this had always been so, Cathy did not find it strange.

I remember such inspections as a child—the reluctant attraction, the fascinated repulsion. It's easy to question some of the parenting choices my own mother and father made, but I believe they took their newborn monster and did the best they could with her. They must have felt this simultaneous love and horror, even while I lay bundled in their arms.

From the cradle to the grave, Cathy's project was to exploit people, manipulate them and insinuate herself into their lives with the sole purpose of spreading poison, madness, and despair around her. I understand her impulse, and I've traveled on her road from time to time. But something in me has made other choices—love most paramount among them—that I imagine must be owed to my parents.

My genetic heritage has made me question whether or not I should ever have children. I worry that they too will be monsters, regardless of how many legs or heads they will have when they are born. I worry that they will be like me, and I worry even more that they will not be like me. I don't know how I could be an appropriate parent to an empathetic child, how I would be able to love and respect it. I have one sister, a tearful, hugging woman, whom I regard with a great deal of disdain. What would I do with a child that needed constant emotional suckling? Maybe I would just be distant—almost certainly, I would be bored.

If I had a sociopathic child, though, I think I could do a good job rearing him or her. I believe my parents did a remarkably good job with me, whether they meant to or not. They set up an ongoing competition for love and scarce resources like time and money among their five children, an active game with relatively straightforward, consistent rules and obvious consequences. They had clear favorites. In fact, on many a weekend afternoon, my siblings would stave off boredom by discussing the relative strengths and weaknesses of each sibling and how they corresponded with the affections of our parents, e.g., Dad likes Scott because Scott will surf with him, but ultimately likes Jim better because Jim indulges his flights of fantasy. It was clear to all how Scott could move up in the rankings by, for instance, supporting my dad's magical thinking—he just didn't care to do so for whatever reason.

I understood my parents' favoritism as a clearly defined meritocracy—a consistent system under which I could learn to operate. I bought into the game and actively participated because I felt like I could play well against my competitor siblings. I did not know all the rules or triggers, but I could learn them, and it was an ongoing challenge because I was not otherwise naturally inclined to care what my parents thought of me. My mother cleaved to the children who showed emotional and musical sensitivities that would encourage and affirm her own, while my father preferred the ones who exhibited innate intelligence sufficient to recognize his intellect but not so great that they questioned his authority. I would always go surfing and skiing with my dad because he would buy me the proper accoutrements—wetsuits, surfboards, surf racks, skis, boots, gloves, poles, and gas for my car—while my sister Kathleen was having to borrow dance shoes and scrounge rides from her friends. My mother always had dreams of our singing together like the Partridge Family, then later upgraded her dreams to a family jazz combo like the Marsalis family. My father always dreamed that we would be like the guitar-playing cool kids he used to envy in high school. I chose to play drums because it fit both of their dreams perfectly, enough that they found the money to buy me a drum set while my sister had to stay home from camp for lack of funds. My parents weren't consistent in terms of providing emotional or financial support for me and my siblings, but their unremitting self-interest made them very predictable; this single vector dominated their every behavior toward us. Getting what we wanted was only a matter of how to appeal to their particular brands of self-interest.

The worst thing that my parents could have done (for me) was to behave in inconsistent ways, or to show us too much mercy. As a child, all I understood was cause and effect. If I felt like I or my siblings could break the rules and still get away with it by crying on cue, then I would have done that instead of

following them. I was as amenable to conditioning as labora-
tory rats, learning to push the levers that gave me treats and to
stop pushing levers that yielded nothing.

I think that sociopaths (particularly young ones) actually feel happier and thrive better in a world of clearly defined
boundaries; when rules are consistently enforced, the child
will just start to take them as a given. I certainly did. I think
simple cause-and-effect rules with clear, predictable outcomes
for compliance or violation encourage the young sociopath
to think of life as an interesting puzzle that can be gamed.
As long as the young sociopath believes that she can acquire
some advantage through skillful planning and execution (and
finds some level of success, which I feel is almost a given), she
will stay committed to the structure of the game you have set
up. It's why sociopaths can be ruthless businessmen fiercely
defending the principles of capitalism.

My favorite teacher had an entirely meritocratic system in
which we could opt out of class time. She had replaced a very
popular teacher in our sixth-grade pre-algebra class midyear.
I didn't like the popular teacher; he had pandered too much to
students and often played favorites. My new teacher initially
struggled to gain the trust of the class. Pre-algebra was the
most advanced math class for our grade and our school was
in a particularly nice part of town, so everyone was very smart
and entitled. The smartest and most demanding of the children (including me) complained that she was going too slow.
In a creative solution, she started giving short quizzes in the
first five minutes of class. If you received a perfect score on
the quiz, you got to go outside on the grass patch just outside
the classroom door and work on your homework instead of
staying inside for the lecture. Every day I would arrive a few
minutes before class, glancing through the material for the day

so I could get a perfect score. Out of the eighty school days left in the year, I only had to stay in for a few lectures, typically due to some small arithmetic error. Those were always very difficult days for me, but I also understood that those were the rules and my teacher applied them exactly and without exception. It felt like a game, and it was a game I liked to play because I outplayed my classmates. The fact that sometimes I lost just meant that it was not an easy game. It was challenging enough to keep my attention and consistent enough to keep my trust.

But if I were confronted with a system in which one lever might sometimes get a shock and sometimes get a treat, I would probably choose not to engage with the system at all, stealing my treats from the other rats instead. The worst thing that parents can do is to be inconsistent. It makes the child sociopath think that the game is rigged; in that case, it doesn't matter what he does, except to the extent that he can out-cheat the cheater (typically the parent). Providing me a system defined by clear incentives, my parents laid out a way for me to gain positive benefits while exercising my sociopathic traits. I didn't have to rely on the soft intangibles of empathy or emotion to get what I needed.

In raising my child, it would be natural for me to follow in my parents' incredibly self-interested footsteps by only fostering those interests in my children that appealed to my own vanity. But there is predictability and honesty to this approach that I believe actually sets up children to thrive in the real world.

And I think that children often prefer emotional detachment from adults in response to their tantrums as opposed to emotional coddling. There's something reasonable and stable seeming about my emotionlessness to children. Especially when children are self-aware enough to acknowledge that there are emotions they can't control (and I think most children are aware of this as soon as they begin acknowledging the emotional worlds of others). It's very calming to have someone not reacting emotionally at all.

My three-year-old niece had a meltdown in church the other day so I took her outside. I knew it was just because she was tired (all of her cousins had slept in the same room as part of a holiday weekend's festivities), maybe a little overexcited with all of the activity and relatives, and maybe a little annoyed about the arrival of her new baby sister. So I just walked with her until she stopped crying, then sat on a curb playing with ants. I didn't talk to her about her feelings or even mention the meltdown. When she got tired of the ants, she insisted we go back into church. I let her boss me around. It was a subtle sign to her that I still took her seriously, even after the tantrum. And then finally after we had settled ourselves into the pew again she asked me to scratch her back, after having acted aloof to me all weekend, and wanted me to go to her Sunday school class with her (I told her I was too tall to fit in the small chairs).

I've discovered that children are aware that they are slaves to their emotions and are a little embarrassed about it the same way twelve-year-old boys are a little embarrassed about their erections. They can't really control them and the last thing they want is more attention being drawn to it. Asking about erections is not good. Tears should have the same rule. Or maybe it's just that the children in my family prefer emotional detachment because that's more what they're used to. Either way, the esteem and affection that my nieces and nephews show me is perhaps proof that I wouldn't be a horrible parent to an empath child after all.

Or maybe I would have little sociopath children. Because

of my own success as a sociopath, I know that if I had equally remorseless, unfeeling children they would have just as much a chance to thrive in life as other children, if provided with the right kind of structure and opportunities to learn how to succeed. They'd be fine. In Steinbeck's description of the sociopath Cathy he explains that "just as a cripple may learn to utilize his lack so that he becomes more effective in a limited field than the uncrippled, so did Cathy, using her difference, make a painful and bewildering stir in her world." I know that any sociopath children of mine would be able to turn their weaknesses into strengths. I would hope that with the proper guidance they could use those strengths not to make a painful and bewildering stir, but for the benefit of their family and the greater world.

My most salient worry would not be how they would treat the world, but how the world would treat them. Would they be outsiders or outcasts? I would hate for them to feel compelled to go underground, never to find acceptance for who they are, to be regarded as hollow, unfinished people—or even the embodiment of evil.

It's hard to parse out the root causes of this disorder. What it would be to know what genes flip which chemical levers that set these subtlest of mental tendencies in early childhood into motion. How do these incipient chemical yearnings mature into full-fledged sociopathy? Geneticists, neurologists, psychiatrists, psychologists, and criminologists are beginning to knit together, from bits and pieces of studies and observation, a complex portrait of a complex human experience.

Budding sociopaths are often categorized as "callous-unemotional" by psychologists who are reluctant to diagnose children as sociopaths or psychopaths too early, feeling that applying that diagnostic label can unfairly affect how the kids and their families are treated. The traits in children are very similar to those in adults: a distinct lack of affect, empathy, and remorse. Callous-unemotional children don't respond to the usual negative cues that teach most people how to behave well. Paul Frick, a psychologist at the University of New Orleans, says, "They don't care if someone is mad at them. They don't care if they hurt someone's feelings. If they can get what they want without being cruel, that's often easier, but at the end of the day, they'll do whatever works best."

That was certainly my experience growing up. I had revelation after revelation that I could get more of what I wanted more easily if I learned how to accommodate the desires of other people. On the playground, you can keep a toy longer if another kid willingly gives it to you than if you take if from him; in high school, you win more popularity by fitting in than by lording your superior intelligence over everyone; in the workplace, you advance more by making your supervisor look good to the boss than you do by undermining your supervisor. As one blog commenter put it:

> Having worked in major corporations for about 3 decades, I know that no matter how you choose to rise through the ranks, there have still got to be people higher who promote you, and they aren't going to do it unless you bring value—to either themselves or the company. If all socios left nothing but a path of carnage and destruction along their career paths, do you think that's hidden from those with the power to move them upward? Even I know that benefiting others in the short term is often

what will benefit me most in the long term—just like
any normal person.

Despite sociopaths' being largely ruled by impulses (or perhaps because they are), they are incredibly sensitive to incentive structures and actively consider both actual costs and opportunity costs in their decision-making. But there are certain consequences that I do not care as much about, particularly the moral judgment of others.

I presumably feel this way because of the wiring of my brain. Magnetic resonance imaging on the brains of psychopathic adults has shown significant differences in the size and density of regions of the brain associated with empathy and social values and active in moral decision-making. These areas are also critical for reinforcing positive outcomes and discouraging negative ones. In callous-unemotional children, negative feedback like a parent's frown, a teacher's chiding, or a friend's yelp of pain may not register the way it would in a normal brain.

The lack of interest in other people's negative emotions could, interestingly, be a matter of attention. Researchers gave a group of callous-unemotional boys a visual test that measures unconscious emotional processing. They flashed a rapid sequence of pictures of faces—fearful, happy, disgusted, and neutral—and measured the boys' preattentive, or unconscious, recognition of the meaning of the emotion behind the faces. When compared with normal kids, the boys were less able to quickly detect fear or disgust, indicating that these callous-unemotional kids are not automatically assimilating threatening or negative cues in their world. They are lacking a fundamental social skill that most other people are born with, and it affects the way their whole emotional palette develops.

A recent study came to the surprising conclusion that children with a certain variation of a gene that affects brain serotonin are more likely to have these callous-unemotional traits if they are also raised poor. In contrast, kids with the same gene who had high socioeconomic status scored very low on sociopathic traits. The lead researcher on the study pointed out that although sociopathy is considered abnormal, these traits may be useful in certain circumstances. "For example, these folks tend to have less anxiety and are less prone to depression," she said, qualities that might be useful in dangerous or unstable environments. It seems possible that kids in bad neighborhoods develop their inborn sociopathic traits as a defense mechanism against a chaotic and unpredictable world.

But these kids aren't doomed to a life of prison or misanthropy. Psychiatrist Lee Robins investigated the roots of sociopathy by conducting a series of cohort studies tracking children with behavioral problems into adulthood. She discovered two important facts. First, nearly every adult who fit the criteria for sociopathy had been deeply antisocial as a child. And second, about 50 percent of the antisocial children who started in her study grew to be fairly normal adults. In other words, all sociopaths were antisocial children, but not all antisocial children become sociopaths. One has to wonder: Did some of those antisocial children simply grow up to be high-functioning, successful sociopaths who were then counted among the "fairly normal adults"? And if so, what in their childhoods made some children take one path, and the others another?

The general consensus has held that sociopathy is an

untreatable disorder, but as evidence mounts that the brain is more plastic, or changeable, than we thought, researchers are beginning to propose that young sociopaths might be susceptible to early intervention. Perhaps children can be trained to develop their vestigial sense of empathy or learn to react appropriately to the emotions of people around them.

As any sociopath knows, people are hardwired to be aggressive and selfish, but it turns out that most of us are also biologically programmed for basic human compassion. Even children from abusive, chaotic homes, the kind who are the most troublesome in school, can learn to listen to that whisper of empathy that seems to be hidden somewhere in them. A Canadian organization is sending mothers and young babies into classrooms to help schoolkids learn the basics of parenting skills. The students try to imagine what the baby is experiencing, so they practice "perspective-taking." The children observe the baby on his stomach barely able to lift his own head and then attempt to understand the baby's perspective by themselves lying on the floor on their stomachs trying to look up. Perspective-taking is the cognitive dimension of empathy, and one that is not familiar or automatic to many of these schoolchildren. A developmental psychologist who has studied the program attests to the larger successes of the program: "Do kids become more empathic and understanding? Do they become less aggressive and kinder to each other? The answer is yes and yes." Or, as Paul Frick says regarding child sociopaths, "you can teach a child to recognize the effects of their behavior." Despite the genetic code written indelibly in our cells, the human mind is amazingly malleable and easily influenced by our experiences.

I am very impressionable. I know that my genes might predispose me to the way I think and interact with the world, but

I also take full responsibility for the amount of control I have over the rest. Every day I am in motion, sensitizing myself or desensitizing myself, constantly reshaping my brain, making and breaking habits, making myself more or less inclined to act or think a certain way.

Everything I have done has changed me, for better or for worse. I didn't realize this when I was a child. I'm lucky that I was raised in a very sheltered, devout religious home. We were not allowed to swear, not even *damn* or *hell.* We could not watch PG-13 movies until we were actually thirteen and we could never watch movies that were rated R. My father had a temper, but my parents never drank, did recreational drugs, or were otherwise out of their heads. My community was so conservative and predominantly born-again Christian that I suspect few of my friends in high school were sexually active—or if they were, I certainly wasn't aware of it.

It's through experiences that normal-gened people can be desensitized to things like killing, and sociopathic-gened people can be sensitized to things like being aware of the needs of others. I was not desensitized to violence. If anything, I was sensitized to music. I learned to be quiet and to listen beyond the surface of things. I was sensitized to spirituality—I was taught to be self-reflective in prayer and other forms of worship. As a middle child and power broker, I cultivated an awareness of the needs of others. Like the children lying facedown on the floor attempting to see the world through a baby's eyes, I was often forced to engage in perspective-taking focused on service and care for others. Even though my mind was not naturally directed to recognizing and responding to the needs of others, my parents, church leaders, and teachers actually did make a difference in making me acknowledge and address these issues.

Not long ago, I read about a Mormon teenage girl who murdered a small child, luring her outside to play, strangling her to unconsciousness, and then slitting her throat to watch the blood drain away. After giving her victim a shallow burial, the girl went home to write in her journal of her breathless excitement and noted that she had to hurry off to church. At her trial, defense counsel demanded that the jury consider the difficult circumstances of the teenager's childhood, characterized by parental abandonment and abuse.

I am not violent. Despite having imagined it many times, I've never slit anyone's throat. I wonder, though, if had I been raised in a less loving home, or a more abusive one, whether I would have also had blood on my hands. It often seems to me that these people who commit such heinous crimes—sociopath or empath—are not so much more damaged than everyone else, but that they seem to have less to lose. It's easy to imagine an alternate universe in which a sixteen-year-old version of me would be handcuffed in an orange jumpsuit, on my way toward scheming for dominion over the juvenile prison population. If I had had no one to love or nothing to achieve, perhaps. It's hard to say.

A well-known recent example of nurture trumping nature is neuroscientist and University of California–Irvine professor James Fallon. Fallon specializes in studying the biological roots of behavior, and he is famous for his work with the distinctive brain scans of killers. While discussing his work at a family function, his mother told him that Lizzie Borden was a cousin of his. Startled by the revelation, he investigated and discovered that on one line of his family there were at least sixteen murderers—"a whole lineage of very violent people," as he described it.

He decided to check the brain scans and DNA of his family

members for indications of sociopathy. He discovered that everyone was relatively normal, except for him—Fallon himself had the brain-scan signature of a killer as well as all of the genetic markers predisposing him to impulsivity, violence, and risky behavior. When he disclosed this information to his family, they were not surprised. "I knew there was always something off. It makes more sense now," his son said. "Everything that you would want in a serial killer he has in a fundamental way." His wife added, "It was surprising but it wasn't surprising . . . he's always had a standoffish part to him." And Fallon, being honest with himself, admitted, "I have characteristics or traits, some of which are . . . psychopathic." He gave the example of blowing off an aunt's funeral. "I know something's wrong, but I still don't care." Why didn't he end up a killer? "It turns out that I had an unbelievably wonderful childhood"—he was doted on by his parents and surrounded by a loving family.

For all these children like me, born with the monster genes of sociopathy, there are many paths to travel. The brain grows and changes in response to many influences. "Brain research is showing us that neurogenesis can occur even into adulthood," says psychologist Patricia Brennan of Emory University. "Biology isn't destiny. There are many, many places you can intervene along that developmental pathway to change what's happening in these children." Rather than waiting for sociopaths to turn violent or criminal and become a burden on the justice system, it seems conceivable that if we notice unusually antisocial traits in a child at a young age, we could prevent them from turning into criminals by redirecting them to a more positive route, through warm and affectionate parenting, as one early study has hinted, or through targeted therapy.

I would not, like James Fallon, describe my parents as doting. I firmly believe that they taught me the skills to manage my sociopathic traits in a productive way, but I also believe that the way I was raised brought those traits to the surface. My father's facile sentimentality made me distrust excessive displays of emotion, and my mother's inconsistent care led me to believe that love could not be depended on. Though I never suffered from trauma or abuse, my parents' own quirks of personality shaped who I am.

Over the last couple of decades, psychiatric researchers have identified a dozen or so gene variants that can increase a person's vulnerability to mood or personality disorders like depression, anxiety, risk taking, and sociopathy, but only if the person suffered a traumatic or highly stressful childhood or life experience. Through complex "gene-environment interactions," it was believed that your "bad" genes could set you up for problems, and life events could then knock you down. Recently, however, a new hypothesis has emerged: These "bad" genes are not simple liabilities. In an unfavorable context, these genes can cause a person problems, but in a positive context, the same genes can enhance a person's life. An article by David Dobbs in the *Atlantic* describes this theory as "a completely new way to think about genetics and human behavior. Risk becomes possibility; vulnerability becomes plasticity and responsiveness. It's one of those simple ideas with big, spreading implications. Gene variants generally considered misfortunes . . . can instead now be understood as highly leveraged evolutionary bets, with both high risks and high potential rewards. . . . With a bad environment and poor parenting . . . children [with these genes] can end up depressed, drug-addicted, or in jail—but with the right environment and good parenting, they can grow up to be society's most creative, successful, and happy people."

This theory matches up with what I've observed in my own

upbringing, and that of other successful sociopaths I know and hear from on my blog. Our genes and childhoods may have made us sociopaths, but we're not destined for lives of unfettered evil. Instead, with the right kind of care, children like us can learn to do great things—even if they never learn to fully empathize with others:

> *I'm no world leader, but I do have a well-paying professional job in a Fortune 500 company rather than languishing in prison, so I guess you could say I am a successful sociopath. I'm as capable as anyone else of learning from mistakes. I certainly never learned empathy, but I'm intelligent enough to learn rules and learn that breaking them often has consequences that are unpleasant. As to wanting to follow the rules, if following them benefits me sufficiently, then I'm fully capable of following them. If breaking them will bring consequences I don't like, then I don't break them. No empathy is involved, simply a logical examination of cause and effect.*

It is becoming increasingly clear that it is possible to be a sociopath and still be successful in normal society. Dr. Stephanie Mullins-Sweatt's research into successful sociopaths confirms this, suggesting that a trait as simple as "conscientiousness" can make all of the difference between a successful and a criminal sociopath.

I believe that sociopathic traits can be managed and even changed, particularly via early childhood intervention. This belief, although still not popular within the psychological community, is finally getting some traction. I believe that the existence of successful sociopaths suggests that this is true, that sociopaths are incredibly malleable and impressionable. Sociopaths are not influenced in the same ways as empaths, but sociopaths are just as susceptible to their own range of outside influence, perhaps even more susceptible. In research involving the propensity of toddlers to share, psychologist Ariel Knafo of the Hebrew University of Jerusalem has researchers spend an hour of quality time with the toddlers. During a snack break, the researcher brings out two bags of a popular peanut-butter-flavored Israeli snack—Bambas. The youngster opens his pack to see the proper number of Bambas, twenty-four, but the researcher opens his to discover only three, to which he exclaims, "Mine has only three!" Some of the toddlers volunteer some of their own Bambas. Interestingly, the toddlers most likely to share are the toddlers who have a gene variant highly correlated with antisocial behavior in children. Leading researcher in child development Jay Belsky explains: "These genes aren't about risk, it's about a greater sensitivity to experience. If things go well for you when you're young, the same genes that could have helped make a mess of you help to make you stronger and happier instead. It's not vulnerability but responsiveness—for better or worse." It's this "for better or worse" aspect that is concerning when considering the possibility of raising a child genetically disposed to sociopathy.

When I consider the possibility of having sociopath children and how I would raise them, I think the ideal situation would be for child sociopaths to be exposed to both a sociopathic parent or adult figure and an empathic person. An empathy role model is important for a sociopath in order to learn to respect how most of the world thinks. Steinbeck describes the origins of the sociopath Cathy's mind-blindness to others:

Nearly everyone in the world has appetites and impulses, trigger emotions, islands of selfishness, lusts just beneath the surface. And most people either hold such things in check or indulge them secretly. Cathy knew not only these impulses in others but how to use them for her own gain.

It is quite possible that she did not believe in any other tendencies in humans, for while she was preternaturally alert in some directions she was completely blind in others.

This description is particularly poignant for me because it provides a readily understood explanation for why Cathy cannot respect the inner worlds of others in a way that would allow her to check her antisocial behavior. All she sees are people's frailties, which, when hidden from the outside world and only acknowledged and indulged in private, drive Cathy to conclude that people are gross hypocrites. She does not respect them, does not even consider their needs and wants worthy of her own consideration, largely because she cannot see the many ways in which empaths are worthy of her admiration and respect: "to a monster the norm is monstrous."

This is why I think it is so important for sociopathic children to be consistently exposed to a loving and admirable empathy figure, in order to realize that empaths are much more than the sum of their basest desires. A sociopathic child would need someone like my friend Ann, who, after I spent decades objectifying all other humans, finally got me to see that empaths were just like me, but different. And after I understood that basic fact, I was finally able to trust that things like "love" and "goodwill" were actual concepts that empaths felt and not just window dressing on lives lived in a collective delusion.

I think that sociopathic children, like the schoolchildren who are learning empathy from babies, should be sensitized to the fact that there are others out there who are different from them, and in fact that most people are different from each other. I think most child sociopaths grow up thinking, first, that everyone is like them, but just not as good or smart or skilled; later they think they're entirely alone and no one else is like them. If children sociopaths grew up realizing that they were different, and more important, that other people are also different from each other, I think they could be taught to respect those differences in a way that would make them uniquely sensitive to the needs of normal people.

I also think a sociopath child should have a sociopath role model in his life. A fellow sociopath would help the child to know that he is not alone, that he is not a monster, "only a variation." A sociopathic role model could help him guide some of his impulses into positive, pro-social activities. Children have legitimate needs and wants, and a sociopath role model might be able to address the special needs and wants of a sociopath child without alienating him with hints of moral repulsion. According to psychiatrist Liane Leedom, the author of *Just Like His Father*, the sociopath child's needs must be acknowledged as legitimate but limited in socially acceptable ways through the use of redirecting the child's attention to acceptable substitutes until the child can learn to meet his own needs "in a way that is productive rather than destructive." It's not a complete cure, but it is probably the best that can be hoped for.

Who knows how children should be raised, really? In a *New York Times Magazine* article titled "How Do You Raise a Prodigy?" Andrew Solomon speaks of a prodigy as "a monster that violates the natural order," who presents his parents with unique difficulties as "bewildering and hazardous as

a disability." Parents fear that they might either fail to cultivate their child's unique gifts or push too hard and break their
child's spirit. These parental anxieties are even greater when
it comes to children who are labeled special or different.

With the benefit of adult hindsight, I believe that my parents remarkably managed to strike a proper balance for me.
I've hated them sometimes, but for the most part, I've loved
them the way one loves the sky or the ocean or home. I recently
read an interview with the virtuoso and former prodigy Lang
Lang in which he described what it was like to grow up with a
tyrannical father: "If my father had pressured me like this and
I had not done well, it would have been child abuse, and I would
be traumatized, maybe destroyed. He could have been less extreme, and we probably would have made it to the same place;
you don't have to sacrifice everything to be a musician. But we
had the same goal. So since all the pressure helped me become
a world-famous star musician, which I love being, I would say
that, for me, it was in the end a wonderful way to grow up."

My hope for a sociopathic child would be that she might
learn to leverage her gifts in order to achieve her own version
of success—to find a sustainable and joyful way to appreciate
a world of infinite possibilities and realities. Sociopathy does
not necessarily equal misanthropy. It hasn't been that way for
me, and I think my parents have had much to do with that, even
if their methods seem draconian or aspects of their personalities seem harmful. They made me feel like there was a place
for me in the world, and to me that made all the difference.

Perhaps if we treat sociopathic children more like prodi-
gies and less like monsters, they might direct their unique
talents toward pro-social activities that reward and sustain
society rather than to antisocial or parasitic behaviors. Perhaps if they feel like there is a place for them in the world, they

would say, as one child prodigy did, "At first, it felt lonely. Then you accept that, yes, you're different from everyone else, but people will be your friends anyway." Perhaps we could make the measured judgment that, even if we could, we wouldn't want to train or love the sociopath out of them, because sociopaths are interesting people who make our world a more diverse, colorful place in ways that we can't predict.

EPILOGUE

A reader of the blog wrote to me:

Hello.

I think I might be a sociopath, but I'm not sure. I don't have a conscience per se, it's more like a logical guide for what is right and wrong. Nothing turns my stomach, no type of immoral behavior enrages me unless I'm on the receiving end. All of my responses, even my "emotional" responses, are calculated and performed.

I know I'm not the smartest person on the planet—VERY WELL, but I feel it. As far as my heart and soul are concerned, there is nobody smarter on this planet, even though the very mind in question knows that's not the case.

I use people when I can, so long as it doesn't hurt them in the process. I'm not sure if that's because I don't want to hurt people or because I'd like to believe I'm not manipulative. Generally speaking, I don't lie about anything except for my feelings.

But I don't go out of my way to hurt people. I actually go out of my way NOT to hurt people. Pretty much my entire life IS an act, and I don't really know who I am . . . but I'm definitely not normal, nor do I fit all of the negative aspects of the sociopath stereotype.

What does this sound like to you? I'm asking because as much as I'm able to make sense of the world around me, I cannot for the life of me make sense of myself. That is the one thing that my mind can't penetrate. I can state facts about what I do, what I don't do, my habits and tendencies, etc, but trying to form an opinion about myself is like walking through a minefield of self-deception and convenient stray thoughts.

This kind of question is common. Many of the people who identify as sociopaths who read and post on the blog are self-diagnosed. There is little advantage to being formally labeled sociopathic by the psychological community, but I believe that a lot of self-understanding can come from deciding for yourself that the label fits you. Here is how I answer these people:

You sound like a sociopath to me, but don't be disheartened. I think you will find that as you continue to learn more about your condition and yourself, the world will begin to seem very right.

Self-deception is a classic denial symptom. Denying the sociopathic aspect of yourself distorts how you see others and impairs your judgment. It is important that you realize that you are different from others—this will help you to avoid hurting them. For instance, most people assume that everyone else is like them and project their own feelings and emotions on others, e.g., "I wouldn't be offended by that comment, so they shouldn't be, either." This is faulty thinking. What you think or feel has nothing to do with what most people think or feel. In fact, it is best to avoid all normative judgments in favor of descriptive ones. Normative judgments hide a million different biases and self-deceptions that will lead you astray.

You are special. You are very smart, I am sure, but better than that, you think in a way that very few other people think. Your success at utilizing the intellect that you have likely lies in your ability to think outside of the box all the time. This is easy for you because you have never been inside the box—you don't even know what it looks like. You can see things that no one else can because you have entirely different experiences coloring your clarity of vision—their blind spots are where you excel and vice versa.

You seek answers. You seek logic and structure. You probably see behavior around you from empaths that you cannot explain. The explanation for their behavior is the most complicated and difficult thing for a sociopath to understand, but in seeking those answers you will learn much about yourself as well. You will also learn that just because we can manipulate others does not mean we choose to do so. Just because we can exploit does not mean we choose to do so. Sometimes you find weaknesses that you do exploit, and sometimes you find flaws in society that you patch. Sociopathy includes both variants. Personal preference, upbringing, and life objectives can all influence why we choose to do what we do. What makes you a sociopath is not that you choose to do certain things, but that you are presented with an entirely different set of choices than a neurotypical person.

I would add that sociopaths are important to society because we are original thinkers. I like ingenuity; it's probably the thing I admire most about humanity. Theo Jansen, the Dutch artist/sculptor/engineer responsible for Strandbeests ("beach animals"), gigantic moving sculptures made out of plastic piping that crawl along the Netherlands' coasts, had this to say about the benefit to society of original thinkers:

> *Mine is not a straight path like an engineer's, it's not A to B. I make a very curly road just by the restrictions of goals and materials. A real engineer would probably solve the problem differently, maybe make an aluminum robot with motor and electric sensors and all that. But the solutions of engineers are often much alike. Everything we think can in principle be thought by someone else. The real ideas, as evolution shows, come about by chance.*

Sociopaths' minds are very different from most people's. Our brain structure is different: smaller amygdala (emotional center), poorer connections between the amygdala and the prefrontal cortex (decision-making, inter alia), what has been described as "potholes" in our brains, and a longer and thinner corpus callosum separating the hemispheres of our brains. What that means is our thought is not as dominated by emotions, nor do emotions drive our decision-making, and we can transfer information between the hemispheres of our brains abnormally fast. In other words, give us a problem to think about and we will naturally process it in a different way than

M. E. THOMAS

people with typical brains. How that plays out in the individual sociopath depends on a lot of different factors, but I have met sociopaths who have both the innocence of children gleefully hurling their bodies into ocean waves and the ruthlessness of single-minded predators under threat. There's something sort of refreshing about our brutal approach to the world. And when we live in a world where "everything we think can in principle be thought by someone else," it might be nice to be around someone who is an entirely different "someone else" than you are.

I like who I am. I like that I am methodical, relentless, efficient, able to capitalize on any situation. I have friends, I value my family, I am a good colleague. Still, I often wonder what other things I may be missing out on in life. Love? Human understanding? Emotional intimacy? Do I experience those things in their fullness? Is my experience of these things a mere shadowy approximation of what is normal or a legitimate human experience in its own right? And if I have in any way chosen this life, have I chosen the better part?

But what are the alternatives? I have sloppily used the term *empath* throughout this book to refer to nonsociopaths, but it is simply not true that every nonsociopath is empathetic. Some have suggested I use the term *normal,* but that is even less correct. The percentage of "normal" people in the population may be an actual minority (i.e., less than 50 percent). Sometimes I think people talk about sociopaths being 1 to 4 percent of the population as if the other 96 to 99 percent are normal, maybe even the opposite of the sociopath. Maybe we believe that if sociopaths have low empathy, then everyone else has robust empathy? Maybe we believe that if sociopaths do not feel guilt, everyone else must? Maybe we believe that if sociopaths frequently engage in crime, then no one else does?

The truth is many people are just assholes. You don't have to be a sociopath to be an asshole, nor is a sociopath an asshole to all people all of the time. When I first started writing about sociopathy on the blog, I hoped to help people realize that sociopaths are natural human variants. I thought at the time that the big challenge would be to try to showcase some of our strengths in a more positive light, to demonstrate that we are not as bad as people might think. Recently I have been thinking that the real problem is not in getting "normal" people to believe that we're better than they think, but in getting them to see that the "normal" ones are actually worse than they believe themselves to be. Sometimes it seems that most people assume that they are that minority of "normal" people instead of thinking that they might also be a little bit "off."

Some people balk at saying that "normal" people might actually be in the minority: "How could the psychological world label half or more of us with a diagnosis?!" But so what if the majority of people qualify for a psychological label? Doesn't that seem equally if not more probable than assuming that half of the people in the world are pretty much interchangeable in terms of brain and emotional functioning?

It is convenient to define normal as whatever you happen to be. No need to confront the possibility that maybe you aren't as empathetic as you seem. Maybe your conscience doesn't have quite the sway that you thought it did. Maybe you are both capable and incapable of much more than you had hoped. Maybe you have a lot more in common with sociopaths than you'd like to think. Maybe it is just one big long spectrum with only a few people at the extremes and the rest huddled closer to the middle. Some have derided self-diagnosed sociopaths as poseurs, clinging to the label as sanctuary from the disappointments of an average existence. Could it be that self-diagnosed sociopaths are just much more honest with themselves than the rest of you who claim, "That's not sociopathic, everyone does that"? Could both be true, that acting a particular way could be both sociopathic and something that everyone does? Or that most people do? Specifically, you—that you sometimes do those things? Does that make you normal, or me?

I don't mean to redefine sociopathy as the new normal, and certainly not "better than normal." Sociopaths are not a race of Übermenschen. We're not out doing good among the populace—standing up for the disenfranchised when everyone else is too afraid—not often, at least, and never as a general rule. Don't get me wrong. I've always loved vigilante-justice movies, but I often root for the bad guy. Society labels the subversive a criminal or revolutionary, not him. He rarely needs to tell himself stories of moral justification in order to engage in his flourishes of elaborate violence. I know I'm not alone in my love of the villain. In him, we see freedom.

Perhaps that is why the sociopath has loomed so large in our fictive spaces—Hannibal Lecter pulling Clarice's strings from behind bars; the talented con artist Tom Ripley infiltrating and destroying the life of his wealthy beloved, Dickie; the perfectly coifed Patrick Bateman traipsing through yuppie New York soaked in blood, real or imagined. They constitute walking manifestations of overblown desire and destructive forces, characterized by the absence of limitations, whether it be empathy, guilt, or fear. Indeed, the most enduring of cold-blooded villains, Dracula, is so limitless that he dissolves into mist. Historically, the diagnosis for sociopathy has in many ways served as an amalgam of miscellaneous reprobate traits, a depository for wayward, antisocial behavior from which its members can be identified and separated from everyone else. In the gothic vampire myth, the existence of the nocturnal creature can be explained, and thus contained, in the realm of the supernatural. In everyday life, however, explanations for the existence of the sociopath are much more elusive.

I wonder if my story is disappointing to you for that reason—that I am not so much myth as man. I do not have secret stories about killing animals (opossum aside), or not that I remember. To the extent that this book is fatally flawed because I do not have a criminal record or shocking or cruel enough examples of my sociopathy, it's a flaw that cannot be mended. Through my website, I've encountered all manner of individuals who exhibit symptoms of or identify as sociopaths or psychopaths—from Bonnie-and-Clyde-type criminals to sensitive teenagers struggling with the difficult notions of empathy and human connection. Despite this heterogeneity, I think there are obvious and substantive differences between the sociopath and the average person.

I have no problem exploring why I do the things I do, but there are no stories about how I am irredeemably depraved. I can only offer my thoughts about how any moral system that could lead to an adjudication of depravity is likely to be flawed, and in ways that won't be immediately obvious to those who have never dared question the foundations for their moral "feelings" about the world. As researcher in the ethics of forensic psychology Karen Franklin told NPR, criticizing the dominant conception of psychopathy:

> *By foregrounding intrinsic evil, [the diagnosis of] psychopathy marginalizes social problems and excuses institutional failures at rehabilitation. We need not understand a criminal's troubled past or environmental influences. We need not reach out a hand to help him along a pathway to redemption. This view of psychopathy, she*

argues, condemns the psychopath as someone who is
not only irredeemable, but so dangerous they 'must be
contained or banished'. An example of circular reason-
ing, it is however enticingly simple.

But sociopathy is not as simple as you have been led to believe. It is not a synonym for evil. Hearing people saying that
we are irredeemable should give you great pause. I hope that
you hesitate upon hearing the suggestion that sociopaths
should have microchips implanted in their brains, or be institutionalized indefinitely, or be shipped off to an island somewhere, and remember that the history of man is marked by
similar acts of hubris and cruelty.

I remember once in law school doing research for a paper
and reading an old statute criminalizing homosexuality.
They're easy enough to find; some of them are still on the
books in democratic countries. The state of Pennsylvania
still has a prostitution law that finds it necessary to specifically include "homosexual *and other* deviate sexual relations"
(emphasis mine). What makes a sexual relation deviate? The
dictionary defines it as "departing significantly from usual
or accepted standards." Interestingly, I once read an old statute in law school that had two notable exceptions to criminal
homosexuality: same-sex relations in prison and in the military. Presumably those same-sex relations are not "deviate"
because "normal" people have historically done them—in the
absence of females, what is a little dalliance between men?

There is a similar double standard currently applied to
sociopaths versus sociopathic behavior. Sociopaths are prone
to violence, but empaths also commit gruesome acts of violence. Those acts are more excusable to juries as long as the
empath shows "remorse." Jurors can self-identify with those

who show remorse because they too may have also committed varying degrees of heinous acts while caught up in the moment that they later anguished over, swearing that they wish it had never happened. It's harder for most people to understand someone who, while recognizing that it was a "bad" thing, went ahead and did it anyway. It's hard for me to not see this as a unique form of hypocrisy to which "normal" people are particularly susceptible when attempting to condemn the behavior of others. Interestingly, once you get people alone, you get a different result. A recent experiment suggests that when single judges sentence sociopaths for whom there is evidence of genetic predisposition to violence and crime, they give lighter sentences than they otherwise would for the reasons that you would expect—sociopaths are less culpable because of their genetic predisposition to committing crimes. As a group, though, people are only a few mental steps away from a sociopath witch-hunt. While only a minority thinks that homosexuality should be criminalized, people have few qualms about unequal treatment of those diagnosed as "sociopaths."

And so the majority goes on deciding what is "normal" and not, who is irredeemable or not, until one day you also get defined as abnormal. But if I look a lot like you, maybe it is because I am. We really should be friends, because if I can be marginalized in a democratic society, so can you. And once you also become a victim of the state, who do you think will be spearheading the revolution? Probably people like me.

One of my favorite parts about writing the blog is meeting strangers who are just like me, down to the most odd and intimate details. I want to accurately represent myself so that when they read the book, they will recognize themselves in my stories. I want to foster a sense of solidarity, a community of like-minded individuals who have a lot to learn from one another. In that way, writing this book has been calculated to achieve a particular effect. It's difficult, though, without having the reader in front of me, to predict whether I have created that desired effect. Perhaps it's like the difference between performing a piece of music to make an audio recording versus performing in front of a live audience. I am unable to gauge the reactions of book readers; I'm blind in a way that I am not accustomed to being. Even on the blog people will comment that they love things I thought were borderline pedantic and hate things that I thought were insightful. That's the true weakness with my manipulations, that I don't understand and never will truly understand the way normal people think—not my closest friends and family members and certainly not strangers, sociopaths or not. I can't test-run a particular passage on myself to gauge how others will feel. I only can extrapolate from what I've learned in past experiences with normal people to try to make general predictions about what will and will not be effective. Writing the book is probably one of the most risky things I've done.

On my blog I actively obscure my identity. Google hosts my Web page. My domain name registration is anonymous. I use gender-neutral pronouns to describe myself. I use Britishisms when I can remember to do so. I have noticed that other sociopaths do this as well—there are several whom I know to be Americans who internationalize their language and their cultural references, the result perhaps of their natural instincts to obscure and befuddle. It's not enough to try to keep your personal information out of reach. One must also actively poison the well with disinformation.

Only one person has come close to identifying me without

my at least tacit permission. I learned a lot from that experience, and I cleaned up my act. I became more careful about who knew what about me and particularly paranoid about what personal information made it online, either under my persona as M.E. or my birth name.

When I decided to write this book, I thought a lot about what that would mean for my public life, the life where I'm not known as M.E. In that life, particularly up until starting the blog, almost no one knew that I identified as a sociopath. At that time, even I didn't care about attaching a label to myself. When I finally decided to accept it and started the blog, I told my immediate family and a couple friends. Since then I've averaged telling about one or two people per year—typically when I have needed their experienced advice in a particular area, about writing, search engine optimization, legal, etc. Or I've just been dying to let them know of some horribly great thing I just managed to pull off, like crushing a bully at work or seducing someone just to ruin them. It can be lonely not having anyone to share your exploits with. About a year ago my mom decided to be open about me with her own siblings. I think she was sort of proud of me and what I have managed to accomplish with my blog and the positive effects on my life from all that self-introspection. There is a difference between being out to people who love you and have various incentives to want to keep you safe, though, and being out to the world.

I decided that if I were to write the book, I would want to be in a glass closet. I knew that I had to be more forthcoming than being totally anonymous; otherwise the book would have little legitimacy. Unless people believe my story, it will lose its effectiveness in terms of educating people and advocating on behalf of myself and others like me. But I also have a separate life and career. I wonder, would I be fired if my employers found this out about me? Not because I'm a bad employee or abusive to students, but just because of my diagnosis? If ever I were sent to jail, I could be denied parole solely based on a psychological profile. Depending on what I was in prison for and what jurisdiction I was in, I could be imprisoned indefinitely. It's a big deal. Although I'm not really planning on becoming a felon any time in the next two years, my level of impulsivity makes that always a very real possibility. Will my friends, employers, or future love interests be able to see past these propensities and judge me solely based on what I have actually done, not just what I am capable of doing? Or will they always be scared that I'm not as under control as I claim to be?

And I have young children in my family. Maybe someday I will even have kids of my own. They share my name. This stigma could reach far past me to those innocents who never asked for it.

I don't mind being an advocate, but I have no desire to be famous. To the extent that the cause needs a face, I don't mind being that face. I don't even mind showing my face. I know that it helps people and personalizes my message. I am a real person. I have a name. I don't even mind your knowing my name. I know that secrets are too enticing, so I don't want there to be any secret. If you're dying to know my real name, please write to me and I'll tell you. My contact information is on my website. The only thing I ask in exchange is that you not disclose my name. Keep it to yourself. Let others find out the same way you had to—directly from me, for themselves.

I'm hoping that this way we can all get what we want. You can find out anything you want to know about me, and my young relatives won't have to grow up with people looking askance at them, wondering if they're also genetically disposed to be monsters. Is it possible to remain in a glass closet in the information age? I'm actually curious to see if it works. Of course, it's risky, but I have a pretty high tolerance for risk. If it does work, maybe I'll write my next academic article on it.

Most sociopaths want to hide their identity, but I don't want to hide forever. My life's goal is not to have to "pass." I want everyone to know who I am. I want to live in the light. Right now it's not safe, though. People don't like sociopaths. There are books and Web pages devoted to detecting and avoiding sociopaths: Don't talk to these people, don't be around them, don't let them ensnare you. I want people like me to know that they aren't alone. And I want everyone else to know that I'm a natural human variant. I want to take off the mask, but not until I change the world to make it a safer place for me.

Acknowledgments

M any thanks to my agent, Emmanuelle Morgen, who saw a book where I had only a blog. To my genius friend, who did all of the heavy lifting. To my editor, Jenna Ciongoli, who was both infinitely patient and unyieldingly exact and without whom the book would be a fraction of what it is. To Lucinda Bartley, whose unparalleled brilliance managed to make it all happen and all worthwhile for me. To Domenica Alioto for pinch-hitting when I needed her most. To everyone at Crown who helped in countless ways: Penny the alchemist, Julie the slugger, Aja the ink slinger, and Matthew the law. To all of the visitors to my blog for their insight, support, and constant entertainment. To my loving family, without whom I would be nothing, and especially to my little relatives for re-minding me to preserve a sense of wonder and openness in the world.

extracts reading groups
competitions books new
discounts extracts extracts discounts
competitions extracts
books new reading groups extracts discounts
events books events
extracts new this reading groups reading groups
interviews
events extracts
discounts
new books events
events new
discounts extracts discounts
www.panmacmillan.com
extracts events reading groups
competitions books extracts new